IARIA

ICDS 2019

The Thirteenth International Conference on Digital Society and eGovernments

February 24 – 28, 2019

Athens, Greece

ICDS 2019 Editors

Lasse Berntzen, University College of Southeast, Norway

Printed from e-media with permission by:

Curran Associates, Inc.
57 Morehouse Lane
Red Hook, NY 12571

Some format issues inherent in the e-media version may also appear in this print version.

Printed by Curran Associates, Inc. (2019)

International Academy, Research, and Industry Association (IARIA)
412 Derby Way
Wilmington, DE 19810

Phone: (408) 893-6407
Fax: (408) 527-6351

petre@iaria.org

Additional copies of this publication are available from:

Curran Associates, Inc.
57 Morehouse Lane
Red Hook, NY 12571 USA
Phone: 845-758-0400
Fax: 845-758-2633
Email: curran@proceedings.com
Web: www.proceedings.com

Table of Contents

ICDS 2019

Forward

The thirteenth edition of The International Conference on Digital Society (ICDS 2019) was held in Athens, Greece, February 24 - 28, 2019.

Nowadays, most of the economic activities and business models are driven by the unprecedented evolution of theories and technologies. The impregnation of these achievements into our society is present everywhere, and it is only question of user education and business models optimization towards a digital society.

Progress in cognitive science, knowledge acquisition, representation, and processing helped to deal with imprecise, uncertain or incomplete information. Management of geographical and temporal information becomes a challenge, in terms of volume, speed, semantic, decision, and delivery.

Information technologies allow optimization in searching an interpreting data, yet special constraints imposed by the digital society require on-demand, ethics, and legal aspects, as well as user privacy and safety.

The event was very competitive in its selection process and very well perceived by the international scientific and industrial communities. As such, it is attracting excellent contributions and active participation from all over the world. We were very pleased to receive a large amount of top quality contributions.

The accepted papers covered a large spectrum of topics related to advanced networking, applications, social networking, security and protection, and systems technologies in a digital society. We believe that the ICDS 2019 contributions offered a panel of solutions to key problems in all areas of digital needs of today's society.

We take here the opportunity to warmly thank all the members of the ICDS 2019 technical program committee as well as the numerous reviewers. The creation of such a broad and high quality conference program would not have been possible without their involvement. We also kindly thank all the authors that dedicated much of their time and efforts to contribute to the ICDS 2018. We truly believe that thanks to all these efforts, the final conference program consists of top quality contributions.

This event could also not have been a reality without the support of many individuals, organizations and sponsors. In addition, we also gratefully thank the members of the ICDS 2019 organizing committee for their help in handling the logistics and for their work that is making this professional meeting a success.

We hope the ICDS 2019 was a successful international forum for the exchange of ideas and results between academia and industry and to promote further progress on the topics of digital society.

We also hope that Athens provided a pleasant environment during the conference and everyone saved some time for exploring this beautiful city.

ICDS 2019 Chairs

ICDS Steering Committee
Lasse Berntzen, University College of Southeast, Norway
Åsa Smedberg, Stockholm University, Sweden
Azi Lev-On, Ariel University, Israel
Jaroslaw Kozlak, AGH University of Science and Technology, Krakow, Poland

ICDS Industry/Research Advisory Committee
Enrico Francesconi, Institute of Legal Information Theory and Techniques - Italian National Research Council (ITTIG - CNR), Italy
Sunil Choenni, Dutch Ministry of Security & Justice / Rotterdam University of Applied Sciences, Netherlands
Korina Velazquez, Comisión Especial de Acceso Digital - Cámara de Diputados, Mexico
Schubert Foo, Wee Kim Wee School of Communication and Information, Singapore

ICDS 2019

COMMITTEE

ICDS Steering Committee
Lasse Berntzen, University College of Southeast Norway, Norway
Åsa Smedberg, Stockholm University, Sweden
Azi Lev-On, Ariel University, Israel
Jaroslaw Kozlak, AGH University of Science and Technology, Krakow, Poland

ICDS Industry/Research Advisory Committee
Enrico Francesconi, Institute of Legal Information Theory and Techniques - Italian National Research Council (ITTIG - CNR), Italy
Sunil Choenni, Dutch Ministry of Security & Justice / Rotterdam University of Applied Sciences, Netherlands
Korina Velazquez, Comisión Especial de Acceso Digital - Cámara de Diputados, Mexico
Schubert Foo, Wee Kim Wee School of Communication and Information, Singapore

ICDS 2019 Technical Program Committee

Chiniah Aatish, University of Mauritius, Mauritius
Habtamu Abie, Norwegian Computing Center, Norway
Ricardo Afonso, Federal University of Alagoas (UFAL), Brazil
Shaftab Ahmed, Bahria University, Pakistan
Mohamad Ibrahim Al Ladan, Rafik Hariri University, Lebanon
Laura Alcaide Muñoz, University of Granada, Spain
Cristina Alcaraz, University of Malaga, Spain
Salvador Alcaraz, Universidad Miguel Hernández, Spain
Charalampos (Harris) Alexopoulos, University of the Aegean, Greece
Alexandre Alvaro, UFSCar - Sorocaba, Brazil
Toshiyuki Amagasa, University of Tsukuba, Japan
Kambiz Badie, ICT Research Institute, Iran
Sebastiano Bagnara, Institute of Cognitive Sciences and Technologies - Italian National Research Council in Rome, Italy
Mortaza S. Bargh, Research and Documentation Centre of the Dutch Ministry of Security and Justice, Netherlands
Ilija Basicevic, University of Novi Sad, Serbia
Najib Belkhayat, ENCG Business School - Cady Ayyad University, Marrakech, Morocco
Lasse Berntzen, University College of Southeast Norway, Norway
Aljosa Jerman Blazic, SETCCE Ltd. / IT association at Chamber of commerce, Slovenia
Mahmoud Brahimi, University of Msila, Algeria
Justin F. Brunelle, The MITRE Corporation, USA
Mikhail Bundin, Lobachevsky State University of Nizhni Novgorod (UNN), Russia
Vinicius Cardoso Garcia, Universidade Federal de Pernambuco, Brazil
Maria Chiara Caschera, CNR-IRPPS, Italy
Sunil Choenni, Rotterdam University of Applied Science (HR), The Netherlands
Yul Chu, University of Texas Rio Grande Valley (UTRGV), USA

Soon Ae Chun, iSecure Lab - College of Staten Island | City University of New York, USA
Kathy Clawson, University of Sunderland, UK
Arthur Csetenyi, Budapest Corvinus University, Hungary
María E. Cortés-Cediel, Universidad Complutense de Madrid, Spain
Marcelo da Silva Conterato, Pontifical Catholic University of Rio Grande do Sul (PUCRS), Porto Alegre, Brazil
Fisnik Dalipi, University of South-Eastern Norway, Norway
Glenn S. Dardick, Longwood University, USA
Lairson Emanuel R. de Alencar Oliveira, Centro de Informática - Federal University of Pernambuco, Brazil
Monica De Martino, CNR-IMATI, Italy
Regina De Oliveira Heidrich, Universidade Feevale, Brazil
Ahmed El Oualkadi, Abdelmalek Essaadi University, Morocco
Rania El-Gazzar, Universty of South-Eastern Norway, Norway
Fernanda Faini, University of Bologna, Italy
Jesus Favela, CICESE, Mexico
Pedro Felipe do Prado, Universidade de São Paulo (USP), Brazil
Schubert Foo, Wee Kim Wee School of Communication and Information, Singapore
Enrico Francesconi, Institute of Legal Information Theory and Techniques - Italian National Research Council (ITTIG - CNR), Italy
Marco Furini, Università di Modena e Reggio Emilia, Italy
Jürgen Fuß, University of Applied Sciences Upper Austria, Austria
Amparo Fuster-Sabater, Institute of Physical and Information Technologies (CSIC), Spain
Héctor Fernando Gómez Alvarado, Universidad Técnica Particular de Loja, Ecuador
Genady Ya. Grabarnik, St Johns University, USA
David J. Gunkel, Northern Illinois University, USA
Huong Ha, School of Business, Singapore University of Social Sciences, Singapore
Stephan Haller, Bern University of Applied Sciences, Switzerland
Myung-Ja "MJ" Han, University of Illinois at Urbana Champaign, USA
Martijn Hartog, Delft University of Technology, the Netherlands
Gerold Hölzl, University of Passau, Germany
Sounman Hong, Yonsei University, Seoul, South Korea
Hana Horak, University of Zagreb, Croatia
Valentina Janev, Institute Mihajlo Pupin - University of Belgrade, Serbia
Haziq Jeelani, Galgotias University, India
Konstantinos Kalemis, National & Kapodistrian University of Athens, Greece
Atsushi Kanai, Hosei University, Japan
Dimitris Kanellopoulos, University of Patras, Greece
Epaminondas Kapetanios, University of Westminster, UK
Georgios Karopoulos, University of Athens, Greece
Sokratis K. Katsikas, Center for Cyber & Information Security - Norwegian University of Science & Technology (NTNU), Norway
Kai Kimppa, Turku School of Economics - University of Turku, Finland
Fernando Kleiman, Ministry of Planning | Brazil Federal Government, Brazil / TUDelft, The Netherlands
Richard Knepper, Cornell University, USA
Ah-Lian Kor, Leeds Metropolitan University, UK
Jaroslaw Kozlak, AGH University of Science and Technology, Krakow, Poland
Toshihiro Kuboi, California Polytechnic State University, San Luis Obispo, USA
Rosa Lanzilotti, University of Bari Aldo Moro, Italy

Azi Lev-On, Ariel University, Israel
Fengqiang Li, Northwestern University, USA
Gen-Yih Liao, Chang Gung University, Taiwan
Chern Li Liew, Victoria University of Wellington, New Zealand
Shuhua Monica Liu, Fudan University, Shanghai, China
Zhengchun Liu, The University of Chicago - Argonne National Laboratory, USA
Giovanni Livraga, Universita' degli Studi di Milano, Italy
Moisés Lodeiro, Universidad de La Laguna, Spain
Justin Longo, University of Regina, Canada
Xudong Luo, Sun Yat-sen University, China
Bonnie MacKellar, St John's University Queens, USA
Christos Makris, University of Patras, Greece
Maryam Tayefeh Mahmoudi, ICT Research Institute, Iran
Panagiotis Manolitzas, Technical University of Crete, Greece
Paloma Martínez, Universidad Carlos III de Madrid, Spain
Riccardo Martoglia, Universita' di Modena e Reggio Emilia, Italy
David Mauricio, Universidad Nacional Mayor de San Marcos, Peru
Elvis Mazzoni, ALMA MATER STUDIORUM - University of Bologna, Italy
Shegaw Mengiste, Universty of South-Eastern Norway, Norway
Alok Mishra, Atilim University, Turkey
Anuranjan Misra, Noida International University, Greater Noida, India
Harekrishna Misra, Institute of Rural Management Anand, India
Jolanta Mizera-Pietraszko, Opole University, Poland
Manar Mohaisen, Korea Tech, South Korea
Manuela Montangero, Università di Modena e Reggio Emilia, Italy
Lourdes Moreno, Universidad Carlos III de Madrid, Spain
John Morison, School of Law - Queen's University, Belfast, UK
Paulo Moura Oliveira, UTAD University, Vila Real / INESC-TEC Porto, Portugal
Javier Muguerza Rivero, University of the Basque Country (UPV/EHU), Donostia, Spain
Debajyoti Mukhopadhyay, Maharashtra Institute of Technology, India
Syed Naqvi, Birmingham City University, UK
Panayotis (Panos) Nastou, University of the Aegean, Greece
Erich Neuhold, University of Vienna, Austria / Darmstadt University of Technology, Germany
Dade Nurjanah, Telkom University, Indonesia
Katsuhiko Ogawa, Keio University, Japan
Adegboyega Ojo, National University of Ireland, Galway, Republic of Ireland
Daniel O'Leary, University of Southern California, USA
Selma Ayşe Özel, Çukurova University, Adana, Turkey
Ingmar Pappel, Interinx Ltd., Estonia
Lahis Pasquali Kurtz, Universidade Federal de Minas Gerais, Brazil
Mirjana Pejic-Bach, University of Zagreb, Croatia
Rimantas Petrauskas, Mykolas Romeris University, Lithuania
Mick Phythian, Centre for Computing & Social Responsibility - De Montfort University, UK
Pedro Luiz Pizzigatti Corrêa, University of São Paulo, Brazil
Nuno Pombo, Universidade da Beira Interior, Portugal
Rajesh S. Prasad, STES NBN Sinhgad School of Engineering, India
Augustin Prodan, Iuliu Hatieganu University, Cluj-Napoca, Romania
Thurasamy Ramayah, Universiti Sains Malaysia, Malaysia

Copyright Information

Managing E-Government Development for Reducing Corruption via Effective Policymaking: Empirical Evidences from Cross-Country Analyses

Prakrit Silal
Management Information Systems Group
Indian Institute of Management Calcutta
Kolkata, India
email: prakrits16@iimcal.ac.in

Ashutosh Jha
Management Information Systems Group
Indian Institute of Management Calcutta
Kolkata, India
email: ashutoshj14@iimcal.ac.in

Debashis Saha
Management Information Systems Group
Indian Institute of Management Calcutta
Kolkata, India
email: ds@iimcal.ac.in

***Abstract*—Internationally E-Government (E-GOV) has been broadly demonstrated as an anti-corruption instrument in extant research, based on the extensive analyses of E-GOV Development Index (EGDI) against Corruption Perceptions Index (CPI). EGDI's effectiveness in combating corruption ideally involves country-specific appropriate policy-driven development along its three constituent components: Human Capital Index (HCI), Telecommunications Infrastructure Index (TII), and Online Services Index (OSI). However, we argue that, while considering EGDI's impact on lowering corruption, existing studies do not consider the heterogeneity among the countries in terms of their EGDI maturity levels. Also, past research does not delve into the analysis of the relative contribution of EGDI components in controlling CPI, which may very well vary with EGDI maturity level. We posit that, unless these determinants are explored, countries would lack in formulating right policies to strengthen the enablers they are currently weak in to fight against corruption. So, this paper aims to understand the exact role HCI, TII, and OSI play individually in alleviating corruption vis-à-vis how these index values vary across cohorts of countries having similar EGDI trajectories. Using longitudinal clustering based on EGDI, we first identify temporal country cohorts and then perform cohort-wise panel regression to analyze the individual effects of HCI, TII and OSI on CPI. As expected, the three components do not contribute uniformly in lowering corruption, and more importantly, each assumes significance only under different contingent internal factors. So, based on our results, we recommend, for each cohort, a set of specific E-GOV development policies targeted for combating corruption, thereby helping countries formulate long-term and short-term measures toward moving up the E-GOV maturity stages too.**

Keywords— E-Government; EGDI; Corruption; CPI; E-Gov Strategies; Longitudinal clustering; Panel regression.

I. INTRODUCTION

Corruption is a social menace that corrugates the foundations of a government machinery, thereby undermining the socio-economic welfare and well-being of the citizens nation-wide. Elbahnasawy [1] defines corruption as "*a manifestation of the principal-agent problem owing to information asymmetry and non-alignment of incentives*". It has proved to be a major barrier for countries seeking to achieve the Sustainable Development Goals (SDGs) set by the United Nations Development Programme (UNDP) [2]. Extant research provides substantial evidence of the negative externalities, such as lowering of economic prosperity, increased environmental degradation, growing resource wastage, increased income inequalities, and growing poverty, propagated by corruption [3]. Taking cognizance of these negative externalities, controlling corruption has become imperative for governments all around the world. E-Government (E-GOV), which advocates the use of Information and Communication Technologies (ICT) in the delivery of public services, has been demonstrated in past studies as an effective anti-corruption tool [4] to reduce information asymmetry and bring transparency in government service delivery [1][5][6]. In literature, E-GOV [5] is defined as "*the use of ICTs to enable and improve the efficiency with which government services are provided to citizens, employees, businesses and agencies*".

Corruption level of a country is usually estimated with the help of the well-known measure, called Corruption Perceptions Index (CPI), published annually by Transparency International [7]. Countries are given a score between 0 and 100, where "0" signifies highest corruption and "100" signifies lowest corruption [7]. On the other hand, E-GOV development of countries is assessed through the measure, called E-GOV Development Index (EGDI), published by the United Nations on a bi-annual basis from 2008 onwards (earlier published annually during 2003-2005) [6]. EGDI is a composite metric consisting of three components: (i) Human Capital Index (HCI) – that assesses the human capabilities (HC) and skill levels, (ii) Telecommunications Infrastructure Index (TII) – which assesses development levels of telecommunications infrastructure (TI), and (iii) Online Services Index (OSI) – which assesses the scope and quality of government's e-services or online services (OS) [6].

Although recent research works [3]–[5] in the "*E-GOV–Corruption*" discourse provide substantial evidence regarding the potential of E-GOV development in combating corruption, we have identified two inter-related research issues that have not been adequately addressed in the literature: (i) how the impact of E-GOV development on lowering corruption varies with the heterogeneity among countries through their temporal EGDI evolutions, due to the differing HC/TI/OS capabilities and differing levels of internal factors, and (ii) how the relative contribution of HC, TI and OS matters in managing corruption at various levels of E-GOV maturity across countries. The previous studies on *E-GOV–Corruption*, therefore, do not consider adequately the context-specific component-wise variations in the *EGDI-CPI* relationship. Hence, the policy recommendations mentioned in these studies are not complete and sufficient to a large extent, rendering such policies not readily operationalizable at the country-level [8][9]. Consequent to such scant research focus and insufficient empirical guidance, countries may incorrectly estimate the exact impact of the three components, namely HC, TI, and OS, in reducing corruption, which could lead to incorrect prioritization and inefficient resource allocation and hence, sub-optimal outcomes thereof [10].

Our primary focus in this paper is on the context-specific role that HCI, TII and OSI play within EGDI in increasing CPI; to be more specific, the relative contribution of HC/TI/OS in reducing corruption. In order to avoid any over-estimation of HC/TI/OS's impact, we have controlled for the effect of governance quality and economic factors on corruption. Towards this, firstly we have taken help of longitudinal clustering technique to group the countries into clusters (referred to as *cohorts* henceforth), based on the similarity of their EGDI trajectories across time; secondly, we have employed panel regression to understand the quantum of individual impact of HCI/TII/OSI on CPI for each of the cohorts. Finally, based on the above findings, we recommend context-aware cohort-specific E-GOV policies to provide guidance regarding the HC/TI/OS prioritization by countries and the enabling factors that the countries should take cognizance of, in order to harness the full potential of E-GOV development in combating corruption.

Therefore, the paper contributes to the "*E-GOV–corruption*" discourse in the following four ways: (i) we account for the heterogeneity among countries in their temporal EGDI evolution, taking cognizance of the dynamic similarities of countries across time, (ii) we identify the individual roles of HC, TI and OS in controlling corruption and the enabling conditions under which the effect of HCI/TII/OSI on CPI is significant, (iii) we combine the above two analyses by relating *country-wise heterogeneity* with *E-GOV-corruption correlation*, and (iv) we recommend, based on our unique combination of analyses, long-term and short-term E-GOV strategies closely aligned with the objective of lowering CPI.

The rest of the paper is organized as follows: The following section reviews the relevant literature, Section III outlines the research framework and methodology, Section IV presents the results and discussions. Section V finally concludes the paper.

II. Literature Review and Background

Since our study draws from two distinct streams of literature: (i) Country-wise heterogeneity, and (ii) E-GOV-corruption discourse, we begin with short introduction of each followed by brief survey of relevant works in each domain.

A. Country-wise Heterogeneity

We extend the definition of a firm's competitive advantage, as defined in the Resource-Based View literature [11], to define country-level heterogeneity as "*the distinct and unique characteristics inherent in countries due to their access to a unique bundle of resources and the subsequent development of capabilities and knowledge, not easily duplicated by other countries.*" In the context of its influence on longitudinal E-GOV development of countries, extant research provides evidence for two broad categories of variables to handle country-level heterogeneity - (i) Internal Capabilities, and (ii) Country-level Governance and Economic factors [3][10][11]. Adapting the definition of organizational capabilities [12], we define internal capability of a country as its ability to derive utility through deployment of valued resources, either in combination or copresence. Borrowing from the arguments in [11], internal capabilities differentiate countries in terms of their absorptive capacity, i.e., their ability to assimilate and make use of available knowledge or technology (including ICT which leads to E-GOV). This, in turn, highlights the importance of internal capabilities in creating unique country-level attributes. At the same time, there exists sufficient empirical evidence of governance and economic factors, such as judicial independence, economic prosperity, institutional strength, and press freedom, having a significant role in fostering E-GOV development in a country [13]. Hence, it becomes imperative that, while using EGDI, one should take country-wise heterogeneity into consideration properly.

However, to the best of our knowledge, no previous study on explaining E-GOV-corruption connect has longitudinally incorporated such country-wise heterogeneity, arising out of the combined effect of internal capabilities and governance/economic factors acting over time. Few studies that try to differentiate among countries, however, either attribute such differences to geographical affiliations [9] or confine to single time-period, thereby ignoring the underlying structural differences among countries over temporal domain. To circumvent these limitations, we invoke longitudinal clustering – a technique that captures the underlying dynamic structural similarities of countries by grouping countries based on some variable (EGDI in this study) over a time-period, as explained in details in Section III.

B. E-GOV and Corruption Discourse

Existing studies in the E-GOV-corruption discourse have demonstrated the ability of E-GOV in lowering corruption at the broader index level [1][5][13], as well as at the individual resource levels, such as Internet diffusion, citizens' educational capability, or mobile phone penetration [8][9]. However, extant studies are silent on taking the country-wise heterogeneity into proper consideration while analyzing the E-GOV-corruption relationship. Furthermore, these studies have missed out on the possibility that the said heterogeneity may stem from the variations in HC/OS/TI capabilities of countries. Extant studies [5][13]–[16], therefore, have not empirically studied the effect of HCI/OSI/TII on corruption. Consequently, the EGDI-corruption relationship has never been explored at the sub-index level (i.e., at the level of HCI, TII and OSI), to the best of our knowledge. However, unless such understanding is explored, countries would be unable to leverage on the strength of their internal capabilities, meanwhile lacking in policies to strengthen the sub-index they are weak in. Moreover, the use of the broad index EGDI masks the inter-country differences in their sub-index prioritizations. For example, Chile and Czech Republic have almost identical EGDI viz. 0.60137 and 0.60695 in 2010 and 2014, respectively [6]. However, there are marked differences at the levels of their EGDI components. While Chile is much superior to Czech Republic in terms of OSI (0.60952 vs 0.37007), it lags Czech Republic in terms of TII (0.27109 vs 0.57532). As existing literature does not clearly spell out the relative contribution of each of the three components of EGDI on CPI, countries, therefore, face decision uncertainties while formulating their E-GOV development strategies. Due to resource limitations, which is a reality in many countries, some countries may choose to provide more emphasis on one or two of the critical components at the expense of other less significant component(s), thereby failing to utilize their limited resources effectively [10].

Our motivation behind delving deeper into the sub-index level comes from the following observation. Despite lack of studies probing HC/TI/OS's effect on corruption individually, there exist empirical evidences that point towards the possibility of each component having its own significant effects in lowering corruption. Education levels and access to education have been shown to lower corruption [13], thereby building a strong case for HCI's significance in increasing CPI. In support of TII, Internet diffusion and cellphone subscription [8] (both being sub-components of TII) have been shown to have significant influence in lowering corruption. In support of OSI, digitalization of government services has been shown to increase transparency, which is an antecedent of reduction in corruption. Furthermore, enablers of E-GOV service usage, such as Internet adoption has been shown to lower corruption levels [8]. We, therefore, posit that the three EGDI components – HCI, TII, and OSI – have significant effects in increasing CPI in their own capacities alone.

III. Research Framework And Methodology

As mentioned earlier, we first account for country-wise heterogeneity by employing longitudinal clustering to group countries with similar EGDI levels. Next, within each group, we use panel regression for testing the effects of HC, TI, and OS in lowering corruption as per the model of Figure 1, which captures the overall structure of the conventional research framework used in this kind of study [3]–[5]. We assume that HCI, TII and OSI (on the left part of Figure 1) are the three basic capabilities derived out of EGDI that contribute to CPI, subject to the internal factors (on the right part) explained below in details.

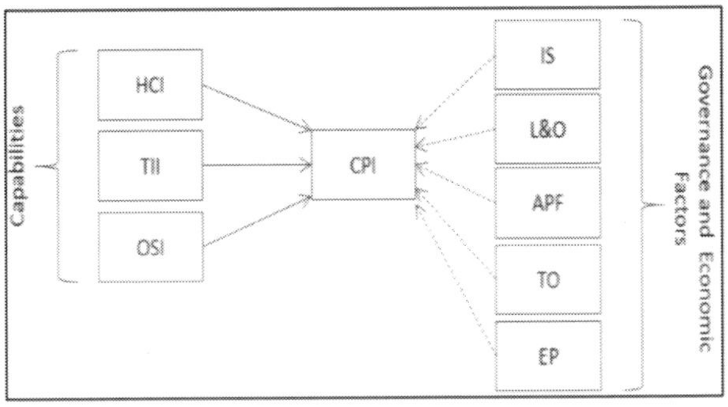

Figure 1. Model for testing EGDI components on CPI

A. Research Model

Our model (Figure 1) aims to draw upon the resource-based view of countries to understand how the unique mix of HC/OS/TI capabilities, subject to governance and economic factors, contribute to corruption control. We control for the effects of governance and economic factors on corruption in order to avoid over-estimation of HC/TI/OS's effects on corruption. Regarding the control variables, though there is no universally agreed upon set as determinants of corruption, based on the existing literature [1], we make use of five control variables, namely Government Effectiveness (GE) [17], which operationalizes Institutional Strength (IS), Rule of Law (RL) [17], which operationalizes Law and Order (L&O), Anti Press Freedom (APF) [18], Trade Openness (TO) [17], and Economic Prosperity (EP) [17], which represent the degree of political and economic freedom enjoyed by the citizens of a country. Causes of corruption have been consistently found, in extant research, to be deeply rooted in these governance (that contribute to political freedom [13]) and economic factors [1][3][13], and have therefore been extensively used as control variables. We consider IS as the variable that captures GE, as shown in Table I, which provides a summary of all variables used in our study.

B. Data Sources

Our study uses a balanced panel dataset consisting of 102 countries with data ranging from 2003 to 2016. The dataset comprises 8 time periods with consecutive time-period data from 2003 to 2005 and alternative year's data from 2008 onwards due to non-availability of EGDI data (the United

TABLE I. Summary Of Variables Used

Sl. No.	Variable	Measure / Description	Scale	Source	Years
1	CPI	Corruption Perceptions Index	0 to 100	Transparency International	2003-2005: 2008-2016
2	EGDI	E-government Development Index	0 to 1	United Nations E-government Global Survey	2003-2005: 2008-2016
3	HCI	Human Capital Index	0 to 1	United Nation E-government Global Survey	2003-2005: 2008-2016
4	TII	Telecommunications Infrastructure Index	0 to 1	United Nation E-government Global Survey	2003-2005: 2008-2016
5	OSI	Online Services Index	0 to 1	United Nation E-government Global Survey	2003-2005: 2008-2016
6	IS	Government Effectiveness	-2.5 to +2.5	World Bank World Governance Indicators	2003-2005: 2008-2016
7	L&O	Rule of Law	-2.5 to +2.5	World Bank World Governance Indicators	2003-2005: 2008-2016
8	APF	Press Freedom from political influence	0 to 100	Freedom House	2003-2005: 2008-2016
9	TO	(Imports + Exports) of goods and services (as % of GDP)	Actuals (%)	World Bank World Development Indicators	2003-2005: 2008-2016
10	EP	GDP per capita (constant 2010 US$)	Actuals ($)	World Bank World Development Indicators	2003-2005: 2008-2016

TABLE II. DESCRIPTIVE STATISTICS OF THE VARIABLES

Variable	Obs.	Mean	Std. Error	Min	Max
CPI	816	47.47	21.72	13.00	97.00
EGDI	816	0.54	0.19	0.09	0.95
HCI	816	0.80	0.17	0.17	1.00
TII	816	0.34	0.25	0.00	0.94
OSI	816	0.49	0.24	0.01	1.00
IS	816	0.36	0.92	-1.53	2.44
L&O	816	0.27	0.96	-1.82	2.10
APF	816	41.77	21.49	8.00	90.00
TO	816	88.63	52.77	20.59	441.60
EP	816	17904.47	21463.99	307.03	108600.93

Nations did not publish the same for the other years). EGDI data contain the three component level data too for HCI, TII and OSI. All the four measures viz. EGDI, HCI, TII and OSI score countries on a scale of 0 to 1, where "0" signifies low and "1" signifies high. The outcome variable, namely corruption, has been operationalized using CPI, published annually by Transparency International [7]. Table II provides the descriptive statistics of all the variables. Our dataset provides a total of 816 observations for every variable.

C. *Methodology*

Our methodology consists of two primary sequential steps: (i) longitudinal clustering based on EGDI trajectory, and (ii) panel data regression within each cluster.

a) EGDI Trajectory based Clustering

Although there are several clustering techniques available [19], our study employs the commonly used *k*-means clustering technique to create longitudinal cohorts of countries in order to capture the dynamic similarities of some countries across time. The *k*-means based algorithm, being an unsupervised learning technique, does away with the need to pre-specify the number of clusters, hence being appropriate for our exploratory study, where the number of clusters is unknown. Some related works have done region-specific studies using single time-period data [9]. However, they have not used any clustering technique per se. So, our paper is the first of its kind to use multi-time period clustering employing *k*-means technique. As mentioned earlier, the factor we have used for the longitudinal clustering is the EGDI trend from 2003 through 2016. We have used the "kml" package present in the open source statistical programming language "R" for conducting the clustering analysis. After testing with various values of *k*, we have narrowed down to four cohorts, namely A, B, C and D, (Figure 2) because four clusters maximize the Calinski-Harabasz Index [20] in the case of EGDI. Table III provides the list of countries included in each cohort post our analysis. Cohort A represents the largest group with 34 countries, while cohort D represents the smallest group with 20 countries.

TABLE III. COHORT WISE COUNTRY LIST

Cohort	Countries
D	Bangladesh, Cameroon, Algeria, Ghana, Gambia, Honduras, Kenya, Morocco, Madagascar, Mali, Mozambique, Malawi, Namibia, Nigeria, Nicaragua, Pakistan, Senegal, United Republic of Tanzania, Uganda, Zimbabwe. (20)
A	Albania, Armenia, Azerbaijan, Bolivia, Botswana, China, Costa Rica, Dominican Republic, Egypt, Georgia, Guatemala, Indonesia, India, Jamaica, Jordan, Kyrgyzstan, Kuwait, Sri Lanka, Republic of Moldova, Macedonia, Mauritius, Panama, Peru, Philippines, Paraguay, Qatar, Saudi Arabia, El Salvador, Thailand, Trinidad and Tobago, Turkey, Ukraine, Vietnam, South Africa. (34)
B	United Arab Emirates, Argentina, Bulgaria, Brazil, Chile, Colombia, Cyprus, Czech Republic, Spain, Greece, Croatia, Hungary, Italy, Kazakhstan, Lithuania, Latvia, Mexico, Malaysia, Poland, Portugal, Romania, Russian Federation, Slovakia, Slovenia, Uruguay. (25)
C	Australia, Austria, Belgium, Canada, Switzerland, Germany, Denmark, Estonia, Finland, France, United Kingdom, Ireland, Iceland, Israel, Japan, Republic of Korea, Luxembourg, Netherlands, Norway, New Zealand, Singapore, Sweden, United States of America. (23)

b) Panel Data Analysis

Compared to only cross-sectional data or pure time series data, panel data includes the inter-individual, as well as the intra-individual differences, besides containing information along both cross-sectional and temporal dimensions. This suits our research requirement perfectly. Moreover, panel data analysis has several advantages including: (i) the ability to model and/or test more complex behaviors and/or hypotheses [21], (ii) the ability to control the effect of omitted variable biases, and (iii) the ability to handle the effect of inter-individual dependencies as well as correlation (aka dependency) across time. This is not possible in other techniques (like Ordinary Least Squares [21]) due to violation of independence assumption [21].

Our research model uses two approaches for fitting the panel data: (i) Within Group Fixed Effects Regression, and (ii) Random Effects Regression [21]. We have used Hausman test [21] to identify the appropriate model for each cohort. Prior to running the models, the dataset was tested for the presence of fixed effects using Chow test, post which the time effect and the individual effects were tested using the Lagrange Multiplier test developed by Breusch and Pagan [21]. The Random Effects model have been run using either the Swamy Arora's Transformation [21] or the Wallace-Hussain Transformation [21]. Heteroskedasticity was tested using Breusch Pagan test [21] and was detected in majority of the models. Therefore, we have calculated heteroskedasticity robust estimates, using Arellano's and White's method [21], for Fixed Effects and Random Effects regression, respectively. The dataset was tested for stationarity using the Augmented Dickey Fuller test [21], where all variables were found to be stationary.

IV. RESULTS AND DISCUSSIONS

We present here our findings, which provide substantial evidence regarding the existence of cohort-wise differences in the EGDI levels, as well as cohort-specific roles of the different EGDI components in lowering corruption.

A. *Cohort-specific Characteristics*

Our findings provide evidence of significant inter-cohort differences regarding their EGDI trajectories. Figure 2 shows the result of the EGDI-based longitudinal clustering, where the vertical axis in the right side of the figure denotes EGDI levels

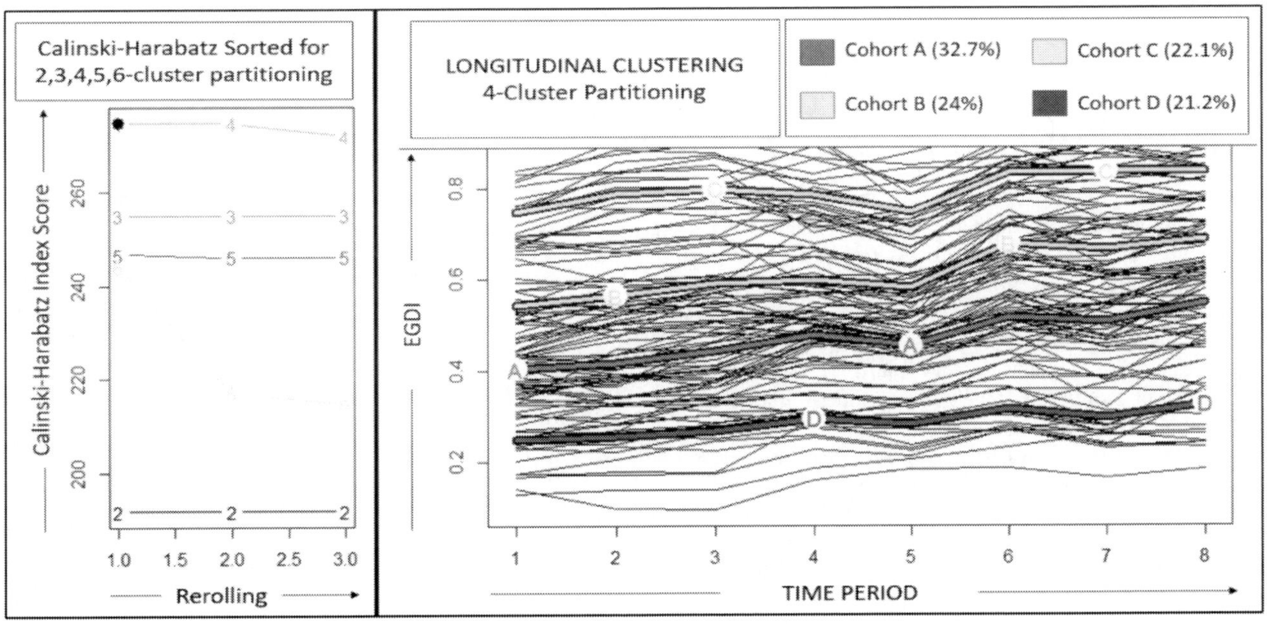

Figure 2. Results of EGDI Longitudinal Clustering

while the horizontal axis denotes the time period. Table IV provides a descriptive summary of the four cohorts (Table III) identified therefrom. Cohort C represents the countries at the higher end of the spectrum across all the variables used in the study, while cohort D represents the countries at the lower end of the spectrum across all the variables. In between, we have cohorts B and A. It can be observed that countries with similar levels of governance levels (IS/L&O/APF), internal capabilities (HCI/TII/OSI), and economic factors (TO/EP) have similar longitudinal EGDI trajectories demonstrated by their automatic affiliation to distinct cohorts (Table IV). Countries are identically clustered for all the variables considered in this study. In other words, cohort D is the cluster with the lowest average value for all the variables, cohort C is the cluster with the highest average value for all the variables, with cohorts B and A in between. Our results provide evidence regarding (i) heterogeneity among countries in terms of their EGDI evolution trajectories, and (ii) the heterogeneity being contingent on the level of internal capabilities and governance quality/economic development levels of countries. As posited, our clustering result provides sufficient evidence of country-wise heterogeneity in EGDI evolution trajectories.

B. EGDI Components and CPI

The panel regression summary indicates some cohort-wise variations in the way EGDI components affect corruption. As observed in Table V: (i) cohorts A and B, both with relatively steeper EGDI trajectories, have TII as the only EGDI component having a significant effect on CPI. Besides TII, governance factors, namely IS, and L&O, are significant for both cohorts, while TO and EP differentiate the two cohorts, (ii) cohorts C and D, both with relatively flat EGDI trajectories have HCI as the only EGDI component having a significant effect on CPI. Besides HCI, IS has a significant effect on CPI for both the cohorts, and (iii) OSI does not have a significant effect on CPI for any of the cohorts. Thus, our findings indicate that the three EGDI components are not uniform in their contribution in lowering corruption. The roles of HCI and TII in lowering corruption assumes significance only under specific contexts, while OSI has no significant effect on CPI.

C. Temporal Analysis of E-GOV Trajectories

In terms of the EGDI trajectory and the relationship between EGDI components and CPI, the four cohorts can be grouped under two broad categories: (i) an unstable transitionary trajectory observed for cohorts A and B, where TII has a significant effect in lowering corruption, and (ii) a stable flat trajectory observed for cohorts C and D, where HCI has a significant effect in lowering corruption. From these observations, we draw short-term E-GOV policy measures for combating corruption. For cohorts with flat trajectories, HCI needs to be given focus in order to lower corruption, whereas

TABLE IV. DESCRIPTIVE STATISTIC OF THE FOUR EGDI TRAJECTORY COHORTS

Cohort	Ave. CPI	Ave. EGDI	Ave. HCI	Ave. TII	Ave. OSI	Ave. IS	Ave. L&O	Ave. APF	Ave. TO	Ave. EP
D	28.89	0.29	0.55	0.08	0.24	-0.61	-0.60	54.10	68.16	1437.98
A	36.29	0.47	0.79	0.21	0.41	-0.10	-0.23	52.51	85.99	7842.92
B	47.47	0.61	0.88	0.40	0.56	0.55	0.38	38.42	89.89	16502.06
C	80.17	0.80	0.94	0.70	0.75	1.69	1.65	18.80	108.96	48621.10
Overall	47.47	0.54	0.80	0.34	0.49	0.36	0.27	41.77	88.63	17904.47

TABLE V. SUMMARY OF PANEL REGRESSION ANALYSIS

Cohort	HCI	TII	OSI	IS	L&O	APF	TO	EP
D	23.061 (***)	ns	ns	4.491 (***)	ns	ns	ns	ns
A	ns	13.368 (***)	ns	9.058 (***)	7.168 (***)	ns	ns	0.0002 (*)
B	ns	9.542 (***)	ns	6.703 (***)	9.375 (***)	ns	0.374 (**)	ns
C	32.046 (***)	ns	ns	10.938 (***)	17.114 (***)	-0.140 (*)	0.031 (***)	ns

*p<0.1; **p<0.05; ***p<0.01; ns: not significant

countries in cohorts where EGDI is transitioning towards mature levels need to prioritize TII in order to lower corruption. As expected, IS has significant effects in lowering corruption for all four cohorts; so overall IS cannot be ignored if corruption control is desired. L&O has a significant role to play only after countries begin the transition, as can be deduced from L&O's insignificance on corruption for cohort D. EP influences corruption only for countries which are at the initial transition stage (cohort A), which highlights the importance of purchasing capacity of citizens to avail the ICT services. For cohorts at higher maturity levels, EP's effect in lowering corruption loses significance. As EGDI levels mature (cohorts B and C), TO and APF, which foster greater transparency in trading practices, as well as information dissemination, start assuming greater importance in lowering corruption.

On a longer term, countries need to plan how they can transition towards cohorts with higher maturity in terms of their EGDI and corruption levels. Although countries need to develop their overall levels for all variables used in this study to gain membership to the next mature cohort, there are certain factors that should receive higher prioritization on a long-term basis as deduced from the panel regression analysis. Accordingly, we have recommended adequate short-term and long-term prioritization of EGDI components, governance and economic factors for each cohort as summarized in Table VI. By focusing on the appropriate factors that have significant effects on corruption, countries could hasten their shift to the next higher mature cohort, while their EGDI strategy being in close alignment with corruption reduction.

TABLE VI. SUMMARY OF RECOMMENDATIONS

Cohort	Short-term Measure	Long-term Measure
D	HCI, IS.	TII, L&O, EP
A	TII, IS, L&O, EP	TO
B	TII, IS, L&O, TO	HCI, APF
C	HCI, IS, L&O, TO, APF	Maintain current levels

V. CONCLUSIONS

The relationship between E-GOV and socio-economic welfare has received major focus in extant research. This line of research helps justify the investments that go into building the requisite infrastructure for E-GOV, and therefore the importance on national E-GOV strategy formulation. Our study also falls in this line of inquiry, where we explore the impact of E-GOV development on corruption, while taking cognizance of associated country level factors, such as IS, L&O, APF, TO and EP. We have found that countries are not homogeneous in their EGDI maturity, and heterogeneity is due to the combined effects of internal capabilities, as well as governance and economic factors. Furthermore, the EGDI components that have significant effects on lowering corruption are different for the different cohorts of countries. So, there is a need for a context-aware prioritization of EGDI components in order to harness the benefits of EGDI in controlling CPI. Towards this, we have derived short-term and long-term E-GOV policy measures, for each of the cohorts, geared towards lowering of corruption, as summarized in Table VI. For instance, let us consider cohort D, which is at the lowest EGDI maturity level primarily due to the absence of adequate capabilities in terms of TII, as well as EP (Table IV). This warrants cohort D to emphasize on TII and EP as part of their long-term policy measures.

Some limitations of this study include unavailability of data for all countries thereby limiting our dataset, and the use of perception-based measures that suffer from subjectivity. Alternative measures could be derived based on the sentiment data mined from social media, or online discussion forums. Our plan for future works goes like this. Additionally, survey instruments capturing perception measures could be administered using these online communities or social media, thus leveraging on new avenues for data collection. We have used the *k*-means longitudinal clustering for grouping the countries. We intend to repeat this work using other clustering methods and compare the results for robustness. Additionally, we wish to further work on uncovering the additional reasons for the decreasing CPI despite increasing EGDI observed for cohort C.

TABLE VII. SUMMARY OF ABBREVIATIONS

Abbreviation	Full form
E-GOV	E-Government
EGDI	E-Government Development Index
CPI	Corruption Perceptions Index
HCI	Human Capital Index
TII	Telecommunications Infrastructure Index
OSI	Online Services Index
SDG	Sustainable Development Goals
UNDP	United Nations Development Programme
ICT	Information and Communication Technologies
HC	Human Capabilities
TI	Telecommunications Infrastructure
OS	Online Services
GE	Government Effectiveness
IS	Institutional Strength
RL	Rule of Law
L&O	Law and Order
APF	Anti Press Freedom
TO	Trade Openness
EP	Economic Prosperity

REFERENCES

[1] N. G. Elbahnasawy, "E-Government, Internet Adoption, and Corruption: An Empirical Investigation," World Dev., vol.

57, 2014, pp. 114–126, doi: 10.1016/j.worlddev.2013.12.005.

[2] United Nations Development Programme, "Sustainable Development Goals," 2018, [Online], Available: http://www.undp.org/content/undp/en/home/sustainable-development-goals.html, [retrieved: January, 2019].

[3] S. Krishnan, T. S. H. Teo, and V. K. G. Lim, "Examining the relationships among e-government maturity , corruption , economic prosperity and environmental degradation : A cross-country analysis," Inf. Manag., vol. 50, 2013, pp. 638–649.

[4] J. C. Bertot, P. T. Jaeger, and J. M. Grimes, "Using ICTs to create a culture of transparency: E-government and social media as openness and anti-corruption tools for societies," Gov. Inf. Q., vol. 27, 2010, pp. 264–271, doi: 10.1016/j.giq.2010.03.001.

[5] S. C. Srivastava, T. S. H. Teo, and S. Devaraj, "You Can't Bribe a Computer: Dealing with the Societal Challenge of Corruption Through ICT," MIS Q., vol. 40, 2016, pp. 511–526.

[6] United Nations Department of Economic and Social Affairs, "United Nations E-Government 2016: E-Government in Support of Sustainable Development," 2016, [Online], Available: http://workspace.unpan.org/sites/Internet/Documents/UNPAN97453.pdf, [retrieved: January, 2019].

[7] Transparency International, "Corruption Perceptions Index 2016," 2017, [Online], Available: https://www.transparency.org/news/feature/corruption_perceptions_index_2016#table, [retrieved: January, 2019].

[8] M.-C. Lio, M.-C. Liu, and Y.-P. Ou, "Can the internet reduce corruption? A cross-country study based on dynamic panel data models," Gov. Inf. Q., vol. 28, 2011, pp. 47–53, doi: 10.1016/j.giq.2010.01.005.

[9] N. Kock and L. Gaskins, "The Mediating Role of Voice and Accountability in the Relationship Between Internet Diffusion and Government Corruption in Latin America and Sub-Saharan Africa," Inf. Technol. Dev., vol. 20, 2014, pp. 23–43, doi: 10.1080/02681102.2013.832129.

[10] H. I. Ergin, "Efficient Resource Allocation on the Basis of Priorities," Econometrica, vol. 70, 2002, pp. 2489–2497, doi: https://doi.org/10.1111/j.1468-0262.2002.00447.x.

[11] T. N. Q. Nguyen, L. V. Ngo, G. Northey, and C. A. Siaw, "Realising the value of knowledge resources and capabilities: an empirical study," J. Knowl. Manag., vol. (in press), doi: 10.1108/ JKM-09-2016-0372.

[12] Y. Wang, L. Kung, W. Y. C. Wang, and C. G. Cegielski, "An integrated big data analytics-enabled transformation model: Application to health care," Inf. Manag., vol. 55, 2018, pp. 64–79, doi: 10.1016/j.im.2017.04.001.

[13] T. Nam, "Examining the anti-corruption effect of e-government and the moderating effect of national culture: A cross-country study," Gov. Inf. Q., vol. 35, 2018, pp. 273–282, doi: 10.1016/j.giq.2018.01.005.

[14] X. Zhao and H. D. Xu, "E-Government and Corruption : A Longitudinal Analysis of Countries," Int. J. Public Adm., vol. 38, 2015, pp. 410–421, doi: 10.1080/01900692.2014.942736.

[15] S. Palvia, A. Anand, P. Seetharaman, and S. Verma, "Imperatives and Challenges in using E- Government to Combat Corruption : A Systematic Review of Literature and a Holistic Model," in *Proceedings of the 23rd Americas Conference on Information Systems, Boston*, 2017, pp. 1–10, Available: https://aisel.aisnet.org/amcis2017/eGovernment/Presentations/9/, [retrieved: January, 2019].

[16] A. Khan and S. Krishnan, "Conceptualizing the impact of corruption in national institutions and national stakeholder service systems on e-government maturity," Int. J. Inf. Manage., vol. 46, 2019, pp. 23–36, doi: 10.1016/j.ijinfomgt.2018.11.014.

[17] The World Bank, "World Development Indicators," 2018, [Online], Available: http://databank.worldbank.org/data/source/world-development-indicators, [retrieved: January, 2019].

[18] Freedom House, "Freedom of the Press," 2018, [Online], Available: https://freedomhouse.org/report/freedom-press/freedom-press-2017, [retrieved: January, 2019].

[19] A. Fahad *et al.*, "A Survey of Clustering Algorithms for Big Data: Taxonomy and Empirical Analysis," IEEE Trans. Emerg. Top. Comput., vol. 2, 2014, pp. 267–279, doi: 10.1109/TETC.2014.2330519.

[20] T. Calinski and J. Harabasz, "A dendrite method for cluster analysis," Commun. Stat., vol. 3:1, 1974, pp. 1–28, doi: 10.1080/03610927408827101.

[21] B. H. Baltagi, Econometric Analysis of Panel Data, 5th Edition. Chichester: John Wiley and Sons., 2013.

One-stop Shop E-government Solution for South-Korean Government Multi-ministry Virtual Employment-Welfare Plus Center System

Sofia Meacham, P.Pratichi Rath, Pritam Moharana, Keith Phalp
Faculty of Science and Technology, Bournemouth University,
Fern Barrow, Poole, Dorset, BH12 5BB, UK
email: smeacham@bournemouth.ac.uk, pratichirath@googlemail.com, pritam.uk@gmail.com, KPhalp@bournemouth.ac.uk

Min Sig Park
Government Complex Seoul of Ministry of the Interior and Safety (MOIS),
Republic of Korea, South Korea
email: minsig@mois.go.kr

Abstract—**In this paper, a one-stop e-Government solution will be proposed for the existing Korean government multi-ministry Employment-Welfare plus system that utilizes latest IT technologies. Since 2001, the Korean government had established 11 initiatives and 31 roadmaps to build e-Government infrastructure. Although this infrastructure has been very successful and well-esteemed in the international society, several improvements are required towards a one-stop shop solution. Currently, the system used by the Korean government is not a one-stop solution with a single point for the citizen to access government services. A Virtual Employment – Welfare Plus Centre (VEWPC) is then introduced to unify the services offered to the citizen. Comparing this VEWS with UK's e-Government solution and review of corresponding literature, several requirements for change towards a one-stop shop solution implementation have been identified. A refined architecture to implement a South Korean e-Government one-stop shop is identified and proposed in this paper. Future plans for the applicability and cost of its adoption are also identified.**

Keywords; e-Government; virtual organizations; one-stop shop.

I. INTRODUCTION

Described simply, e-Government is the application of the tools and techniques of e-Commerce to the work of government. These tools and techniques are intended to serve both the government and its citizens. It can also be described as the complete process transformation of the Governance using the implementation of Information and Communication Technology. Its primary objective is to bring faster and transparent service delivery, information sharing, accountability and people participation in governments' decision-making process [1].

After the economic crisis in 1998, over the past 20 years, the South Korea government is continuously engaged in reforming the government structure by integrating large departments performing similar public service functions. This has led to building up an e-government structure providing improved administrative services with better efficiency.

Since 2002, with the help of ICT functions, an online platform in the form of the one-stop shop is established to make numerous public services easily accessible through the website "Government 24". This online service allows citizens to request and receive many civil petitions without having to visit administrative agencies [2].

The current structure of the South Korean Government welfare service system and functions of its different building blocks are greatly influenced by New Public Management (NPM) and Joined-up Government (JUG) organization structure by integrating multiple ministerial departments to provide a single platform based public services. This presents both problems and challenges to form a collaborated system to combine the employment and welfare services under a virtual organizational platform [3].

Based on the data collected in previous case studies, literature review and comparative analysis along with the results from the interviews and surveys, it is possible to draw the architecture of the current system to distinguish between the key elements and considerations necessary to design the architecture of the one-stop shop center.

Finally, based on this high-level architecture description, it can be concluded that the one-stop shop virtual government organization is a conceptual model of the manpower management system that utilizes business process data in the information system.

In this paper, we have viewed the high-level architecture as a three-layered functional architecture in order to elaborate the different infrastructural functions: layer one the customer, layer two local welfare service centres and layer three as the virtual environment of the ICT infrastructure with integration of e-Governance policy.

However, this can possess both limitations and challenges to implement conceptualized architecture using multi ministerial policies. Therefore, a comprehensive evaluation and further research are required to this paper in the areas of producing a detailed collaboration model for the above system.

The remainder of this paper will cover an overview of the system, including its requirements, in Section 2. In Section 3, the designs of the system will be defined and presented. Section 4 will detail the implementation of the overall system, including the classifier, interfaces, and explainability. Section 5 will present reflections and evaluations of the system, and Section 6 offers conclusion and suggestions for future work and research directions.

II. E-GOVERNMENT EVOLUTION IN SOUTH KOREAN GOVERNMENT

This case study has been constructed in a collaborative project between South Korea Government Department and Bournemouth University. The main aim is to propose improvements in the existing South Korea Government business processes and infrastructures.

The evolution of e-government implementations within the South Korean Government ministries is briefly described in the following subsections.

A. *Service-Centred Government Policy*

After the economic crisis in 1998, over the past 30 years, South Korea government is continuously engaged in reforming the government structure by integrating large departments performing similar public service functions. This has led to building up an e-government structure providing improved administrative services with better efficiency. Since 2002, with the help of ICT functions, an online platform is established to make numerous public services easily accessible through the website "Government 24". This online service allows citizens to request and receive many civil petitions without having to visit administrative agencies.

South Korea Government has implemented a 3.0 strategy in the form of 'Government 3.0' in 2013 [4], to integrate the administrative services provided by the various administrative agencies into one window, and the provision of these services is well appreciated by the public. The main elements of this strategy were based upon (i) to set-up and promote an administrative reform in the form of the e-government, (ii) open information on all administrative agencies and (iii) collaborate and share information between administrative agencies. This strategy eventually has led to the formation of the 'Employment Welfare Plus Centre', which handles the employment and welfare related public services that have been carried out in various institutions autonomously.

B. *The Level of e-government*

In 2001, the Korean government had established 11 initiatives and 31 roadmaps to build e-government infrastructure. These initiatives include 11 systems, with an online administrative service system, an electronic procurement system, a financial information system, a home text system, and an electronic approval document system. The roadmaps include improved governments' working methodology, innovating administrative services and innovating information resource management.

In [5] presents the Government 24 online portal providing public services, such as apply and print official documents using the internet from home or offices, without a need of visiting the government agencies. It uses the cloud-based Government Integrated Data Centres (GIDC) gateway comprising of 20,000 information systems from 44 ministries. The cloud system has proprietary government-private cloud services that could provide central government agencies with information resources quickly and efficiently to support government agencies' smart service. With the advent of ICTs and integrated government services, South Korea is implementing a 'smart government' in which ordinary users can easily and freely access government services regardless of delivery channels.

Based on these achievements, Korean e-Government ranked No. 1 in the E-Government Development Index (EGD) and E-Participation Index in the United Nations Global E-Government Survey for 2010, 2012 and 2014 [6]. Therefore, Korean e-governmental effectiveness is widely recognized in the international society and a similar range of e-government systems are being introduced to developing countries [2].

C. *Workforce Management Strategy and Public Body Reform*

As part of the reformed South Korea government, Ministry of the Interior and Safety (hereafter MOIS) is responsible for the manpower management, through setting up an upper threshold for a total number of employment and operating the manpower demand within that threshold. The review of the workforce for legal amendments and manpower threshold for upcoming projects in the coming years is assessed by the MOIS and confirmed with the Ministry of Strategy and Finance (hereafter, MOSF) every year. Ministry of Personnel Management (hereafter, MPM) administers the recruitment, independence, and professionalism of the personnel workforce.

III. EMPLOYMENT-WELFARE PLUS CENTRE (EWPC) – ONE-STOP SHOP SOLUTION

To introduce the implementation of JUG and NPM concept, the South Korean government has formed Employment - Welfare Plus Centre (EWPC) that links employment services and welfare services to alleviate the budget burden caused by the surge in welfare costs in 2014.

A. *EWPC Managers and staff*

The Employment - Welfare Plus Centre is an administrative service delivery system that eliminates blind spots in employment and allows the social safety net to be linked to employment. EWPC has been established in more than 100 geographically distributed centres, between 2014 and 2017, depicting the one-stop shop model that provides a combination of employment, welfare and financial services to the public easily and comfortably.

B. EWPC Architecture

The implementation of EWPC is modeled in two ways, first by adding welfare-related services to the existing employment centres and second by creating the new centres with linked welfare and employment-related public service.

EPWCs are affiliated to the Ministry of Employment and Labor, they are controlled and monitored by employees from the ministries and agencies related to employment and welfare policies [7]. Thereby, the centre is subdivided into employment, welfare support, finance, and culture departments and other welfare-related functions [8]. The centres' management consultation is done by the steering committee and the complex employment welfare case (if any) is managed by the Working Group and the Case Management Group.

Figure 1 presents the typical architecture for Employment-Welfare Plus Centre.

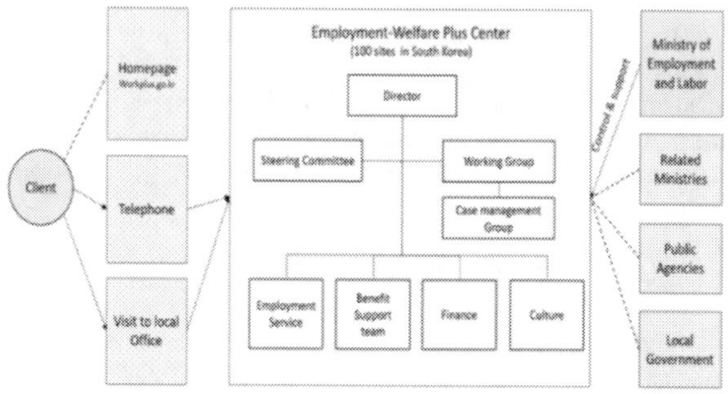

Figure 1. Architecture for Employment-Welfare Plus Centre

An individual seeking the government services should be able to find the relevant information using the online portal (Workplus.go.kr), then call further to gain information or visit the EWPC in person for an additional consultation [9].

Also, there is a separate online portal (Work.gov.kr) on job searching and job advertising for job seekers, which is not connected to EPWC. This is the problem with not having a true one-stop shop where employment-related services are integrated into one platform.

C. EWPC Functions and Clients

The main functions offered by the EWPC to their various clients including job seekers, benefit seekers, women with career break, veteran soldiers, retirees, and low-income earners are as follows:

(i) *Employment services*: Provides comprehensive employment services such as job-hunting and re-employment support to help the livelihood of the unemployed, employment stabilization project supporting job creation and vulnerable classes.

(ii) *Training services:* Provides employment support services for job seekers (interview technical coaching, cooperative interviews, etc.), job search, recruitment events, etc.

(iii) *Women with career break:* Provides job counseling, vocational education and training, and internship for women with career breaks.

(iv) *Services for veteran soldiers:* Supports career counseling, employment and start-up support for soldiers who have completed long-term service.

(v) *Benefit support services:* Provides counseling social welfare services, receiving welfare applications, linking public and private for welfare support.

(vi) *Finance Support Services:* Provides services such as low-interest funds, credit recovery support, and illegal financial meltdown counselling services for ordinary people, small businessmen and low-income people who are experiencing economic difficulties [8].

D. EWPC Business Process

Based on the type of the required public services, the main functions of the Employment Welfare Plus Centre can be categorized as follows:

(i) *Employment Services:* Available for clients who are unemployed and do not require any welfare services

(ii) *Employment and Welfare Services:* Available for clients who are unemployed and require welfare services as well, such as housing benefits, low-income support etc.

(iii) *Welfare Services:* Available for clients who are able to work, however, requires other forms of welfare services. They also receive the employment services [8].

The list below describes the business process flow for availing different types of services in the EWPC, in its current state: client seeking employment or welfare public services can do so by, (i) visiting the centre directly, (ii) receiving an initial interview on employment services, welfare services only or both the services, (iii) deciding and implementing a suitable service. Record of these activities is stored in the local information database.

E. EWPC Performance

After the implementation of the EWPC, in 2016, there are remarkable improvements in public welfare services to the client such as:

(i) The number of employed workers per centre increased from 653 to 731, an increase of 12%.

(ii) Employment-welfare services linkage per centre increased from 118 to 212 [8].

(iii) Different service paths are set for clients seeking an initial consultation, giving the benefit of availing employment services in more than one field within the visit to the centre.

(iv) Reduction of time and cost by not visiting more than one service centres.

(v) The collaboration of organizations to solve clients' problem by not only taking their own problem but also, by taking into account their surrounding circumstances.

The EWPC is expanded quantitatively to 100 centres within three years of introducing the system, however, the gap in the service quality is huge due to a large variation in workloads in each region and lack of legal platform as a government organization.

The above information was provided and evidenced by one the authors- Min Sig Park through confidential performance information collected from South Korea Government Ministry of the Interior and Safety (MOIS) where he is the director.

There is a need to increase manpower as the physical integration and expansion of the centre is steadily increasing. In addition, there is segregation of work due to the operation of a separate government system internally by dispatching agencies. The current integrated service on employment and welfare is to achieve the original purpose, that is expanding the employment rate and saving the cost of welfare. Therefore, it needs innovation of the operating system for the present centre by utilizing IT.

F. Problems Areas in Employment Welfare Service System-Comparison with UK's system

This section presents a comprehensive comparison between the Korea Employment Welfare Service System with the corresponding UK system. The choice for the comparison was by the definition of the project as the Korean Government representative who is an author in this paper, Min Sig Park, was tasked to start an appropriate study comparing the two countries to start with from his Government employer. More countries and examples should be considered in future research.

Both countries used the e-government architectural concept to establish and promote national government reforms by adopting a top-down approach. The innovations are prioritized in areas directly affecting people's lives. In both countries, recent administrative reforms trends are being pursued in the form of an open government using data and digital technology.

Compared to the UK, Korea has lack of interconnectedness and consistency between national plans for government innovations. There is not enough and specific systematic approach towards offering the consultation to government officials who are promoting government innovations and/or related guidelines that the public officials should pursue.

Both countries are evaluated as e-government powerhouse by the international community to provide one-stop service to the people using government portal viz, GOV.UK for UK and Government 24 for Korea. The UK has continued its efforts to build an e-government centred on the integration of the people's services through the council. However, South Korea has pursued e-government centred on building service systems and data centres. Therefore, the UK has established GOV.UK as a national government gateway to provide a single administrative service, however, South Korea is providing services through Government 24, which is a representative government gateway.

In terms of the workforce management, both countries require to consult with the financial authorities when they increase the government workforce. The two countries have established a long-term plan for government personnel and carrying out planned and systematic workforce policies. In the UK, government organizations and manpower management are managed by the Cabinet Office. However, in South Korea, the Ministry of the Interior and Safety oversees organization and manpower management, while the Ministry of Personnel Management is in charge of human resources development such as recruitment of manpower. Unlike the UK, which is reducing its workforce by establishing and implementing a workforce reduction plan, South Korea is restricting workforce growth by adopting a quorum system to maintain the upper limit of the workforce.

In terms of the organizational architecture of the e-government system and business processes, both countries use face-to-face interviews as the primary medium to converse with their clients due to the nature of the public services offered. However, Korea does not have an online system for a remote application like the UK where online applications can be made through GOV.UK which is the governments' single gateway.

The UK is well structured in partnership with local government, local communities, employers, and so on. In the case of Korea, the centre staff is dispatched to the relevant ministries, local government, and related organizations to collaborate. The UK is integrated with the job search website GOV.UK, but the Korean Worknet operates independently of the centre.

Typically, the clients in both countries organization system are either unemployed or like to seek other benefits. The clients for Jobcentre Plus in the UK are job seekers, students, graduates, and the disabled people, however, the clients of Employment Welfare Plus Centre in South Korea are job seekers, women with career interruptions, retirees, veterans, disabled people, and social disadvantage. In the UK, the benefits are directly implemented because the benefits agencies are integrated into the early stages. However, the Korean centre only enforces employment-related benefits directly, and the benefit only functions in consultation and acceptance.

In terms of business processes, both organizations are conducting face-to-face interviews for the initial assessment and conducting job search programs for job seekers with benefits. The UK provides consultation and employment welfare services through the integrated government gateway GOV.UK, telephone, and visit, whereas, South Korea has the drawback of not having an integrated online gateway but provides counseling and employment welfare services through telephone or institution visits. The client seeking unemployment benefit needs to go through initial interviews, however, in South Korea, an unemployed client does not need to go through the initial interviews. In the UK centre, professional counselors as a work coach are in the process of customizing their work. However, South Korea Centre is engaged in consultation with employees dispatched from ministries related to employment counseling.

In terms of the performance, the UK centres are making a visible contribution to reducing unemployment benefits and increasing labour supply. There are direct and indirect effects on saving the welfare budget and increasing the national treasury. In South Korea, it is estimated that outcome will take time because the centre has been in operation for only three years.

The below is the summary of the main problem areas in the current South Korea Welfare System:

(i) lack of connectivity between national strategies
(ii) single gateway does not fully integrate to online service level
(iii) workforce management using information management is not available
(iv) no one-stop shop for employment welfare services
(v) no linkage or integration with government 24, the government gateway
(vi) a high proportion of manual work processes
no visibility on the performance

IV. SURVEY WITH KOREAN GOVERNMENT EMPLOYEES AND MANAGERS

This paper uses in-depth interviews and focus group interviews among various qualitative research methods to obtain user's requirements. These interviews were conducted online and in person by Min Sig Park as part of his role in the Korean Government and as part of the research project with Bournemouth University in order to provide a comprehensive analysis of an e-government solution for South Korea Government. Since, VEWPC is an information system that processes the current business process, business management, and manpower management in a virtual space. Thus, to understand the system better, in-depth interviews are required including MOIS mid-level managers and staff who manages government organizations and personnel in off-line activities [10]. In addition, focus group interviews were conducted in order to grasp the various requirements of the staff working at the site. All the interviews were recorded with the consent of the interviewee. This survey uses an open questionnaire to identify the diverse experiences and opinions of the interviewees.

The following section describes the results without incorporating the authors' related research. The final proposed system in this paper, incorporates all elements from the survey and the research.

A. *Survey Findings*

a) EWPC Supervisors and Employees

The results are extracted from the survey conducted by the Ministry of Employment and Labor departments, as part of the "Development Plan for the EWPC" projects. This describes three aspects of service linkage, manpower management and information system operation.

TABLE 1. EWPC SUPERVISORS AND EMPLOYEES SURVEY RESULTS

Service Linkage Aspect	Due to the reorganization of the employment centers into employment and welfare centers, the main clients of the center are the unemployment seekers. The lack of integration between the welfare and unemployment services brings diversity and complexity to the centre, which leads to poor services
Personnel Management Aspect	As a result of the employment and welfare linkage there is a surge in workforce requirement demanding new workers to cater the service demands. Centers vary in workload, workforce composition, service objects and jurisdictions leading to difficulty in coordinating work among internal employees.
Information System Operation Aspect	Due to the separated information system of employment and welfare services, it is difficult to compare, collaborate and share information of employees resulting in data redundancy and administrative inefficiency. This possesses one of the major concerns for the development of employment and welfare linked services.

b) Workforce management

The summary of the results listed below are extracted from the survey conducted with the employee responsible for workforce management across the centers.

TABLE 2 – EWPC MANAGERS AND STAFF SURVEY RESULTS

Information systems operation status	Most of the staff supported the idea of using information system for workforce management and management of the organization. This consists of workload information, staffing information and accuracy of data around that information. However, due to lack of integrated infrastructure and difficulties of collecting those data, most employees are not actively utilizing the information data.
Workforce analysis functions	Staff agreed that the annual workload prediction and work assignments are important in the calculation of manpower to identify the annual workload trend. Besides, analysis based on the accurate identification of

	the current workload and manpower problems are equally important.
Factors and benefits while introducing the new system	Many of the interviewees agreed for the implementation of the virtual government organization concept, but there can be unforeseen side effects due to the emergence of this fictitious virtual organization. The consideration of many factors is vital such as information security, details of comprehensive services and consideration for vulnerable groups accessing those data. However, the introduction of this virtual system can create new services beyond the existing business domain, communication between employees can be greatly improved along with proper organization management.

The above surveys led to the realization that an IT integration through a new virtual organization approach was emerging within the South-Korean government.

V. Virtual Employment-Welfare Plus Center (VEWPC) System

The employment welfare service system is not a simple interorganizational collaboration system but a virtual service that is built around a multi-ministry collaboration system to combine employment and welfare services to provide fast and personalized employment-welfare services. In addition, it presents a model to develop an organization and workforce management system for efficient management of the organization and employees related to the employment-welfare service.

A. *VEWPC Architecture – Functional Requirements*

The architecture supports the model to build a collaborative system using the virtual space to provide employment-welfare services that are performed jointly by multiple ministries. The intended users and audience of this architecture can be categorized into two parts. The first categories are the users and audiences related to the collaboration system comprising of government officials and supervisors who provide employment-welfare services. It also includes unemployed customers seeking the employment- welfare services. Second category of users are the users of the organization and the employee's management system related to the employment-welfare service. This includes the managers managing the relevant ministry officials providing the employment-welfare services. In addition, government officials in related ministries can also be seen as users because they need to update matters related to their duties.

The stakeholders of the virtual employment-welfare plus center are the various sponsors, customers, and users. The sponsors include the Ministries of Employment and Labour (MOEL) in South Korea and the Ministry of the Interior and Safety (MOIS) which is in charge of the management of government organizations and employees. The customers are the people seeking support in terms of employment and welfare public services from the government. Finally, the users are employees and staff who work for MOEL and MOIS [10].

The VEWPC is a collaborative system built by integrated online employment-welfare service to manage the workforce efficiently. In addition, it identifies the number and workload of the employees who are using the existing information system and utilize it in the management of the workforce using the newly developed information system.

The section below discusses the architecture of the Korean Virtual Employment-Welfare architecture and the business process flow associated with it.

The center consists of an online platform (web portal), employment-welfare service system, workforce management system and the related seven support systems. The customers seeking unemployment support services or welfare services, get support from this center through the portal. Then, after going through an initial assessment and database cross-check of seven administrative agencies the center evaluates customers' current situation, needs and comes to a decision of providing the support to that customer. The Workforce Management System comprehensively analyses the operational speed and performance of the ministries and agencies that operate to support the virtual center. The system also helps managers to determine the relocation, reinforcement and reduction of workforce.

Figure 2 shows the database diagram for the Virtual Employment-Welfare Plus Centre. The main frame of the databases is made up of two parts. One of the databases (DB) stores information related to the welfare services and another one stores workforce management related information. The employment-welfare service server is composed of employment information DB, local job DB, woman's re-employment DB, veteran employment DB, local welfare DB, microfinance DB, and self-sufficiency DB. Also, the workforce management server consists of personnel management DB, system metadata DB, payroll DB, organization and workforce DB, individual business record DB, and user profile DB.

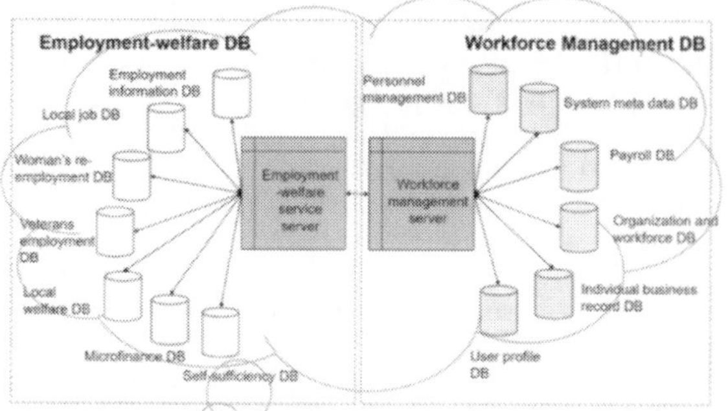

Figure 2. Database Model for the Virtual Employment-Welfare Pulse Centre

The process flow as the use cases represent in providing the public service can be described as follows:

1) the system receives enquiries seeking employment and welfare support from a citizen, 2) the inquiries are cross-checked by the employees of multi-ministries or agencies in government, 3) the employee decides and provide a suitable solution based on the decision, 4) the system record individual business performance, 5) the system analyses relationship between workforce and workload, 7) the administrative staff determine which action is appropriate based on the workload demand, 8) the administrative staff and managers take suitable actions to re-deploy, increase and reduce workforce accordingly.

In this arrangement, the citizen creates a personal account to use the public service. The actors are the citizens requesting employment and welfare public services from the government. The requests can be directly made via the online portal or by visiting the service center or by sending a letter. The employees enter the request details manually into the system. The employees do not work in one center but work individually in different ministries, responsible for different tasks. The meetings with customers and reporting activities are not automatically managed by the system.

One of the functional requirement of the system is to monitor the business process of employment-welfare service and employee's workload 24/7 to identify the processing time it takes to handle inquiries and be able to support flexible working hours for the employees.

B. *VEWPC Non-Functional Requirements*

The non-functional requirements, which can be implemented as improvement areas to realize a true one-stop shop virtual employment-welfare service system are shown below:

Usability and humanity requirements: The system should consider the work process, results, and working style of the employees. In addition, the system should be designed with usability heuristics in mind.

Performance requirements: The system should measure the individual workloads and the workload of the organization. It should also be able to calculate the manpower demands based on criteria set by the workforce policy standards.

Operational and environmental requirements: The system should have an integrated web portal and easy to use a mobile app for employees to enter the business progress remotely from an off-site location. The working times can be set for this remote working arrangement.

Maintainability and support requirements: The system should provide real-time information about new appointments and retirements of employees.

Security requirements. The system should include employees' personal and business performance information along with employees' task schedule information as workload changes. Therefore, managers and employees should have different access rights to this sensitive information.

Cultural requirements. The system should be customized based on the way of working such as, administrative policies and regulations, administrative culture etc.

Legal requirements. Government organizations should limit the basic rights of the people or impose obligations on them, so the establishment of the government in a virtual environment should be done carefully. This should be examined together with the implications of legal issues and public confidence in government organizations.

C. *VEWPC Architecture Modeling*

Based on the literature reviews and the specific case study requirements, we have transformed the existing Virtual Employment-Welfare System architecture into SysML Block Definition Diagram. Although SysML is not the traditionally used formalism for business processes, we have selected this in order to integrate the business processes world with the corresponding systems architectures. More diagrams from this project towards a completed model-based approach will be part of our future plans. This can help to prototype the model for one-stop shop based solution architecture. Due to the limitation of accessing the government technical information, Figure 3 is an approximate view of the existing architecture

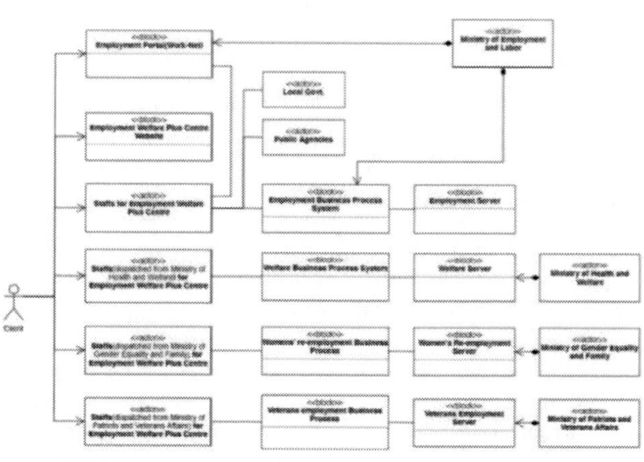

Figure 3. Block Definition Diagram for Korea Virtual Employment-Welfare Plus Center

As mentioned in the earlier section, in South Korea, the integrated information system has not yet implemented except for the *Work-Net* online platform for customers seeking employment services established by the Ministry of Employment and Labor. This *Work-Net* is not an exclusive business process information system of the EWPC, but an employment portal operated by the Ministry of Employment and Labor.

The inquiries submitted by the client are handled by the staff dispatched by the related ministries. The tasks are carried out by using the existing information infrastructure of their respective departments. This is the drawback of lack of integration of the information system between different ministerial departments and business processes, although, the work gets carried out at an integrated place. This demands to design a new model for a true one-stop shop virtual employment and welfare service system.

VI. PROPOSED ONE-STOP SHOP ARCHITECTURE

The architecture of the one-stop e-government, the virtual government organization in the public sector, is similar to the one-stop shop architecture described above.

The generic model of one-stop e-government, presented by [11], is based on a client-centered approach, concurrent access point, channel multiplicity, versatility, and security. Alo, Liu described that the model of one-stop e-government comprises of integration of information resources, system-based application construction and infrastructure construction [12].

Figure 5 shows the prototype architecture for one-stop shop Employment and Welfare Plus Center in South Korea based on the previous literature review of Liu and Dias & Rafeal, the comparative analysis results of the UK and Korea and the results of the survey.

In 2005, the South Korea has integrated servers of 44 central government ministries and local governments. Recently, G-Cloud has been introduced to optimize data management, analysis and services, and to protect data resources from the hacking. Thereby, the South Korean government needs a foundation for the information resource infrastructure and resource integration needed to build a one-stop shop.

Thereafter, the reorganization of the back office is required to build a one-stop shop, which is not yet done. Also, it is necessary to integrate work processes using information systems and collaborations of related ministries and agencies to provide employment welfare services. Therefore, it is designed that the government officials of each ministry or agency access the Employment-welfare service system through the platform that handles the inquiry related to employment welfare. A data exchange system should be designed separately to exchange data between existing related information systems. With the help of business process integration, it is possible to process work from a distance which provides the less expected number of employees required at the center.

The customers who need employment welfare services should access the platform and submit an inquiry once, and then the Employment-welfare service system and related public officials should be able to process the inquiry. The information system then automatically handles the tasks that are handled manually, and the center staff only needs to perform the face-to-face meeting with clients in a complementary manner.

Finally, all the work processes and performance are managed by the workforce management system. If necessary, it can reallocate the work and personnel to increase or decrease the manpower.

Figure 4 shows the high level of architecture in more detail and allows for the construction of a customized regional center that reflects regional characteristics. This architecture includes a detailed server deployment plan which has improved the efficiency of data management by providing a regional server (database) under the main sector server. In addition, to implement the customized one-stop shop as a virtual governmental organization, a Virtual Online Window is integrated into the existing Work-Net and GOV.KR.

"LAYERED" PROPOSED ARCHITECTURE

The proposed architecture for the one stop shop Employment and Welfare system can be represented as three-layered high-level architecture. In this section, we discuss each of these sections with a view to integrate and consolidate the information data for easier workflow and knowledge management.

The first layer of this architecture depicts the citizen seeking the welfare support services should access the online platform and submit the inquiry. To implement the customized one-stop shop as a virtual governmental organization, the primary step is to integrate the Virtual Online platform with the official portal of the South Korean Government. This portal provides public services [5], an employment portal operated by the Ministry of Employment & Labor (Work-Net), telephone consultation services and employment & welfare hub.

The second layer presents the Employment Welfare Plus Centre architecture. For instance, if the client seeking employment, welfare or both services are unable to find the required information and avail the services using the online

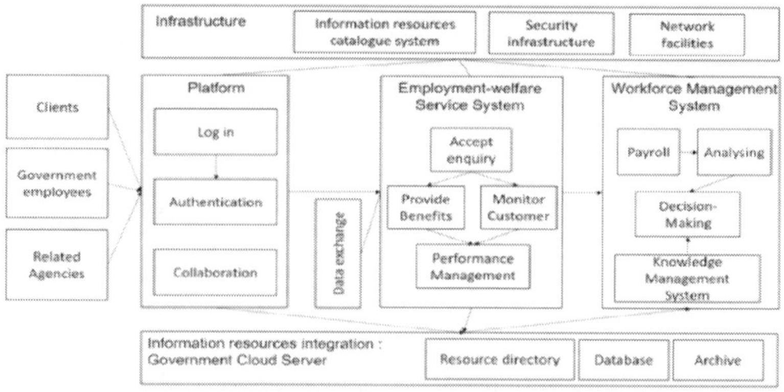

Figure 4. Conceptual Architecture of one-stop shop.

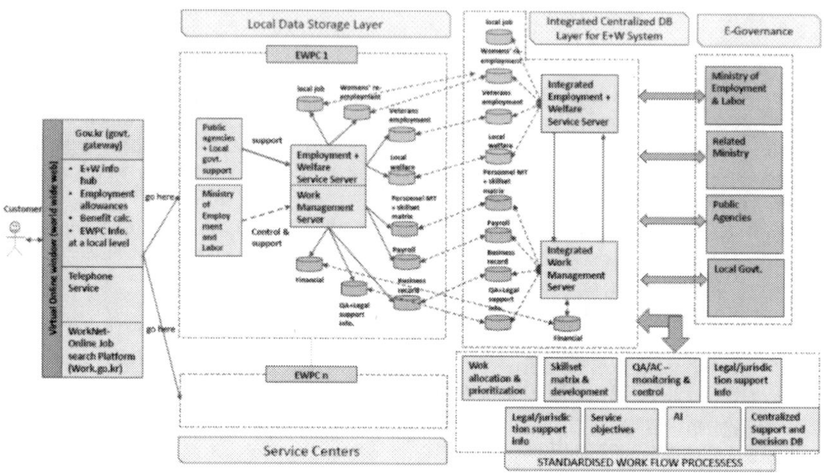

Figure 5. The Architecture of one-stop shop.

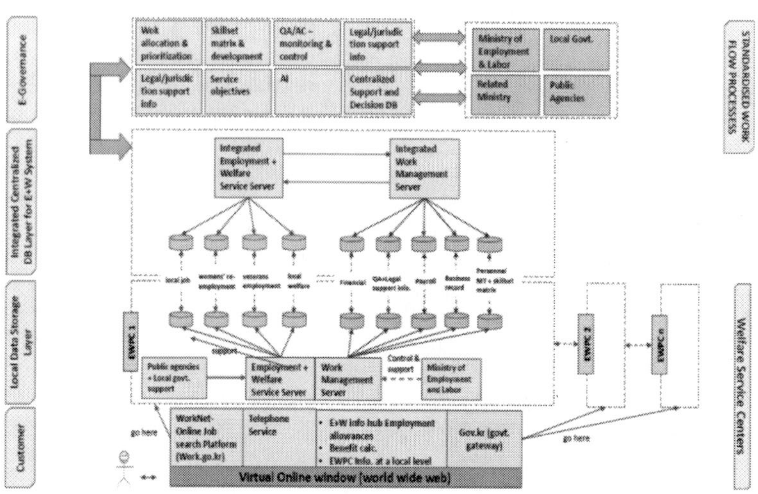

Figure 6. Intention-Based Design for one-stop shop Conceptual Architecture.

web portal information hub and telephone services are required to visit the walk-in welfare-employment center. An inquiry submitted by the client is checked and accepted by the Inquiry Process Department. Following to this, the client seeking employment services is required to attend an initial interview with the government employee consultants available at the centre. Once, the enquiry acceptance, processing and validation are completed, a suitable employment service is decided and implemented to the client's inquiry.

An unemployed person who seeks a welfare service receives an employment service can also avail the welfare benefits. However, there is an option where an unemployed person can choose to take the employment service only by opting-out the welfare services. In contrast to this, welfare service recipients can receive both welfare and employment services, if they have a valid working ability, otherwise can only choose to avail welfare services.

After a certain period of time, the client is required to visit the local walk-in centre for further consultation to evaluate the status of the provided services and eligibility criteria associated with the initial inquiry. Furthermore, a check is required to identify if there is any change of circumstances since the recording of the last update. If there is no change in personal circumstances and the eligibility criteria are met, then the provision of the services is also continued. In the instance where there is a change, then the client is advised for an in-centre consultation to re-evaluate and check if the eligibility criteria are met or not and accordingly to avail the services.

Information related to eligibility criteria, provided services, decisions and any special notes are stored in centers' local Employment & Welfare Service Server Database against the unique ID.

Information related to financial data such as employees' payroll, business record, personal skillset matrix is stored in the localized Work Management Server. Databases in various Employment Welfare Plus Centres are located in many geographically dispersed locations.

These information data are integrated into centralized server system, creating the 3rd layer of the proposed high-level architecture. Here, we would propose a federated or hybrid technology or similar for efficiency, scalability and security as well as service-oriented architecture implementations. This is to be further investigated in future studies.

Centralized database not only acts as an information storage system but also a platform for decision making and governance for policies and regulation. These policies and directives will be adopted from different ministries which are responsible for providing the services and its functional operation. Thus, creating a true one-stop architecture which can be easily and efficiently managed and controlled.

The following points describe the main components that are catered to by the database:

- An integrated hub for policies, directives and regulation governed by different ministries, localized public agencies, local government and ministry of employment and labor
- Support and decision-making process for legal and jurisdiction compliance
- An integrated workforce management system facilitating: work allocation and prioritization, employee skillset evaluation and development program, service levels classifications and monitoring, QA/QC monitoring and control
- Archive of information

VII. Conclusion

In this paper, we have presented a virtual organization solution by introducing a one-stop shop solution to the Korean government case study. The required collaboration model presented by the Korean government case study is very complicated as it involves several ministries and models of collaboration and therefore a Virtual Organization (VO) approach is required that will take into account all contributing factors. In this paper, an initial conceptual model of the proposed architecture has been proposed.

In the proposed architecture, a hybrid approach that combines centralized and localized information storage and handling decision making has been followed. Despite the main requirement for a centralized VO approach, it has been proposed that a major part of the data processing and decision-making stays at the local level, therefore, leading to a hybrid architectural model. This optimizes the overall decision-making process by assigning to the local resources for data processing and storage, while, the complex decision making, involving multi-ministerial policies and related influences is handled by the centralized e-Governance layer. This has been tailored to the specific case study requirements in order to optimally solve South Korea Government e-government requirements.

The work was evaluated through feedback from Korea Government as was submitted to the Ministry of Interior and Design for evaluation as the outcome of the collaborative project with Bournemouth University. According to this feedback the virtual organization approach of the proposed architecture would add a major advantage to the existing structure. It would provide a simplified and faster model of decision making led by an integrated & centralized e-Governance policy platform (VO solution).

Initial draft cost analysis was also performed which demonstrated that this was a beneficial solution which required medium and feasible investment. This particular solution was preferred comparing to riskier alternatives which incorporated, for example, block-chain solutions and were also proposed and discussed during the project.

Future plans also include the design development of a complete model-based approach using SysML and other formalisms in order to incorporate the business processes and virtual organizations' requirements with system architecture descriptions. In this work, we have started from a high-level description of the problem and the proposed architecture. In order to proceed with the implementation of such a complex architecture, a top-down model-based approach has been identified as a requirement that will incorporate business logic with IT. For the time being, the SysML language has been identified a standard and more accepted platform both requirements and solutions.

Although there are several steps required until the successful conclusion of this study, the initial feedback from the South Korean government is encouraging and promising for the adoption of Virtual Organization approaches in real-world applications.

REFERENCES

[1] Mogaha, "Government of Koreae Best Practices," Seoul: Ministry of Government Administration and Home Affairs in South Korea, 2016.

[2] M. Howard, "E-government across the globe: How will "e" change government?" e-Government 2001, 90, 80.

[3] C. S. Chung, "The Introduction of e-Government in Korea: Development Journey, Outcomes and Future1," Revue Gestion et Management Public , vol. 3, no. 4, pp. 107-122, 2015.

[4] S. G. Lim, "Achievement and Challenges of Government 3.0:. 2015-34 ed. Seoul: Korea Institute of Public Administration," 2015.

[5] Government 24 online portal. [Online] Available from: www.gov.kr/portal/main [Accessed 30 5 2018].

[6] United Nations DESA, *UNITED NATIONS E-GOVERNMENT SURVEY 2014 E-Government for the Future We Want, New York: the United Nations.* [Online] Available from: https://publicadministration.un.org/egovkb/portals/egovkb/documents/un/2014-survey/e-gov_complete_survey-2014.pdf [Accessed 13 01 2019].

[7] MOEL, *Ministry of Employment and Labor in South Korea.* [Online] Available from: https://www.moel.go.kr/english/main.jsp [Accessed 26 5 2018].

[8] Employment Welfare Plus Center in South Korea, *Emplyment Welfare Plus Center.* [Online] Available from: http://workplus.go.kr/index.do [Accessed 29 5 2018].

[9] Korea Employment Information Service, *Worknet.* [Online] Available from: http://www.work.go.kr/seekWantedMain.do [Accessed 30 5 2018].

[10] MOIS, *Ministry of the Interior and Safety.* [Online] Available from: http://www.mois.go.kr/eng/a01/engMain.do [Accessed 26 5 2018].

[11] G. P. Dias and J. A., Rafael, "A simple model and a distributed architecture for realizing one-stop e-government," Electronic Commerce Research and Applications, vol. 6, no. 1, pp. 81-90, 2007.

[12] H. Liu, "Model and architecture of one-stop government system: A solution of systemic interoperability," In Information Management, Innovation Management and Industrial Engineering (ICIII), 2013 6th International Conference, vol. 1, pp. 75-79, 2013.

Digital Interactions Strategy: A Public Sector Case

Samantha Papavasiliou and Carmen Reaiche
Entrepreneurship, Commercialisation and Innovation Centre (ECIC)
University of Adelaide,
Adelaide, Australia
e-mail: samantha.papavasiliou@adelaide.edu.au, carmen.reaiche@adelaide.edu.au

Peter Ricci
Data Science
Australian Taxation Office (ATO),
Adelaide, Australia
e-mail: peter.ricci@ato.gov.au

Abstract— **The public sector's role as mandatory service provider is to produce effective services for users, and to make compliance uncomplicated and straightforward. However, at present, public sector services appear to not meet these user expectations. The purpose of this research is to explore ways to enhance digital adoption in the public sector by further understanding who these users are, when and why they seek assistance, and the various potential outcomes post-assistance. Evidence to support this research will be provided via a case study from the Australian Taxation Office. This research project will be presented in three sections. Firstly, the researchers describe a conceptual model they have created, which places the user at the centre of the research and policy direction. Secondly, results and some critical findings will be presented, of a pilot study which was conducted to test the model on a small scale. Thirdly, the researchers will outline planned extended research which proposes to validate the pilot findings and explore the service users in greater detail. The extended research utilises additional demographic data to better understand the greater system dynamics. This research is ongoing and forms part of a PhD dissertation.**

Keywords- Mandatory Systems; Digital Service; Digital Ecosystems.

I. INTRODUCTION

Increasing digital service adoption and the provision of a better digital client experience is vital to any successful government digital service platform. To achieve this success, research needs to identify and understand the users, including understanding why users seek assistance, and leverage points to maximise the users' capacity to complete their interaction. A recent study conducted by the Australian Digital Transformation Office [1] suggests that there is evidence that further research is required to address how to maximise digital service adoption. Improved understanding of issues users may have with specific public sector digital services has become increasingly important in Australia, with changes to service provision from in-person/call centre to digital. This research seeks to address knowledge gaps regarding who the users are, why they need assistance and where self-service assistance can be provided. This research will be based on a case study conducted by the Australian Taxation Office (ATO). Through consultation with the ATO staff and examining company and academic literature, a clear gap was identified between what was known about mandatory digital service use and the users required to use them. Currently, standard methods for evaluating government services include interviewing or surveying users about services provided. This often results in biased results, as users often display expected behaviours [2]-[4]. Accordingly, research thus far has ignored a multitude of factors that impact adoption, and failed to identify barriers to adoption within a mandatory environment, and how different experiences with digital services can impact long-term adoption and when and why users seek assistance.

The creation of the Digital Continuity Policy 2020 mandated digital first platforms for all public sector services [5], causing significant challenges to service providers and users. For the purposes of this research, mandatory users are defined as citizens who meet certain characteristics, which including earning an income in Australia, and submit an annual income tax return to the ATO. Research into digital adoption does not engage with the concept of mandatory services and the impacts of digital first policies on users required to engage with digital services to comply with legislative requirements [6]. To address these concerns, analysis techniques should be holistic and adaptive, in order to incorporate an understanding of how a variety of factors can prevent or encourage users to go digital. This research utilises a holistic approach to analyse factors impacting users through the application of Systems Thinking and the testing of a conceptual model for analysing stakeholders/users in a multidimensional manner.

This paper is divided into six sections. Section one contains the introduction, section two presents the literature reviewed, section three discusses the research significance, section four outlines the research methods undertaken, section five highlights the results to date, and section six offers some conclusions.

II. LITERATURE REVIEW

Citizens expect digital services to be useful, accessible, easy to use and functional [7]. The goal of eGovernment is to create additional public value, by increasing stakeholder inclusiveness and encourage equal access to services [8].

The purpose of utilising e-government is to provide transparency and cooperation, improve government process, and provide digital services [9], all of which require continuous monitoring and assessment [8]. Furthermore, more needs to be done to understand the structural inequalities that affect the use of digital services, to prevent the issues becoming more intense and ingrained [10]. There is also a concern that social inequalities may be perpetuated online, given that those who are already in more privileged positions are more likely to use the medium [11]. These important factors highlight the value of researching barriers which prevent individuals from accessing government services.

The most common definition of adoption refers to continuous use of a digital service or innovation [12]. For digital services to be sustainable, they should be appealing and useful [13]. Shareef et al found in their research that perceived usefulness, perceived ease of use, perceived security and perceived reliability positively impact an individual's intention to adopt digital services [14]. Hargitti argued that not all online activities are equally important to enhancing one's human, financial and social capital [15]. This research determined that there is a strong relationship between level of education and type of digital services used [15]. Access to technology no longer determines inequalities alone – exposure to experiences which increase the digital participation and literacy are vital [15].

Research highlights four kinds of barriers to digital access: (1) lack of elementary digital experience due to lack of interest, (2) no computer access, (3) lack of digital skills, and (4) lack of significant usage opportunities [16]. Further barriers identified within the literature include lack of internet access, lack of awareness, language, user friendly websites, lack of trust, and security fears [9]. Researchers still need to understand the digital divide within the social, psychological, cultural and non-technological access context [17]. The challenge going forward is to determine the resources and functions that can be developed and provided to support positive user behaviour [7]. eGovernment aims to provide information and public services to citizens and encourages citizens to participate in different platforms [7].

Existing research does not focus on the multitude of factors impacting users' capacity to adopt and participate in a mandatory digital ecosystem, and there is little discussion around how digital adoption in mandatory spaces is different from adoption in other contexts. A thorough review of the literature identified the factors within a user's environment which have a significant impact on a user's capacity or willingness to adopt digital services within a mandatory space. For this research project, numerous different ecosystem styles were analysed, including digital, business, technology and innovation ecosystems.

Through the creation of a testable conceptual model, it is proposed that through the use of client-centric research, policy can better understand and support different stakeholders/users.

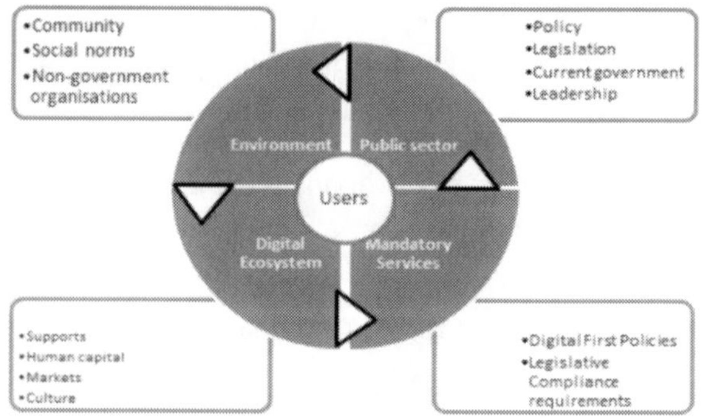

Figure 1 Conceptual Model with the User at the Centre

This conceptual model was created through the application of numerous stakeholder analysis techniques, combined with an analysis of the environment (based on Systems Thinking analysis) and digital ecosystems literature. The proposed conceptual model is highlighted in Figure 1. The four elements which capture the system are the Environment (including interactions with other people), Digital Ecosystem (including how digital products are accessed), Mandatory Services (including how they are different to voluntary services), and Public Sector (including the elements that make the services mandatory). Along with results of further research, this will be used to build an in-depth model.

III. SIGNIFICANCE AND RESEARCH GAP

This research will extend current understanding about the variety of factors impacting mandatory digital service adoption, bridging a gap in knowledge. The conceptual model in Figure 1 tests how policy can put the user at the centre, and help develop a better understanding of the user. Understanding digital adoption in the mandatory space should include how, why and when users adopt digital services, and in contrast when, how and why they do not, and in the latter case how they fulfil their mandatory compliance obligations. This research is based on understanding the outcomes of those users who actively seek assistance when using digital services, mapping the links between non-digital and digital issues, while also measuring outcomes. The application of a Systems Thinking approach will be applied to provide a more transparent view of the system, to understand the process holistically, per individual components and key interactions within the system. Therefore, the overarching aim of this research is to understand areas which may require intervention or can be leveraged to assist citizens adopt public sector mandatory digital services. This research proposes the model in Figure 1 to be tested through the collection and analysis of supporting data.

Previous research has applied a client-centric view to researching digital adoption; however, based only on voluntary digital services or those provided by the private sector [18]-[22]. Prior research has identified that there are a number of socioeconomic, cultural and intrinsic values that influence whether or not an individual will accept digital services [23]-[26]. This has been, to a certain degree, ineffectively applied to public sector research on digital adoption [1]. When mandatory digital services *have* been researched, the outcomes commonly revolve around acceptance of e-government services; results are based on survey responses specifically related to trust and innovation factors [27]-[31]. Previous research does not appear to have addressed the issues around adoption in a mandatory space, why users do and do not adopt these services, and how they comply with legislative obligations when they do not utilise digital services. Research has not included in-depth exploration about why users seek assistance when utilising digital services from the supplying entity and the outcomes post seeking assistance. This is critical for successfully adopting and sustaining commitment in mandatory digital systems. Previous models too, fail to explore the issues and environments associated with mandatory digital service adoption. The application of the proposed model helps fill some of these gaps and provide greater clarity on these potential blockers.

IV. Approach

The research approach used in this research has been exploratory in nature, allowing for ongoing developments as the findings developed. The researchers initially had a liberal set of goals, with the intention of allowing the data collected to further refine the specific questions, direction and analyses. The data collection was implemented in two phases. First, a pilot study was conducted to determine the validity of the proposed model for stakeholder/user inclusiveness. The second phase involved the data collection for the extended research Only the pilot results are included in this paper, with plans in place to examine the second phase with different analysis techniques.

A. Data

Two qualitative datasets were collected during the pilot and extended research period. The pilot study was conducted over a 3-week period (July 2017) to validate the conceptual model. This was conducted by 2 researchers, located in an ATO shopfront environment (in-person assistance) in South Australia; 234 cases were collected. The second and more extensive dataset was collected by 11 ATO officers over 4 weeks (July 2018). Data was collected from numerous ATO call centres across Australia, with 3990 valid cases collected. From the 3990 cases collected, additional quantitative data was obtained. This data includes three years' worth of results for callers' including their income, income type, occupation and how they lodged their tax return. This data was joined to the qualitative data to provide a richer picture of the callers, specifically identifying why they sought assistance and how that impacted their lodgement. All data was anonymised to ensure confidentiality and anonymity of participant data.

B. Methods

Two qualitative methodologies were applied to explore the data – firstly, Gioia's method for qualitative rigour and secondly, a Systems Thinking Approach. This enabled the researches to find structure in unstructured qualitative forms, as it is a systematic approach. Firstly, the Gioia method [32] [33] requires the researcher to step back, and then categorise the accounts into three different phases (First, Second and Third order). The first order, 'Concepts', is the 'voice of the user' (also known as 'voice of the customer'). The second order, 'concerns and statements', identifies specific sentences from participants which are then grouped together to discover the themes and patterns in events and accounts. These create Themes that are more generalised underlying explanatory dimensions, to test consistency and patterns [32] [33]. Finally, the third order 'aggregate dimensions', identifies the generic themes encompassing all of the first and second order data [32] [33]. Significance was measured through counting occurrences of first, second and third order elements to identify themes and patterns throughout the different accounts. The patterns in the text were then linked by connections, highlighting key features and emergent concepts or themes that require further analysis.

Secondly, Systems Thinking analysis was applied to systematically identify and order findings into their respective components of the process [34]. This helped to identify the points within the process and system that are causing the most issues and where support can be implemented. Systems Thinking was used to visually convert the findings into simplified figures that highlight key emergent findings. Our analysis will focus on profiling participants to identify relationships between why users seek assistance, their demographics and how/if they lodged a tax return.

V. Results

Results from the pilot demonstrate that there are many components of the system which are hindering the successful adoption and use of ATO digital services for users lodging tax returns. Specifically, without support many taxpayers would have been unable or would have struggled to lodge their documents.

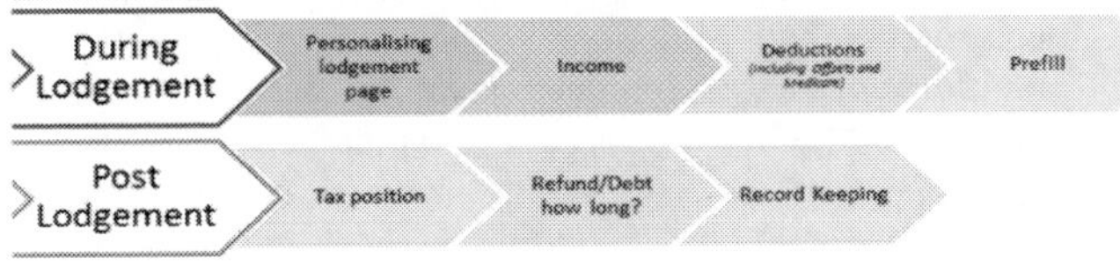

Figure 2 Pilot results - Lodgement Process Assistance Points

As highlighted in Figure 2, this is the first view of the system where intervention points are possible. Lessons learnt from this research demonstrate that, on average, taxpayers who sought assistance required it for more than one element of their tax return. Systems analysis demonstrates that there are more than one intervention points pre/during/post lodgement that should be leveraged for education and assistance. However, this research does understand that not everyone will be able to lodge digitally, and not everyone who needs help seeks help. For the purpose of client experience, it is important to recognise that negative experiences within the system will impact willingness to obtain assistance and advice in the future.

Descriptive analysis of the pilot data indicates that of the individuals who sought assistance utilising digital platforms for lodgement, the most frequent age group was 18-29 year olds (53.5%). This finding was unexpected. The other significant trend within this data was the high frequency of the pilot population seeking assistance who were in different life transitions (25.65%) (e.g., rental properties, deductions, income sources, retirement, etc.). Of the pilot population, those who had self-reported language barriers (17% of those seeking assistance) were more inclined to utilise paper solutions for lodgement rather than digital means. There is a concern that this will deter them from utilising digital means, and future research will determine whether or not digital or non-digital lodgement patterns are habitual, and if there are identifiable clusters of the population or demographics that are more inclined to behave in this manner.

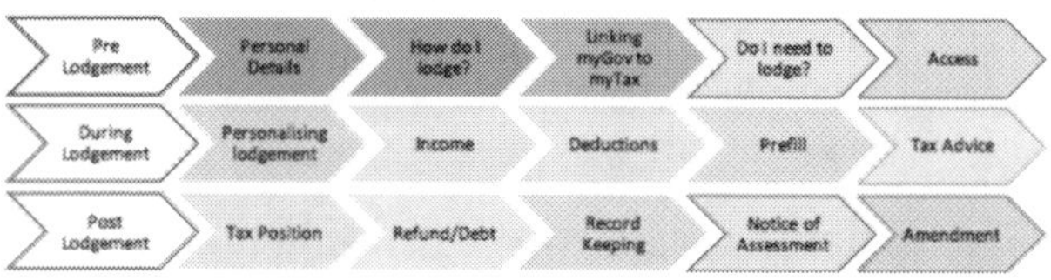

Figure 3 Extended research - Lodgement Process Assistance Points

Results from the extended research are still under development; however, preliminary results show how detailed follow-up research can improve the level of detail of the lodgement process systems view diagram, as shown in Figure 3. The current findings show that this process of analysis provides a more transparent view of the system, identifying the issues and points of the system that can be leveraged. This research has highlighted the links between digital and non-digital components of the tax system, e.g., understanding of tax and needing assistance. Figure 3 highlights the level of complexity associated with digital services in mandatory environments, especially when considering how adoption is impacted considerably by a multitude of factors. Implications of the extended lodgement process in Figure 3 are still under exploration.

This research is ongoing with additional research underway, including modelling of key outcomes, with a number of analytical techniques being explored. As is, the research continues to justify and validate the model outlined in Figure 1. Suitable methodologies to support the quantitative data analysis are currently being explored. This research can be applied to other areas of the public sector, especially those areas that have or are introducing mandatory digital services. With the transition of private sector entities to digital first platforms, the financial services sector, for example, could benefit from this style of research.

VI. Conclusion

This research seeks to understand the different barriers affecting adoption of mandatory digital services. The preliminary results highlight findings that need to be explored in further detail. The conceptual model will assist in identifying the interactions between the different elements outlined within the model, as well as increased details built within a systems view. Through ongoing data analysis and future papers, this model will be tested further. Future research will identify specific areas of assistance that are required going forward.

References

[1] L. Reichelt, *Gov.AU is a 'Mental Model' of Government* [Online]. Avaliable from: https://www.dta.gov.au/blog/gov-au-is-a-mental-model-for-government/ 2016. Retrived 10 November 2018.

[2] A. Furnham, "Response Bias, Social Desirability and Dissimulation", Personality and Individual Differences. Vol. 7 (3), pp. 385–400, 1986. doi:10.1016/0191-8869(86)90014-0

[3] A. J. Nederhof, "Methods of Coping with Social Desirability Bias: A Review", European Journal of Social Psychology. Vol. 15 (3), pp. 263–280, 1985. doi:10.1002/ejsp.2420150303

[4] M. T. Orne, "On the Social Psychology of the Psychological Experiment: With Particular Reference to Demand Characteristics and Their Implications", American Psychologist. Vol. 17 (11), pp. 776–783, 1962. doi:10.1037/h0043424

[5] National Archives of Australia 2015, *Digital Continuity 2020* [Online]. Avaliable from: www.naa.gov.au/Information.management /Digital.Continuity.2020. Retrived 10 November 2018.

[6] R. Bell and L. Nicol, *Digital Disruption: What do Governments Need to do?* [Online], 2016, Avaliable from: https://www.pc.gov.au/research/completed/digital-disruption Retrived 10 November 2018.

[7] S. Sawalha, M. Al-Jamal and E. Abu-Shanab, "The Influence of Utilising Facebook on e-government Adoption", *Electronic Government*, vol.15(1), pp.1-20, 2019. doi: 10.1504/EG.2019.096573

[8] E. Siskos, M. Malafekas, D. Askounis and J. Psarras, "E-government Benchmarking in European Union: a Multicriteria Extreme Ranking Approach" Proceedings of the 2013 Conference on e-Business, e-Services and e-Society, 2013, pp.338-348. doi: 10.1007/978-3-642-37437-1_28

[9] E. Ziemba, T. Papaj and R. Zelazny, "A Model of Success Factors for E-Government Adoption – The Case of Poland", *Issues in Information Systems*, vol.14(2), pp.87-100, 2013. doi:10.18517/ijaseit.7.4.2518

[10] J. Van Dijk and K Hacker, "The Digital Divide as a Complex and Dynamic Phenomenon", *The Information Society*, vol.19(4), pp.315-326. doi: 10.1080/01972240309487

[11] E. Hargitti and G. Walejko, "The Participation Divide: Content Creation and Sharing in the Digital Age", *Information, Community and Society*, vol.11(2), pp.239-256, 2008. doi: 10.1080/13691180801946150

[12] E.M. Rogers, *Diffusion of Innovation*, New York: Free Press, 1995.

[13] E. Ziemba, "The Contribution of ICT Adoption to Sustainability: Households' Perspective", *Information Technology and People*, 2018. doi: 10.1108/ITP-02-2018-0090

[14] M. A. Shareef, Y. K. Dwivedi, S. Laumer and N. Archer, "Citizens' Adoption Behaviour of Mobile Government (mGov): A Cross-Cultural Study", *Information Systems Management*, vol.33(3), pp.268-283, 2016. doi: 10.1080/10580530.2016.1188573

[15] E. Hargitti and A Hinnant, "Digital Inequality: Differences in Young Adults' Use of the Internet", *Communication Research*, vol.35(5), pp.602-621, 2008. doi: 10.1177/0093650208321782

[16] J. Van Dijk, *The Network Society, Social aspects of New Media*, Sage: Thousand Oaks, 1999.

[17] J. Van Dijk, "Digital Divide Research, Achievements and Shortcomings", *Poetics*, vol.34, pp.221-235, 2006. doi: 10.1016/j.poetic.2006.05.004

[18] M. Saal, S. Starnes and T. Rehermann, *Digital Financial Services: Challenges and Opportunities for Emerging Market Banks* [Online], 2017, Avaliable from: https://www.ifc.org/wps/wcm/connect/4e45d83f-e049-41d3-8378-2e388ffc1594/EMCompass+Note+42+DFS+Challenges+updated.pdf?MOD=AJPERES Retrived 10 November 2018.

[19] K. Sousa, H. Mendonca, J. Vanderdonckt, E. Rogier and J. Vandermeulen, "User Interface Derivation from Business Processes: A Model-Driven Approach for Organisational Engineering" Proceedings of the 2008 ACM Symposium on Applied Computing, 2008 pp. 553-560. doi:10.1145/1363686.1363821

[20] S. Barquin and H. V. Vinayak, *Digital Banking in Asia: What do Consumers Really Want?* [Online]. 2015. Avaliable from: http://zenithinfobank.com/wp-content/uploads/2015/04/Digital_Banking_in_Asia_What_do_consumers_really_want.pdf

[21] M. Hiltunen, L. Heng and L. Helgensen, "Personalised Electronic Banking Services", *Designing Personalised User Experience in eCommerce*, pp. 119-140, 2004. doi:10.1007/1-4020-

[22] D. R. Raban, "User-Centred Evaluation of Information: A Research Challenge", *Internet Research*, vol. 17(3), pp.306-322, 2007. doi: 10.1108/10662240710758948

[23] X. Luo, H. Li, J. Zhang and J. P. Shim, "Examining Multidimensional Trust and Multifaceted Risk in Initial Acceptance of Emerging Technologies: An Empirical Study of Mobile Banking Services", *Decision Support Systems*, vol. 49(2), pp. 222-234, 2010. doi:10.1016/j.dss.2010.02.008

[24] K. Kelton, K. R. Fleischmann and W. A. Wallace, "Trust in Digital Information", *Journal of the American Society for Information Science and Technology Banner*, vol. 59(3), pp. 363-374, 2007. doi: 10.1002/asi.20722

[25] B. Suh and I. Han, "The Impact of Customer Trust and Perception of Security Control on the Acceptance of Electronic Commerce", *International Journal of Electronic Commerce*, Vol. 7(3), pp 135-161, 2003. doi: 10.1080/10864415.2003.11044270

[26] M. S. Abbasi, F. H. Chandio, A. F. Soomro and F. Shah, "Social Influence, Voluntariness, Experience and the Internet Acceptance: An Extension of Technology Acceptance Model within a South-Asian Country Context", *Journal of Enterprise Information Management*, vol. 24(1), pp. 30-52, 2013. doi: 10.1108/17410391111097410

[27] L. Carter and V. Weerakkody, "E-government Adoption: A Cultural Comparison", *Information Systems Frontiers*, vol. 10 (4), pp. 473-482 2008. doi: 10.1007/s10796-008-9103-6

[28] L. Carter and F. Belanger, "The Utilisation of E-government Services: Citizen Trust, Innovation and Acceptance Factors", *Information Systems Journal*, vol 15(1) pp. 5-25, 2005. doi: 10.1111/j.1365-2575.2005.00183.x

[29] F. Belanger and C. Lemuria, "Trust and Risk in E-Government Adoption", *The Journal of Strategic Information Systems*, vol. 17(2), pp.165-176, 2007. doi: 10.1016/j.jsis.2007.12.002

[30] M. Warkentin, D. Gefen, P. A. Pavlou and G. M. Rose, "Encouraging Citizen Adoption of E-Government by Building Trust", *Electronic Markets*, vol. 12(3), pp. 157-162, 2010. doi:10.1080/101967802320245929

[31] K. De-Ruyter, M. Wetzels and M. Kleijnen, "Customer Adoption of e-service: An Experimental Study", *International Journal of Service Industry Management*, Vol. 12 (2), pp.184-207, 2001. doi:10.1108/09564230110387542

[32] D. A. Gioia, K. G. Corley and A. L. Hamilton, "Seeking Qualiative Rigour in Inductive Research; Notes on the Gioia Methodology", *Organisational Research Methods*, vol. 16(1), pp. 15-31, 2012. doi:10.1177/1094428112452151

[33] D. A. Gioia and .K Chittipeddi, "Sensemaking and Sensegiving in Strategic Change Initation", *Strategic Management Journal*, vol. 12(6), pp. 433-448, 1991. Doi: 10.1002/smj.4250120604

[34] D. Cabrera, L. Colosi and C. Lobdell, "Systems Thinking", *Evaluation and Program Planning*, vol.31(3), pp.299-310, 2008. doi: 10.1016/j.evalprogplan.2007.12.001

Effects of the Digital Divide in E-Participation Development in the UN Countries

Explanatory Factors of E-Participation for UN Countries

Rosario Pérez-Morote
Business Administration and Management Department
University of Castilla-La Mancha, UCLM
Albacete, Spain
email: rosario.pmorote@uclm.es

Carolina Pontones-Rosa
Business Administration and Management Department
University of Castilla-La Mancha, UCLM
Albacete, Spain
email: carolina.pontones@uclm.es

Esteban Alfaro-Cortes
Applied Economics Department
University of Castilla-La Mancha, UCLM
Albacete, Spain
Email: esteban.alfaro@uclm.es

***Abstract*— E-government offers citizens the potential for greater access to their representatives and confers policy makers the possibility to make G2C relationships more inclusive. However, the real translation into governance outcomes will depend on policy makers' consideration of the environmental complexity and the singular characteristics of the target population. This paper analyses the relationships between e-participation development and the variables associated to the digital divide in a sample of 178 countries for the period 2008-2016. The authors use a multiple linear regression model and the UN's E-participation Index as the dependent variable. The test of the hypotheses shows the significant and positive effect of telecommunications infrastructure and age and a significant negative effect of education and rural condition. Results reveal that Gender and Political freedom and Democracy are not influential.**

Keywords- E-participation; UN's E-participation Index; digital divide; linear regression

I. INTRODUCTION

E-government (EG) can be an instrument to improve the relationship between people and their government. In the achievement of public governance, EG aims at increasing participation in decision making and making public institutions more transparent and accountable. From the perspective of the principal-agent theory, EG provides citizens with a basis to decide, participate and engage with government actions, which in turn may strengthen their trust and reinforce Government-to-Citizen (G2C) relationships, increasing public authorities´ legitimacy [25][26]. However, Dawes [10] pointed to a multi-dimensional digital divide that posed challenges to governments trying to provide equitable access to information and services as well as opportunities to broaden participation in political processes.

Although recognizing the growing interest and literature in the field, there is a relative low number of papers focused on the analysis of citizen e-participation from a quantitative perspective. In this context, our article wants to contribute to the existing research and enhance the understanding of the drivers affecting e-participation dynamics. With that aim, the UN's E-participation Index (EPI) is taken as indicator for e-participation in order to study its evolution over the period 2008-2016 in a sample of 178 countries. EPI measures the availability of e-participation tools on national government portals [48]. This legitimized index remains meaningful in that it enumerates the diverse levels of the online activity of civil participation. The index has been used in previous research [15][18][50].

In this research, panel data is used to conduct ordinary least squared linear regression model in order to test hypotheses as to the relationship between the evolution of EPI and that of economic and socio-demographic variables of the context, which relate to the digital divide (telecommunication infrastructures, education, location, age, gender, and political freedom and democracy).

Apart from the introduction section, the paper is structured in six more sections. Section 2 corresponds to literature review, in Section 3 we propose the model and the hypotheses developed, Section 4 describes the methodology applied, in Section 5 we show the main results, Section 6 corresponds to the discussion of the results and finally we present the main conclusions in Section 7.

II. LITERATURE REVIEW

A broad line of research have described and measured the attributes of government websites trying to assess their maturity in terms of EG development [9][12][13][19][22] [36][39]. Generally, these researches have also investigated the factors affecting that development, considering politic, socio-economic and demographic variables, mainly.

A less abundant amount of publications have studied, from a quantitative perspective, the potential of EG to permit citizen participation [33][34][35]. Pina, Torres and Royo [29] in their web maturity assessment in UE local governments, obtained similar results: democratic participation and citizen dialogue presented the lowest scores. For their part, Pina, Torres and Acerete [28], Bonsón, Torres, Royo and Flores [4], Girish, Yates and Williams [15], Zhao, Ning and Collier [50] or Jho and Song [18] analyzed EG development in terms of e-participation and connected it with economic, socio-demographic, cultural and information society factors, among others.

III. CONCEPTUAL MODEL AND HYPOTHESES DEVELOPMENT

The main objective of this section is on the one hand to clarify the concepts of the E-participation and the Digital Divide and on the other hand, to raise the research hypotheses.

A. *E-participation and the digital divide.*

Generally, E-participation is defined as the use of ICT to support democratic decision [23][24]. Following Reddick [33], our research considers different forms of participation in government ranging from the one-way interaction (managerial), two-way interaction directed from government (consultative), and finally the highest form of e-participation of the two-way interaction directed from citizens to government and vice versa (participatory).

According to the UNDESA 2016 EG Survey [48], the digital divide refers to the gap among individuals, households and businesses at different socio-economic levels with regard to both their opportunities to access ICTs, and their use of the Internet for a wide variety of activities. It also refers to disparities between developed and developing countries, as well as within and among groups in a country, especially countries with greater rural populations. In general, it could be said that the digital divide refers to the unequal access of citizens to ICT, and uneven possession of skills and experience required for using it. It can take many forms and be described variously in terms of gender, location, skills, and income [1].

B. *Determinants of e-participation: hypotheses.*

From the above, it can be drawn that EG-enabled citizen participation is influenced by socio-economic and demographic and political factors that, in turn, might be associated to the existence of a digital divide [7][37]. A research question arises and leads us to investigate if governments are considering this digital divide when designing their national portals. In particular, are the variables associated to the digital divide an influential factor for the inclusion of participation tools in the webs?

Using the EPI as indicator of web maturity in terms of citizen participation, the relationship between e-participation and telecommunications infrastructure, education, age, location, gender and political freedom and democracy will be explored.

Experience suggests that the implementation of EG demands significant investments in technical and administrative infrastructures. Holzer and Kim [16] indicated that economically advanced countries had more emphasis on citizen participation, compared to less developed countries. Similarly, Siau and Long [36] and Das, Singh and Joseph [9] identified significant differences in EG development for countries with different levels of telecommunication infrastructure. Akin to them, the analysis of Jho and Song [18] showed that the level of ICT is a crucial variable in determining the level of e-participation. After this reflexion the first hypothesis in this research is set out:

H1. The investment in telecommunications infrastructure is associated with EG-enabled citizen participation.

The literature on the digital divide has claimed that internet use relates to higher educational levels [3][6][38][48]. Similarly, authors like Kim [22] refer to the need of knowledge and skills for the use of the EG-related technologies. Developing countries' lower literacy rates hamper the necessary changes that must take place for the appropriate development of EG projects, leading to their failure [8]. According to this idea, the second hypothesis is set out:

H2. Education is associated with web-enabled citizen participation

There are large regional and rural/urban differences with regard to access to and possession of information technology [2]. Rural population is often associated with lower levels of EG usage and, subsequently, e-participation.

Educational levels might be one factor behind this fact, considering that education is frequently concentrated in large cities. Taipale [38] reached this conclusion when observed that rural people, who would benefit most from EG services, are not using them, while in cities that have been able to maintain office services, people also use e-services. Taking the above into account, our third hypothesis is as follows:

H3. Location is associated with web-enabled citizen participation

The age of the population has been studied in connection with levels of political participation, citizen engagement and trust [30]. Specifically, within the abundant research on EG, it is easy to find publications that have investigated its relationships with the age factor. Literature on the digital divide points to older populations facing significant disadvantages in the use of EG compared to younger people [11][14]. The following hypothesis investigates the relationship between age and e-participation:

H4. Age is associated with web-enabled citizen participation.

Previous research has been inconclusive regarding the existence of a relationship between gender and EG. Although many discard this connection [3][6][32][38][49], other works confirm a positive relationship between masculine gender and use of EG. Some studies point out to the fact that women in many parts of the world lack an equal access to ICT services [1]. To contribute to this debate, a fifth hypothesis is drawn:

H5. Gender is associated with web-enabled citizen participation.

The approach of deliberative democracy or pluralist democracy addresses citizens as active participants and as co-producers of policies [28]. In this regard, digital government has the power to increase citizen input to government [20]. However, unless civil liberties are widely permitted, e-government would not perform beyond a billboard as one-way communication with the public, and citizens might be afraid of voicing their opinions and monitoring government programs and services. To contribute to this debate, the last hypothesis is set out:

H6. *Political freedom and democracy are associated with web-enabled citizen participation.*

IV. METHOD

The research has used secondary data drawn from the E-Government Survey, published biannually by United Nations. The Survey is the most extensive world survey on EG to date, covering 191 countries [48]. Other data sources used are the World Bank and the World Bank Group.

A panel data has been complied for the period 2008-2016, for a group of 178 countries. The number of cases observed is 890. The high number of countries studied and the longitudinal character of the analysis allows our research contribute to understanding the e-participation development factors on a global scale. Figure 1 shows the variables analysed, their correspondent indicators and the data source.

Variable	Indicator	Description	Source
E-Participation	E-Participation Index (EPI)	UN e-Participation indicator	UNDESA (2008, 2010, 2012, 2014 and 2016)
Technology and telecommunications infrastructure	Telecommunications Infrastructure Index (TII)	UN telecomunication infrastructure indicator	UNDESA (2008, 2010, 2012, 2014 and 2016)
Education	Human Capital Index (HCI)	UN education indicator	UNDESA (2008, 2010, 2012, 2014 and 2016)
Location (rural vs urban)	%Rural	% rural population vs total population	WB (2006, 2008, 2010, 2012 and 2014)
Age	%. Pop>65	% population > 65 years vs total population	WB (2006, 2008, 2010, 2012 and 2014)
Gender	% Female	% women vs total population	WB (2006, 2008, 2010, 2012 and 2014)
Political freedom and democracy	Voice Account Rank	WBG freedom and democracy indicator	WBG (2006, 2008, 2010, 2012 and 2014)

Figure 1. Variables, indicators and source

In order to study the e-participation, the EPI has been selected as the dependent variable. As it was explained before, the EPI is elaborated by the UN within the EG surveys [40] [41][42][43][48].

As regards the independent variables, the first one is the level of telecommunications infrastructure of a country, which is measured by the Telecommunications Infrastructure Index (TII), also extracted from the UN's EG surveys, yet the primary data source is the ITU. The second independent variable is the level of education of a country's population, measured by the Human Capital Index (HCI), which is extracted from the UN's EG surveys as in the previous cases. Data to measure the next three independent variables have been extracted from the World Bank. The predictor variable Location reflects the percentage of rural population over the total population. The variable Age takes as indicator the percentage of population above 65 years over the total population of a country. The variable Gender is measured by the percentage of females over a country's total population. Political freedom and Democracy makes up the last independent variable, measured by the indicator "Voice Account Rank". This is one of the Worldwide Governance Indicators calculated by Kaufmann, Kraay and Mastruzzi in 2010 [21] for the World Bank Group.

In addition to this, the variable Year has been included as a controlling factor in order to reflect the variations derived from the economic scenarios.

V. RESULTS

The ordinary least squared multiple regression model for EPI has been conducted using R statistical program [31]. Figure 2 offers the results for the Ordinary Least Squares (OLS) model.

```
Call:
lm(formula = f1, data = base)

Residuals:
   Min      1Q  Median      3Q     Max
-57.599 -12.397  -1.517  11.401  60.349

Coefficients:
                  Estimate Std. Error t value Pr(>|t|)
(Intercept)      22.103613  14.215708   1.555   0.1205
TII               0.555048   0.064551   8.599  < 2e-16 ***
HCI              -0.090973   0.042739  -2.129   0.0337 *
%Pop>65           0.352334   0.168725   2.088   0.0372 *
%Rural           -0.252103   0.042882  -5.879 6.74e-09 ***
%Female           0.205721   0.303203   0.678   0.4977
VoiceAccountrank  0.006618   0.037604   0.176   0.8604
Year              2.359904   0.300548   7.852 1.80e-14 ***
---
Signif. codes: 0 '***' 0.001 '**' 0.01 '*' 0.05 '.' 0.1 ' ' 1

Residual standard error: 18.48 on 621 degrees of freedom
  (261 observations deleted due to missingness)
Multiple R-squared: 0.5697, Adjusted R-squared: 0.5648
F-statistic: 117.4 on 7 and 621 DF, p-value: < 2.2e-16
```

Figure 2. Linear Model

From the results, it can be observed that about 68% of the countries in the sample started the period with an EPI value of 22 ± 14 points and increased almost 2.36 % every year.

The seven variables included explain a 56.4 % of the variance of EPI, according to its adjusted R squared. The beta coefficients shows the significant positive influence of Year, TII and %Pop.>65 and the significant negative influence of HCI and %Rural. The 95% confidence intervals for their coefficients are [0.43, 0.68] for TII, [0.17, -0.00] for HCI, [0.02, 0.68] for %Pop.>65 and [-0.33, -0.17] for %Rural.

VI. DISCUSSION

In this section, our results will be explained and discussed against literature of reference in the general field of EG and in the particular area of e-participation.

Focusing on our results, the variable Year positive influence reflects that, in a good proportion of the sample, EPI improves over the time for the period considered.

The coefficients for TII (beta 0.55) are statistically significant at the 0.05 level and indicate that throughout the period 2008-2016, there is a strong connection between the telecommunications infrastructure of a country and the level of e-participation allowed on national government portals. When holding all other variables constant, a one-unit increase in a country's TII increases a country's score on the EPI by 0.55. Consequently, hypothesis 1 is verified. This positive and significant influence of technology and telecommunications on the specific topic of e-participation has not been confirmed by any of the works consulted, yet Jho and Song [18] identified a positive effect of a country's online population over EPI. Notwithstanding, Siau and Long [36], Pina et al. [28] and Das et al. [9] concluded TII was influential on EG development in general.

As regards the second predictor variable, Education, measured through Human Capital Index, it results significant with a beta value of -0.09. According to the digital divide phenomenon, educational levels affected positively e-participation, but with a different sign. Our second hypothesis is confirmed but not in the expected way. One possible explanation would be that education solely is not enough to increase e-participation, meaning that governments need to work to make citizens aware of the benefits of using EG [17].

Following the results, the indicator used to measure Location, % Rural population, shows a significant negative influence in EPI (beta -0.25) along the period of study, confirming our third hypothesis that belonging to rural areas is associated to lower levels of e-participation and vice versa. These results support the digital divide paradigm [48] that conveys that rural areas are generally associated with low levels of ICT and telecommunications [39] and education [38], which, in turn, generate barriers for EG access and usage. Besides, our results are consistent with those obtained by previous research [15][22].

As far as the variable Age is concerned, the results point to a significant and positive influence of the percentage of population over 65 in EPI (beta 0.35), at the 0.05 level. In other words, when holding all other variables constant, a one-unit increase in a country's %Pop.>65 increases a country's score on the EPI by 0, 35. This strong connection confirms our fourth hypothesis, although in a different sense from the expected according to the digital divide approach, which claims that older populations face significant disadvantages in the use of EG compared to younger people [11][14]. On the contrary, our results suggest that ageing relates to increased e-participation in government portals. Piewtrosky and Van Ryzn [27] could not confirm that older people demanded more transparency from Governments. The authors have not found previous works that tested the effect of ageing on the specific area of e-participation, with the exception of Reddick [33], who also pointed to the not significant effect of age in the participatory model constructed by the author.

Focusing now on the values obtained for the indicator percentage Female, used to measure the effect of Gender. The results do not permit to verify the fifth hypothesis. This contradicts the existence of a digital divide between men and women, in the sense that women in many parts of the world lack an equal access to ICT services [1] or men are more prone to use EG services than women [5]. Reddick [33] also discarded a statistically significant influence of the gender in e-participation.

Finally, political freedom and democracy come up as not significant according to our research. It is surprising that civil liberties are not required for the full development of EG. It cannot be confirmed that countries that do not guarantee civil liberties and democracy are associated with low levels of EPI. Consequently, our last hypothesis is rejected. Previous work is inconclusive about this issue. Girish et al. [15] and Jho et al. [18] have studied the topic in relation to EPI. The former detected a significant and negative influence for the political freedom variable coupled with a positive coefficient for democracy aspects. As Das et al. [9] pointed out; the evidence that EG can develop without significant dependence on governance alerts us that the type EG that is being developed is primarily for the billboard.

As a synthesis of the above, Figure 3 collects the test of the hypotheses put forward in this research.

Hypothesis	Expected sign	Result
H1. The investment in telecommunications infrastructure is associated with EG-enabled citizen participation.	Positive	Confirmed
H2. Education is associated with web-enabled citizen participation.	Positive	Not confirmed
H3. Location is associated with web-enabled citizen participation.	Negative	Confirmed
H4. Age is associated with web-enabled citizen participation.	Negative	Confirmed (positive)
H5. Gender is associated with web-enabled citizen participation.	Negative	Not confirmed
H6. Political freedom and democracy are associated with web-enabled citizen participation.	Positive	Not confirmed

Figure 3. Summary of the test of the hypothesis

VII. CONCLUSIONS

From the test of the hypotheses, some practical implications may be drawn:

In general, it is important for governments to identify demographic groups with unequal access to the benefits of EG services. This will provide them with the ability to target future policies and initiatives to narrow the digital divide and increase the population that can actively engage with public services.

The positive and significant coefficient of the TII permits to verify the first hypothesis. In this regard, inclusive EG polices should be supported with investment plans in ICT in order to raise the number of people with Internet access.

The results for the HCI predictor were significant but unexpected. It could be argued that education is only a minimum requirement but does not imply use of EG. Governments must consider this fact and implement policies to increase awareness about the benefits of the use of EG for citizens.

The percentage of rural population over all population resulted significant with a negative influence on EPI. Interpretation of this finding advises policy makers to pay appropriate regard to the special condition of the rural population, normally associated to reduced government size and budget to develop e-participation tools.

The results for the older population go against the existence of a digital divide due to age. However, interpretation must be careful. More aged countries are also associated to higher degrees of life expectancy, ICT infrastructure and education, which may be behind these results. It seems that the elderly living in developed countries are increasingly adopting EG, reducing the digital divide.

As regards for the gender, the results lead to discarding an influence of this variable in the level of e-participation. Similar conclusions apply for the "voice account rank".

Civil liberties and democratic institution are not necessarily associated to EPI scores, which seems incoherent with the foundations and objectives of EG and e-governance in particular.

REFERENCES

[1] E. Abu-Shamad and N. Al Jamal, "Exploring the Gender Digital Divide in Jordan", Gender, Technology and Development, vol. 19, no. 1, pp. 91-113, 2015.

[2] F. Amagoh, "An Assessment of E-Government in a West African Country: The Case of Nigeria", International Journal of Public Administration in the Digital Age (IJPADA), vol. 2, no. 3, pp. 80-99, 2015.

[3] F. Belanger and L. Carter, "The impact of the digital divide on e-government use", Communications of the ACM, vol. 52, no. 4, pp. 132-135, 2009.

[4] E. Bonsón, L. Torres, S. Royo and F. Flores, "Local e-government 2.0: Social media and corporate transparency in municipalities", Government Information Quarterly, vol. 29, no. 2, pp. 123-132, 2012.

[5] J. Choudrie and Y. Dwivedi, "A survey of citizens' awareness and adoption of e-government initiatives, the Government Gateway: A United Kingdom perspective", In EGovernment Workshop'05 (eGOV05), 2005.

[6] S. E. Colesca and L. Dobrica, "Adoption and use of e-government services: The case of Romania", Journal of applied research and technology, vol. 6, no. 3, pp. 204-217, 2008.

[7] M. Crutcher and M. Zook, "Placemarks and waterlines: Racialized cyberscapes in post-Katrina Google Earth", Geoforum, vol. 40, no. 4, pp. 523-534, 2009.

[8] D. Dada, "The failure of e-government in developing countries: A literature review", The Electronic Journal of Information Systems in Developing Countries, vol. 26, no. 7, pp. 1-10, 2006.

[9] A. Das, H. Singh and D. Joseph, "A longitudinal study of e-government maturity", Information and Management, vol. 54, pp. 415–426, 2017.

[10] S. S. Dawes, "Governance in the digital age: A research and action framework for an uncertain future", Government Information Quarterly, vol. 26, no. 2, pp. 257-264, 2009.

[11] T. Friemel, "The digital divide has grown old: Determinants of a digital divide among seniors", Media and Society, vol. 18, no. 2, pp. 313-331, 2014.

[12] I. Gallego, L. Rodríguez and I. M. García, "Are determining factors of municipal E-government common to a worldwide municipal view? An intra-country comparison". Government Information Quarterly, vol. 27, no. 4, pp. 423-430, 2010.

[13] J. L. Gandía and M. C. Archidona, "Determinants of web site information by Spanish city councils", Online Information Review, vol. 32, no. 1, pp. 35-57, 2008.

[14] M. Geana and A. Greiner, "Health information and the digital divide", Journal of Management and Marketing in Healthcare, vol. 4, no. 2, pp. 108–112, 2011.

[15] J. Girish, D. J. Yates and C. B. Williams, "Understanding the impact of political structure, governance and public policy on e-government". In System Science (HICSS), 45th Hawaii International Conference, pp. 2541-2550. IEEE, 2012.

[16] M. Holzer and S. T. Kim, "Digital governance in municipalities worldwide. A Longitudinal Assessment of Municipal Websites Through the World". The E-Governance Institute, National Center for Public Productivity, Rutgers, the State University of New Jersey, Global e-Policy e-Government Institute, Graduate School of Governance Sungkyunkwan University, retrieved: August, 2017.

[17] P. T. Jaeger and K. M. Tompson, "E-government around the world: Lessons, challenges, and future directions", Government Information Quarterly, vol. 20, no. 4, pp. 389-394, 2003.

[18] W. Jho and K. J. Song, "Institutional and technological determinants of civil e-Participation: Solo or duet?", Government Information Quarterly, vol. 32, no. 4, pp. 488-495, 2015.

[19] S. Jorge, P. M. Moura, A. F. Pattaro and R. P. Lourenço, "Local Government financial transparency in Portugal and Italy: a comparative exploratory study on its determinants". In 13th Biennial

CIGAR Conference, Bridging Public Sector and Non-Profit Sector Account, pp. 9-10, 2011.
[20] E. Kamarck, "Government innovation around the world", 2004.
[21] D. Kaufmann, A. Kraay and M.Mastruzzi, "The Worldwide Governance Indicators: A Summary of Methodology, Data and Analytical Issues", World Bank Policy Research Working Paper No. 5430. (Available at http://papers.ssrn.com/sol3/papers.cfm?abstract_id=1682130, retrieved: June, 2018.
[22] C. K. Kim, "A Cross-national Analysis of Global E-government". Public Organization Review, vol. 7, no. 4, pp. 317-329, 2007.
[23] A. Macintosh, "Characterizing e-participation in policy-making". Proceedings of the 37th Annual Hawaii International Conference on System Sciences, IEEE, 2004, pp. 10.
[24] R. Medaglia, "E-Participation research: Moving characterization forward (2006–2011)", Government Information Quarterly, vol. 29, no. 3, pp. 346-360, 2012.
[25] A. J. Meijer, "Publishing public performance results on the Internet: Do stakeholders use the Internet to hold Dutch public service organizations to account?". Government Information Quarterly, vol. 24, no. 1, pp. 165-185, 2007.
[26] G. Misuraca, C. Codagnone and P. Rossel, "From practice to theory and back to practice: Reflexivity in measurement and evaluation for evidence-based policy making in the information society", Government Information Quarterly, vol. 30, pp. 68-82, 2013.
[27] S. Pietrowsky and G. G. Van Ryzin, "Citizen Attitudes toward transparency in local government", The American Review of Public Administration, vol. 37, no. 3, pp. 306-323, 2007.
[28] V. Pina, L. Torres and B. Acerete, "Are ICTs promoting government accountability?: A comparative analysis of e-governance developments in 19 OECD countries", Critical Perspectives on Accounting, vol. 18, no. 5, 583-602, 2007.
[29] V. Pina, L. Torres and S. Royo, "E-government evolution in EU local governments: a comparative perspective", Online Information Review, vol. 33, no. 6, pp. 1137-1168, 2009.
[30] R. D. Putnam, "Bowling alone: The collapse and revival of American community", New York: Simon and Schuster, 2001.
[31] R Development Core Team. R, "A Language and Environment for Statistical Computing". R Foundation for Statistical Computing, Vienna, 2018.
[32] C. G. Reddick, "Citizen interaction with e-government: From the streets to servers?", Government Information Quarterly, vol. 22, no. 1, pp. 38-57, 2005.
[33] C. Reddick, "Citizen Interaction and e-government. Evidence for the managerial, consultative, and participatory models. Transforming Government", People, Process and Policy, vol. 5, no. 2, pp. 167-184, 2011.
[34] R. A. Rodríguez, L. Welicki, D. A. Giulianelli and P. M. Vera, "Measurement framework for evaluating e-governance on municipalities websites". Paper presented at the Proceedings of the 2nd International Conference on Theory and Practice of Electronic Governance, 2008, pp. 381-387.
[35] R. Sandoval-Almazán and J. R. Gil-García, "Are government internet portals evolving towards more interaction, participation, and collaboration? Revisiting the rhetoric of e-government among municipalities", Government Information Quarterly, vol. 29, pp.72-81, 2012.
[36] K. Siau and Y. Long, "Factors Impacting E-Government Development", Journal of Computer Information Systems, vol. 50, no. 1, 98-107, 2015.
[37] M. Stephens. Gender and the Geoweb, "Divisions in the Production of User-Generated Cartographic Information", GeoJournal, vol. 78, pp. 981–996, 2013.
[38] S. Taipale, "The use of e-government services and the Internet: The role of socio-demographic, economic and geographical predictors", Telecommunications Policy, vol. 37, no. 4, pp. 413-422, 2013.
[39] C. J. Tolbert, K. Mossberger and R. McNeal, "Institutions, Policy Innovation, and E-Government in the American States". Public Administration Review, vol. 68, no. 3, pp. 549-563, 2008.
[40] United Nations. Department of Economic and Social Affairs (UNDESA), Division for Public Administration and Development Management, "United Nations e-Government Survey 2008. From e-Government to Connected Governance", 2008.
[41] United Nations. Department of Economic and Social Affairs (UNDESA), Division for Public Administration and Development Management, "Leveraging e-government at a time of financial and economic crisis", 2010.
[42] United Nations. Department of Economic and Social Affairs (UNDESA), Division for Public Administration and Development Management, "E-Government for the People", 2012.
[43] United Nations. Department of Economic and Social Affairs (UNDESA, Division for Public Administration and Development Management, "E-Government for the future we want", 2014.
[44] United Nations Public Administration Network (UNPAN), (2014). http://www.unpan.org/Library/MajorPublications/UNEGovernmentSurvey/tabid/646/Default.aspx, retrieved: January, 2018.
[45] United Nations, "Transforming our world: the 2030 Agenda for Sustainable Development. 2015". A/RES/70/1. sustainabledevelopment.un.org, retrieved: March, 2018.
[46] United Nations, Department of Economic and Social Affairs (UNDESA), Population Division. "World Population Prospects: The 2015 Revision", DVD Edition.
[47] United Nations Public Administration Network (UNPAN). http://www.unpan.org/EGovernment/UNEGovernmentSurveys/PreparatoryProcessof2016UNEGovernmentSurvey/EGovernmentSurvey2016OnlineConsultationForm/tabid/1789/language/en-US/Default.aspx, retrieved: December 2017.
[48] United Nations. Department of Economic and Social Affairs (UNDESA). Division for Public Administration and Development Management. "E-Government in support of sustainable development".2016.
[49] J. Van Dijk, W. Pieterson, A. Van Deuren and W. Ebbers, "E-services for citizens: the Dutch usage case". In International Conference on Electronic Government, pp. 155-166, 2007 Springer, Berlin, Heidelberg.
[50] F. Zhao, K. Ning and A. Collier, A, "Effects of national culture on e-government diffusion—A global study of 55 countries", Info Information and Management, vol. 51, pp. 1005–1016, 2014.

Towards a Smart City Blueprint Template

Christian Pfister
baeriswyl tschanz & partner ag
Bern, Switzerland
e-mail: christian.pfister@btpag.ch

Stephan Haller, Eduard Klein
E-Government Institute, Bern Univ. of Applied Sciences
Bern, Switzerland
e-mail: { stephan.haller, eduard.klein }@bfh.ch

Abstract— **A common approach transforming a city into a smart city is to study successful transformation approaches. However, there is no recommended adaptation process for smart city transformation, thus often resulting in manual, project-based and costly efforts. In this paper we propose a methodology, tools and a process which guides through the documentation and transformation process when transferring smart city innovation to other cities. Considering public value as main result of the smart city value chain, an adaptation of the business canvas to a smart city canvas allows a holistic view on the most important aspects during smart city transformation. Moreover, a blueprint template is proposed together with a process which has proven to be a valuable tool for the adaptation of successful smart city concepts to other cities. The approach has been validated in the context of a large-scale smart city innovation project.**

Keywords- Smart City; Blueprint Template; Transformation Process; Public Value.

I. INTRODUCTION

An increasing number of cities use data from citizens and devices in order to use resources efficiently and design smart services, thus becoming a smart city. Although there is no shared definition of smart city available, in [1] a taxonomy of pertinent smart city application domains is elaborated. Instead of just automating routine functions for individuals, buildings or traffic systems, a smart city should monitor, understand, analyze and plan its situation in order to increase efficiency, equity and the quality of life for its inhabitants in real time [2]. Often, smart cities are seen as a composite of various networks, which continuously collect data regarding the movement of people and materials and use them for decision-making. Cities, however, can only be smart if they have intelligent tools which are able to integrate and synthesize data for a specific purpose.

It is common to use smart city platforms to process sensor data, open (government) data, social media data, as well as data from third party providers and private users. Many smart city projects describe the need for such a platform [3][4] as a valuable driver in the promotion of smart city innovation.

Within the CPaaS.io research project [4], the developed smart city platform had to be validated through several large-scale use cases from different contexts such as (high) water management, (sports) event management, emergency medical care, smart parking and public transportation [5]. Instead of starting from scratch for every use case, the authors searched for ways to re-use knowledge and experiences from prior use cases.

Although there exist information frameworks for the creation of smart cities (e.g., [6]), to date there is no common process or even a recommendation for developing a smart city project beyond the commonly acknowledged trinity data – platform – smart applications. Often, the wheel is re-invented, although the transformability of use cases and applications from city to city would be possible thereby re-using experience and know-how. The following research question was used as guidance throughout the research: "How can successful smart city concepts be used for smart city transformation?". Or, more precisely: "Which are appropriate methods, tools and processes for performing and documenting smart city transformation?". This paper proposes a blueprint process and a template covering technical and organizational aspects.

Since every city has specific characteristics, smart city applications are not transferable without adaptation to its context. To support the documentation and adaptation of smart city applications, a blueprint approach is proposed, guiding through the problem-solving cycle and assisting in the abstraction and concretization process of a smart city application and thus in the adaptation process.

The blueprint template covers important categories along the value chain [7] of smart city applications. The objective of the blueprint template is to create a description of the system without enforcing specific implementation methods. It considers processes, architecture views, hardware, software, possible project and communication plans. Further aspects support the creation of public value within a smart city application as well as the operation and optimization of an application set in place.

To simplify the adaptation of a smart city blueprint, a so-called *One-Pager* shows the most important aspects of the blueprint. The One-Pager guides through the development of the blueprint and shows which aspects need to be re-evaluated when adapting an existing blueprint to another city.

The paper is structured as follows: After presenting the research design conducting our findings in Section 2, the tools and processes are introduced in Section 3, where the derivation of the smart city value chain is also discussed, and the blueprint template based on it is justified. In Section 4, the checklist-based adaptation process is presented, and in Section 5, the validation of the approach is discussed within the context of a practical, large-scale smart city innovation project.

II. Research Design

The development of the blueprint template and process was conducted in a classical three-step approach: analysis, design and validation. In the analysis phase, relevant literature was searched on smart city blueprints, on public value of governmental initiatives, on the value chain of smart city applications, on the future of smart cities and on specification guidelines in the smart city context. The literature research was conducted in various online resources in spring 2018. However, in none of the papers a blueprint template, framework or specification guidelines for smart city applications was presented.

Additionally, papers on best-practice methodologies on innovation creation, architecture guidelines, specification guidelines, business model creation and operation models were searched in the same way for importance on the planned template design.

During the design phase, a generic grid was suggested based on the value creation of smart city applications according to [8]. The definition of vision, mission and strategy is an adaptation of the Business Model Canvas from [9] with focus on the generation of public value.

As a result, a four-phase blueprint template is suggested considering the phases initialization, conception, realization and deployment and operation, as common in project management [10], accompanied by a process guiding users through the development of a blueprint instance.

During the third step the blueprint template process is validated against use cases of the CPaaS.io project [4], in which the authors of this paper participate. This validation process is still ongoing, initial results are promising as they confirm the usefulness of the tool in capturing information and some of the cities we are in contact with have expressed interest in using such templates for their upcoming application implementations. These activities will help us to improve the blueprint template further.

III. The Smart City Blueprint Template

The blueprint template covers important categories along the value chain of smart city applications. The objective of the blueprint template is to create a description of the system without enforcing specific implementation methods. It considers processes, architecture views, hardware, software, and possible project and communication plans. Further aspects support the creation of public value within a smart city application as well as the operation and optimization of an application set in place.

A. Value Chain of Smart City Applications

In business, the concept of a value chain is commonly used. Porter [7] defined five primary activities of a company that lead to profit: sourcing logistics, production, distribution logistics, marketing and sales, and customer services. In addition, he defined the following supporting activities: infrastructure, human resources, technology development, and procurement. A city however has different goals compared to a business-oriented company: While a company's primary goal is to increase profits, a city strives to create public value. Introduced by Moore [11], the concept of public value describes the value an entity contributes to society, e.g., increasing the quality of life for its population, supporting transparency and democratic processes, or other useful services a city may provide to residents or enterprises. Such services are especially important where market mechanisms alone are not providing the desired service levels, like in health care or public transportation [12].

So how could a value chain for a smart city be defined? The base currency for a smart city is data, which leads to information and insights, and thus to new services and better and faster management of city processes. Laaboudi and D'Ouezzan [8] postulate that the value chain of a smart city consists of the following elements:

- Data Collection: Data collection from a wide range of devices such as mobile devices, sensors, home applications, vehicles or data from 3rd party applications via interfaces.
- Data Carriage: Network technologies like fiber, wireless, telecommunication infrastructure or Low-Power Wide-Area Network (LPWAN) or other connectivity components to transfer the collected data.
- Data Storage: Data centers, cloud or other storage capabilities to store the collected data.
- Data Analytics: The heart of the value chain that brings smartness into a smart city application. Dedicated platforms are used for standardization, communication of information and transforming data into linked data with semantic context.
- Data Marketplace: Exposing data, authenticating users, authorizing access as well as possible billing or booking capabilities. The marketplace is a central element to open data strategies for cities.
- Application Layer: The application layer is dedicated to creating, developing and improving a smart city application. It represents the tools and services, as well as APIs for the city and the users.

All these elements need to be considered when creating a smart city application generating public value. However, not every element may be essential for value creation in every smart city application, some applications may only address a few elements. Usually however, most elements of the smart city value chain need to be addressed.

Regarding supporting activities, the following can be identified: sourcing of vendors (hardware and software), governance and risk management, data protection and security, as well as financing. Thus, the model of Porter is adapted as shown in Figure 1.

Sustainable and optimal development of a smart city application is based on a city's vision with focus on public value, a network of organized actors, a set of codes and technologies and values that governs all stakeholders. In this sense, governance is needed around a common vision for the transformation of cities.

B. Structure of the Smart City Blueprint Template

The smart city blueprint template consists of four parts (see Figure 2) which relate to the four typical phases of most projects [10] plus a *One-Pager* giving a summary and overview of the blueprint and its use case. In the following, we will describe these parts in more detail.

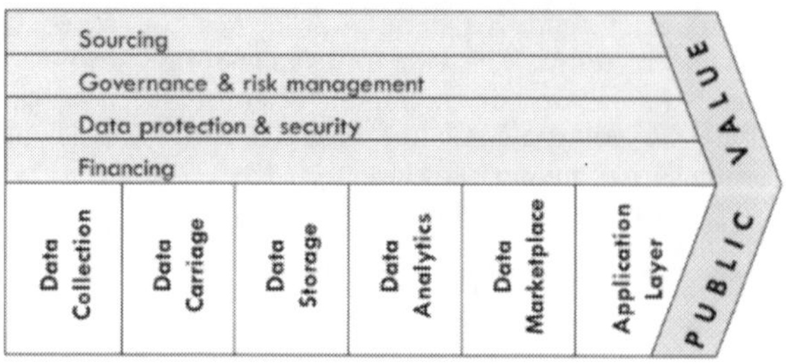

Figure 1. Smart city value chain (adapted from [7, 8]), generating public value based on data usage and on supporting activities.

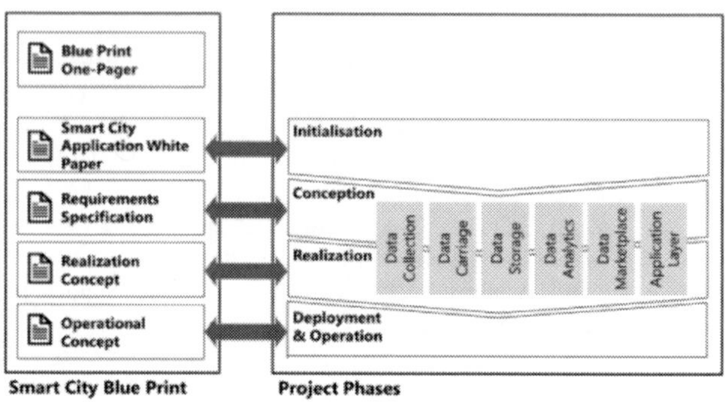

Figure 2. Structure of a smart city blueprint and relationship to project phases

C. Smart City Application White Paper

The Business Model Canvas defined by Osterwalder and Pigeur [9] is a well-recognized tool in the business world for the creation of innovation and the associated development of new business fields. With few adjustments due to the different goals for business and cities discussed above, a similar conceptualization for the smart city context is proposed (see Figure 3).

Contrary to the business model canvas, in the smart city canvas the focus is on the *public* value proposition, and on beneficiaries instead of customer segments. For the same reason also the customer relationships and channels elements of the Business Model Canvas are replaced with a single relationships element which is used to capture all stakeholder relationships, both positive and negative, as Smart City projects typically involve a multitude of different stakeholders.

This smart city canvas is the central piece and starting point of the smart city application white paper within the initialization phase (see Figure 2). In addition to the canvas, the white paper should provide an overview of services, standards and technology, especially on IT topics. This includes user descriptions, case studies and market research results.

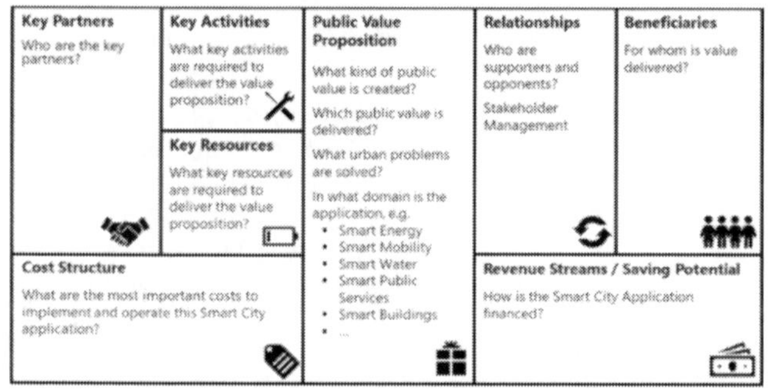

Figure 3. The smart city canvas is an adaptation of the business model canvas of Osterwalder and Pigeur [9]

D. Requirements Specification

The following specification guidelines are based on the IREB Standard, which includes a toolset of different methodologies for the management of requirements [13]. The requirement specification should begin with the description of the planned system, giving an overview of the application to be created. Furthermore, it should be ensured that the system boundary and the system context are defined before the requirements are collected. This is relevant for the definition and understanding of the requirements of the system under consideration.

To structure the requirements catalogue in a uniform and retrievable manner, they are categorized according to the elements in the value chain of smart city applications. Such a split is also helpful when developing the application, as each part may possibly be developed as a separate component. As a first step, it is thus advisable to identify which elements of the value chain are affected and play an important role in the application at hand. Table I provides a simple but useful tool for such analysis, also listing initial questions to help elicit requirements. In addition, for each element a sentence template for how to formulate the requirements has been defined. For example, the sentence template for the Data Collection element looks as follows:

The system can/should/must collect data from <source> about <topic>.

Sentence templates are an easy-to-learn and easy-to-use approach to reduce linguistic effects [13] – an important issue in multi-stakeholder projects as smart city applications typically are – and are also commonly used in agile approaches like SCRUM.

E. Realization Concept

An important step for the realization concept is listing selected technology toolsets for realizing the application. Similar tables as used in the requirements specification (cf. Table I) can also be used for summarizing the technology options, however, instead of listing requirements, possible solutions are listed here, thus spanning a solution space from which elements can be selected during a transfer and adaptation project. In addition to technology options, the realization concept must also tackle the issues of project methodology, development road map and architecture.

TABLE I. CHECKLIST TO DETERMINE THE APPLICATION REQUIREMENTS ACCORDING TO THE SMART CITY VALUE CHAIN

Value Chain Element	Requirements	Element affected?
Data Collection	**Is the planned application dependent on collecting data?** What types of data are required to implement the smart city application? Where, how (e.g., sensors) and by whom (e.g., 3rd parties) is the data collected?	☐ yes
Data Carriage	**Is the transfer of data needed for the application?** All functional and non-functional requirements related to data transmission.	☐ yes
Data Storage	**Is persistent storage of data relevant to the application?** How is the data stored? How sensitive is the data? How fast must the data be retrievable? Does the data have to be stored in a certain form? Which semantic standards or guidelines must be observed?	☐ yes
Data Analytics	**Does the application require the data to be analyzed in order to provide value?** How must data be aggregated? Which data is relevant for the analysis? What does the data curation processes look like?	☐ yes
Data marketplace	**Is it intended to sell data?** Who should have access to the collected data? How is the operator of the application remunerated for providing the information? What are the price models and payment modalities?	☐ yes
Application Layer	**Is an interface / API necessary to provide another application with information?** Which interfaces are required? Are actuators required for the application? Is a user interface provided? What actions are users or actuators performing?	☐ yes

Project methodology

Identifying a project methodology for implementing a use case is crucial for the realization concept. There are various project methodologies in use, from classical waterfall-like models to agile approaches like SCRUM. In this context, it is important to decide, to what extent citizen participation should be encouraged, and if co-creation approaches are useful.

Since smart city projects are mostly highly complex projects with multiple stakeholders and sometimes unproven technology, agile project methods are very suitable, as they are designed to deal with changing requirements, to integrate a balanced set of stakeholders and use a controlled, iterative procedure to offer an appropriate, situational response. On the other hand, government agencies often have regulations and standards how public projects have to be executed (e.g., HERMES in Switzerland) that mandate more classical, waterfall-like models of project management.

Project Roadmap

According to Galati [14], smart city planners should develop a realistic path to move from the concepts of their smart city architecture to achieving the application objectives. When planning the roadmap, project managers must consider that there may be delays in projects and that unexpected obstacles may arise. Furthermore, all expenditure should be meticulously managed and monitored. The roadmap in the realization concept must give the necessary, high-level guidance, possibly also coordinating with other smart city applications being developed in parallel. The selection of common platforms, which should be used in a given setting is a typical element of such a roadmap.

Architecure

A sound architecture of the overall smart city application landscape is crucial, since any newly developed application needs to fit into the landscape. In particular when a common smart city platform is already deployed or is planned to be, a common architecture like the functional architecture developed in the context of the CPaaS.io project becomes very useful. The realization concept must address how the application is integrated into the existing landscape. Using views and perspectives as defined by Nick Rozanski and Eoin Woods [15] is recommended to describe the application architecture. Of particular importance for smart city applications are the following perspectives: security, regulation, performance and scalability, usability, availability and resilience, as well as evolution.

Operational Concept

According to [16], the following aspects should be considered when defining an operational concept:

- Determination of operational requirements
- Description of the system technology
- Description of the organizational plan
- Description of business processes
- Treatment of disorders
- Description of safety aspects

The IT4IT operating model [17] proves to be well suited within the realization concept due to its flexibility, because it can be integrated into existing operating models such as ITIL and COBIT but focuses on the clear embedding and obligation to integrate new applications and suppliers into the operating model. The great benefit of IT4IT as a reference architecture for the IT function lies in its application as a guide.

For a smart city application landscape, it is important to think about the transfer and operation of the platform in advance. By using the IT4IT reference model, a future-proof operation of the application is achieved in view of necessary extensions. In [17], a template is given according to which IT4IT could be implemented.

F. Smart City One-Pager

For orientation, the extensive information described in the previous sections is summarized in the so-called smart city blueprint One-Pager, as shown in Table III. It forms the basis for any transfer, as a city official interested in a specific application can quickly gauge if that blueprint is relevant for his or her city, and if yes, it provides an initial list of issues that need to be tackled, and thus to an initial roadmap and project plan. An example of a One-Pager is discussed in section V.

IV. Adapting an Existing Smart City Blueprint

Developing a blueprint for a targeted city is guided by an adaptation process (see Figure 4), starting with the selection of an appropriate existing One-Pager. The next step focuses on the gaps between that One-Pager and the targeted implementation, where those aspects are identified that must be validated against the blueprint template of the targeted implementation. Finally, the blueprint can be enhanced (e.g., with new options for the realization phase), adapted or completed in an appropriate way.

In Figure 4, the adaptation process is modeled in BPMN notation. Note that it is crucial to take the technical possibilities as well as the cultural context of a city or its region into account.

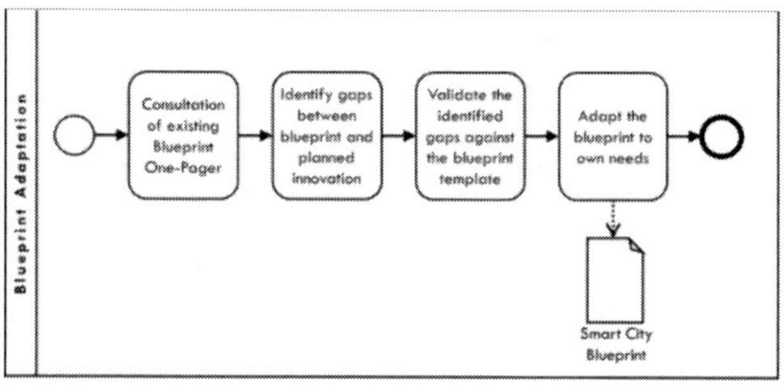

Figure 4. Adaptation process of a smart city blueprint during smart city transformation.

Checklists can assist in identifying existing gaps between the blueprint and the needs of the city that wants to adapt a blueprint. An initial version of such a checklist is given in Table II, referring to sections in the One-Pager. It might be necessary to continuously update this initial checklist with the experience gained in the actual blueprint adaptation processes.

V. Smart City Blueprint Validation

The smart city blueprint template provides a tool to guide developers of smart city applications in the initial process, giving a structure for a project plan and listing all aspects that should be considered. Using the blueprint template already at this early stage allows also capturing important information and experiences gained along the way, and thus provides the basis for the transfer to another city.

To validate the practical use, the first step is to fill out the template for selected use cases, leading to concrete blueprints. In a second step, we need to adapt these blueprints to the requirements and the context of other cities and use this adapted template in the implementation of the use case in the respective city, thus verifying that the blueprints significantly facilitate and speed up the implementation process.

In Table III, a preliminary One-Pager is shown for the Amsterdam water management use case from the CPaaS.io project, illustrating the basic use of the blueprint template. Currently, this blueprint and blueprints for other use cases are being detailed and completed. Several cities show interest in using this blueprint approach in their smart city activities, where its usefulness can be demonstrated. Specific interest exists also in using the Smart City Canvas and the One-Pager. For example, we are currently talking to a larger Swiss city to use and adapt the smart parking blueprint originally developed for the implementation in the city of Murcia, Spain. Furthermore, the water management use case shown in Table III has raised the interest of some cities in Japan. The questions listed in Table II will guide this adaptation process.

TABLE II. CHECKLIST FOR BLUEPRINT ADAPTATION

Section	Checklist questions
Vision	• Does the value proposition cope with the needs of urban environment?
Requirement Specification	• Are there any additional special security risks? • Are frameworks in use, which are not applicable for us? • Are sourcing and vending partners considered who are not suitable for us? • How is the project financed?

Realization	• Is it possible to use the project methodology used for implementation?
	• Can the implementation period be similar or is a massively shortened implementation period targeted?
	• Can the same software be used?
	  ○ Yes
	  ○ No → Does the software intended for use have the same functionality as the one used in the other city?

Tools & Technologies	• Is data collected independently or obtained from existing systems that cannot be used by us? Do we depend on the same data? • Is the technology used for data transmission available in our region and does it operate in the same frequency band? • Does the data storage meet our expectations regarding queries and does it have sufficient protection mechanisms against external access? • Is the syntax and semantics used sufficient for data analysis? • Is recorded content made available to other parties and does the marketplace support your requirements for data transfer or provision? • Should the end application be structured as it is used in the other city? Can the software and any actors involved also be used?
Operation	• How can the smart city application be operated after introduction? • What does the organization look like?

VI. Conclusion and Future Work

With the presented blueprint approach, a methodology, tools and a process are available for documenting and transferring smart city innovations to other cities. Based on well-proven concepts, such as Osterwalder's Business Model Canvas, Jenny's project phase concept and Pohl's work on specification, the proposed smart city value chain together with the blueprint template are well suited for specifying a holistic picture of a specific smart city implementation. Moreover, the proposed checklist guides through the adaptation process and helps identifying gaps between an existing blueprint and the needs of a city that is aiming at adapting the blueprint.

To date, all the proposed concepts are developed and documented, and have been validated in the context of a smart city innovation project [4]. By capturing the information of the use cases in the project, we could validate that these tools can not only be used to capture information about specific use cases, but that the structure of the tool is helpful in doing so. Currently, the approach is applied for various other city contexts and use cases for validation purposes, in order to evaluate and possibly adapt the proposed tools and processes. Respective stakeholders from different cities have shown specific interest in the Smart City Canvas as well as the One-Pager. This will enable the next step of validation, applying and adapting an existing blueprint in the context of another city.

ACKNOWLEDGMENT

This work is supported by the Horizon 2020 EUJ-02-2016 Research and Innovation Action CPaaS.io; EU Grant number 723076, NICT management number 18302.

TABLE III. SMART CITY BLUEPRINT ONE-PAGER FOR AMSTERDAM WATER MANAGEMENT USE CASE

Smart City Blueprint One Pager						
Value Proposition – Creation of Public Value		Extreme rainfall and periods of continued drought are occurring more and more often in urban areas. Because of the rainfall, peak pressure on a municipality's sewerage infrastructure needs to be load balanced to prevent flooding of streets and basements. With drought, smart water management is required to allow for optimal availability of water, both underground as well as above ground.				
Requirement Specification						
Ownership / Contact		WaterNet (water utility)				
Affected Value Chain Elements:	Data Collection	Data Carriage	Data Storage	Data Analytics	Data Marketplace	Application Layer
	[x] yes	[x] yes	[x] yes	[x] yes	[ ] yes	[x] yes
Supporting Activities						
	Sourcing	LoRa Network (The Things Network), Polderdak (water buffers)				
	Governance & Risk Management	tbd				
	Data Protection & Security	Remote-control access to valves must be secured, data transmission over secure channels				
	Financing	Government-level funding				
Realization						
Project organisation		Led by WaterNet				
Roadmap		Prototyping individual sites, then boader roll-out				
Architecture		PaaS (Platform as a Service), using CPaaS.io / FIWARE components (e.g., FogFlow for distributed edge computing				
Chain link specific tools and technologies used:						
	Data Collection	Data Carriage	Data Storage	Data Analytics	Data Marketplace	Application Layer
	1. Water-level sen-sors (in buffers as well as in sewage systems) 2. Weather data	LoRaWAN transmissionon (EU 863-870MHz ISM band)	Storing the Data in the FIWARE Orion context broker	Control water buffer valves based on fill levels, expected weather data, and status od sewage system.		FIWARE APIs (NGSI-10)
Operation						
Currently in prototype stage, determining parameters for continuous operation.						

REFERENCES

[1] P. Neirotti, A. de Marco, A. C. Cagliano, G. Mangano, and F. Scorrano, "Current trends in Smart City initiatives: Some stylised facts," *Cities*, vol. 38, pp. 25–36, 2014.

[2] M. Batty *et al.*, "Smart cities of the future," *The European Physical Journal Special Topics*, vol. 214, no. 1, pp. 481–518, 2012.

[3] Nokia, *Nokia - Smart City*. [Online]. Available from: https://networks.nokia.com/smart-city. [retrieved: January 2019].

[4] CPaaS.io, *City Platform as a Service - Integrated and Open: Horizon 2020 EU-Japan Research & Innovation Action*. [Online]. Available from: https://www.cpaas.io/. [retrieved: January 2019].

[5] CPaaS.io, *Use Cases of the CPaaS.io project*. [Online]. Available from: https://cpaas.io/?page_id=280. [retrieved: January 2019].

[6] J. Jin, J. Gubbi, S. Marusic, and M. Palaniswami, "An Information Framework for Creating a Smart City Through Internet of Things," *IEEE Internet Things J.*, vol. 1, no. 2, pp. 112–121, 2014.

[7] M. E. Porter, *Wettbewerbsvorteile: Spitzenleistungen erreichen und behaupten = (Competitive Advantage)*, 8th ed. Frankfurt am Main: Campus-Verlag, 2014.

[8] K. Laaboudi and S. D'Ouezzan, "White Pater: Smart City Value Chain," 2016. [Online]. Available from: http://www.e-madina.org/wp-content/uploads/2016/11/White-Paper-e-Madina-3.0-Value-Chain-of-Smart-cities.pdf. [retrieved: January 2019].

[9] A. Osterwalder and Y. Pigneur, *Business Model Generation: A Handbook for Visionaries, Game Changers, and Challengers,* 1st ed. New York, NY: John Wiley & Sons, 2013.

[10] B. Jenny, *Projektmanagement: Das Wissen für den Profi,* 3rd ed. Zürich: Vdf Hochschulverlag, 2014.

[11] M. Moore and S. Khagram, "On creating public value: What business might learn from government about strategic management," John F. Kennedy School of Government, Harvard University, Cambridge, MA Working Paper no. 3, 2004. [Online]. Available from: http://www.hks.harvard.edu/m-rcbg/CSRI/publications/workingpaper_3_moore_khagram.pdf. [retrieved: January 2019].

[12] A. C. Neuroni, S. Haller, W. van Winden, V. Carabias-Hütter, and O. Yildirim, "Increasing Public Value Creation for Smart Cities Using an Ecosystem Approach," in *Setting Foundations for the Creation of Public Value in Smart Cities*, M. P. Rodriguez Bolivar, Ed.: Springer, 2019.

[13] K. Pohl, *Requirements engineering: Grundlagen, Prinzipien, Techniken,* 2nd ed. Heidelberg: dpunkt-Verlag, 2008.

[14] S. R. Galati, "Funding a Smart City: From Concept to Actuality," in *Smart Cities*, S. McClellan, J. A. Jimenez, and G. Koutitas, Eds., Cham: Springer International Publishing, 2018, pp. 17–39.

[15] N. Rozanski and E. Woods, *Software systems architecture: Working with stakeholders using viewpoints and perspectives,* 2nd ed. Upper Saddle River, NJ: Addison-Wesley, 2013.

[16] H. Mourgue d'Algue, G. Eicher, and B. Kruschitz, *Hermes 5.1: Projektmanagementmethode für alle Projekte : Referenzhandbuch,* 1st ed. Bern: Eidgenössisches Finanzdepartement EFD Informatiksteuerungsorgan des Bundes ISB and Vertrieb BBL Verkauf Bundespublikationen, 2014.

[17] M. Andenmatten, "IT4ITTM – das agile Betriebskonzept der IT der Zukunft," *HMD*, vol. 54, no. 2, pp. 261–274, 2017.

Quality of Life Index Analysis for the Case of Romanian Regions

Ilie Cristian Dorobăț, Octavian Rinciog, George Cristian Muraru, Vlad Posea
Faculty of Computer Science
Politehnica University of Bucharest
Bucharest, Romania
Email: ilie.dorobat@stud.acs.upb.ro, {octavian.rinciog, vlad.posea}@cs.pub.ro, murarugeorgec@gmail.com

***Abstract*—The analysis of the quality of life has become an increasingly complex process through which a number of economic, political and social factors are examined in order to identify the necessary measures to be taken for the social inclusion of disadvantaged people, to reduce the poverty rate of the population and to increase the living conditions. Through a detailed analysis of the determinants of living standards, we identified the progress that Romania has made since 2007, the year of accession to European Union, until 2016, the year for which the latest open data sets are available. Thus, an important discrepancy it has been identified between the level of quality of life from the region that has obtained the highest score, the region which covers the Romanian capital has been excluded, and the one which has obtained the lowest score. With an income difference of 28% and with four times higher of foreign investments attracted in the Central Region against the North-Eastern Region, the identification and adoption of administrative politics become imperative for ensuring a unitary development of the eight Romanian regions of economic development.**

Keywords-quality of life index; quality of life dimensions; open data quality; QoLI Framework.

I. INTRODUCTION

Measuring the quality of life represents an important instrument in determining the level of development of a determined region, as an increased value of life satisfaction reflects at the same time the individual's and the society's economic welfare, individual's satisfaction, which reflects not only in his/her good emotional state, but also in the assessment of the local economy by the increase of productivity, capital attraction, increases of workplaces, etc.

For an identification as accurate as possible of the level of the quality of life it is necessary not only to use the economic dimensions, which consider the rate of income and expenses, or other financial elements, but also to turn towards the factors which measure the citizens' safety level, the medical facilities' capability to ensure public interest healthcare, the education level accessible to citizens, the individuals' satisfaction and other social factors which might have significant influence both on the economic welfare and on the social welfare of individuals belonging to a certain society.

On the same hand, even though the data sets come from official sources, for calculating the level of the quality of life, an analysis of the former must be realized in order to ensure a level of data quality as high as possible by correcting possible errors present in the analyzed data sets.

For the atomization of the calculation of the quality of life index, the QoLI Framework represents an authentic solution as it absolves the analysts from the application of complex sets of formulas in order to determine the level of quality of life of a determined community. Through this framework, the analysis becomes easier, involving only the preparation of the date which will be used to realize the calculation and to interpret the results obtained after applying the calculation formulas over a sphere of eight economical-social dimensions and of two supplementary indicators, the net medium income and the level of resident population. Thus, the quality of life indicator calculated using the QoLI Framework becomes a robust indicator, which has in mind both the financial nature factors which influence the purchasing power of individuals and the social nature factors as well, which affect the physical and emotional state of the population.

The present case of study aims at realizing a study relative to the level of the quality of life in Romania centered on the economic development areas for the period 2007-2016, the year of accession of Romania to the European Union (2007), respectively the last year for which statistics are available. For this reason, we will briefly present the most important indexes for measuring the quality of life used after 1990, followed in Section III by a focus over detailing the economic and social dimensions which make up the formula for calculating the Quality of Life Index (QoLI).

Section IV is reserved to presenting the used open data sources, followed on the next section by a focus on the process of ensuring the quality of data by identifying and suggesting solutions for rectifying the sensitive aspects regarding the increase of the data's quality. The framework's structure implementation will be presented in Section VI, while in Section VII it will be presented the result of the calculation of the QoLI for the laps of time analyzed so that the following section exposes a series of findings regarding the approached subject will be revealed.

II. STATE OF ART

One of the most used metrics for determining the level of development of a country [1], the Human Development Index (HDI) [2], has its origins in year 1990, when the United Nations Development Programme launched a formula for calculating the rate of the welfare of the population using the following three factors:

a) the population's health status and longevity;
b) the level of knowledge the citizens have access to;

c) the population's life standard reflected through the rate of its income.

The recognition of the multi-dimensional nature of the factors that affect the quality of life has determined the identification of a new index, the World Health Organization Quality of Life (WHOQOF) [3], which treats more dimensions than the HDI:

a) physical domain;
b) psychological domain;
c) level of independence;
d) social relationships;
e) environment;
f) spirituality, religion, personal beliefs.

Although HDI and WHOQOF are two indexes useful in determining a country's level of development, the European Union's Statistical Office (Eurostat) proposed that in official reporting, to measure the quality of life using the following relations [4]:

a) material and living conditions;
b) productive or main activity;
c) health;
d) education;
e) leisure and social interactions;
f) economic and physical safety;
g) governance and basic rights;
h) natural and living environment;
i) overall experience of life.

As far as the quality of the data is concerned, in the literature [5] [6] [7] can be distinguished the following four central dimensions which ensure a level of data quality as high as possible: i) data accuracy - measures the degree of representativeness of the data from the database in relation to the elements from real life which they represent; ii) data consistency - is the data's property of respecting the integrity constraints; iii) information completeness - measure the capacity of the database to offer complete information at the user's queries; iv) data currency - reflects the degree of update of the data.

III. Quality of Life Indicators

Although the Gross Domestic Product Index (GDP) is one of the most used indicators for determining the level of development of a country [8], it is limited as it measures the quality of life only from a financial perspective. Therefore, scientists headed towards the identification of all factors which might have a significant influence over the population's quality of life, such as social indicators, measures for the increase of the population's welfare, economic measure [9], etc. As Eurostat itself specifies [4], the dimensions of the quality of life are grouped according to the functional capacities the citizens should have in order to identify a decent living.

A. Material and Living Conditions

The Material and Living Conditions (MLC) is a dimension which reflects the living conditions of a population, not only from a material point of view, but also from the perspective of the place where they live in. If the pay grade is a component which highlights the rate of standard living, MLC includes other relevant factors to be taken into account, such as the purchasing power of a household, the relative poverty rate, poverty risk and severe material depravation, etc. These distinctive factors reflect, on the one hand, the difficulty of satisfying the basic needs of a decent living, and on the other hand, the capacity of a population to afford expenses in order to support a decent living, such as contacting mortgage loans, paying bills, purchasing household appliances, tacking voyages inside and outside the frontiers of the country, etc.

B. Productive or Main Activity

As the time spent at work represents a significant lapse of time at which the individual renounces so that he/she might obtain benefits for him/herself, it represents an important factor in determining the self-respect. Thus, through a fair remuneration of the work undergone and through the evolution of the social status, individuals may feel their work appreciated, and their mental health is enriched by professional life success [10]. Therefore, the Productive or Main Activity (PMA) dimension is particular one as it measures the quality of life from the perspective of the individual's social status.

C. Health

Health is another determining factor in calculating the rate of the quality of life because it directly affects the life of the individuals. This dimension can be calculated from the perspective of several factors, such as the quantity of fruits and vegetables consumed, the quantity of alcohol consumed (with a negative effect on the quality of life), the population's degree of access to healthcare and the medical facilities' capacity of ensuring public interest healthcare both from the point of view of the available infrastructure and of the existing qualified personnel, the rate of incidents (with a negative influence), average life expectancy, as well as other factors which directly affect the individual's health quality.

D. Education

An important factor which has a significant contribution in determining the quality of life is represented by the level of education of the population, because a group with a high educational level may have access more easily to well-paid employment, which contributes to the possibility of accessing higher quality healthcare and to the increase of the living conditions. Moreover, the high level of education of the population is reflected in the governing and lawmaking, in creating a friendly environment both from the point of view of social interaction and from the point of view of nature preservation.

E. Leisure and Social Interactions

The fifth dimension which can measure the population's quality of life, the Leisure and Social Interactions (LSI), is closely linked both to factors which facilitate the social interactions in environmental areas, such as museums, spectacles and to factors which are found in sports environments, such as the number of sports facilities.

F. Safety

Another dimension which has a significant influence over the quality of life of the population is represented by Safety. As the Law no. 51/1991 on National Security of Romania defines national security as a state of social, economic and political stability, we can look at the safety term as being a state of stability both social and economic. Therefore, the Safety dimension considers the individual analysis of the economic security (of the measures the society or individuals take for ensuring the individual economic security in case of loss of employment, variation of monthly expenses, mortgage and other exceptional situations) and of the physical security (of the factors that reflect the physical insecurity of a population, as the crime rate, the percentage of the population with a definitive penal sentence, etc.).

G. Governance and Basic Rights

The dimension Governance and Basic Rights (GBR) represents that series of factors which influence the life of population from the perspective of the governing and law making, but also from the perspective of the equality of opportunity no matter the political, religious or cultural background of the individuals in a society.

H. Natural and Living Environment

The dimension Natural and Living Environment (ENV) considers the calculating of the level of standard living of the population considering the quality of the environment where the individuals live by analyzing a series of factors, such as the level of pollution of the area, the measures taken to combat pollution, the degree of the population's access to basic services (drinking water systems, electrical power supply systems, etc.).

IV. Open Data Sources

From a simple perspective, by the term open data it can be seen as being that concept which defines the freedom of use, reuse and distribute data. Nevertheless, some data suppliers may have different perspectives regarding what it can be understood by openness [11], in the sense that the use, reuse, reworking, redistribution and reselling might have terms and conditions by their own, so that, even though the access to data is free, their use in one way or another, might be restricted.

The collection of statistical was made through the API's offered by the National Institute of Statistics of Romania (INSSE) [12], which allows the selection of open data sets according to topics, years and economic development area both in XLS format but also in CSV format. For the analyzed period, there have been identified data sets referring to the eight main topics, as the level of income and the average expenses of a household, the living standard of the population, the GDP value, the average number of employees and of unemployed workers, the population's state of health, the level of development of the healthcare and educational system both from the state and private area, the number of leisure places, data regarding the measure for assistance and social protection, the rate of green spaces per head of population, the dimension of the drinking water supply system and a two data sets referring to the level of the average net income and the level of resident population which permits to calculate the main topics indicators as they have been presented in Table I.

Due to the fact that INSSE does not make available a set of public data regarding the result of the parliamentary elections, these data were extracted using the portal of the Permanent Electoral Authority of Romania [13], where we identified two PDF files containing information regarding the turnout at the parliamentary election dated year 2008 and 2012, and one HTML file dated year 2016.

V. Open Data Quality Assessment

Considering that the open data is a concept that enforces the existence of a free license for accessing the data, the open data quality may be expressed as it is expressed the quality of the data regardless their licenses, as being that state of the data which allows their use by consumers [14] [15]. The most frequently mentioned dimensions of this property [16] [5] in the literature being accuracy, completeness, consistency and timeliness. Therefore, the rate of the quality of data is directly related to the accuracy of the presented elements.

TABLE I. Data Sources

Dimension Name	Dimension Indicator Name
Material and Living Condition (5 CSV files)	Household income rate Poverty Rate Poverty Risk Deprivation Rate
Productive or Main Activity (4 CSV files)	Researchers Rate GDP Rate Employment Rate Unemployment Rate
Health (17 CSV files)	Infrastructure Rate Medical Staff Rate Food Consumption Rate Injured Rate Natural Population Growth Rate Life Expectancy
Education (5 CSV files)	Teaching Staff Rate Infrastructure Rate Abandon Rate
Leisure and Social Interactions (3 CSV files)	Museums Rate Cinematographic Performances Rate Sports Sections Rate
Economic and Physical Safety (8 CSV files)	Family Support Allowance Rate Social Assistance Rate Social Canteens Rate Pension Rate Convicts Rate Crime Rate Offences Rate Police Solved Offences Rate
Governance and Basic Rights (1 CSV file, 2 PDF file, 1 HTML file)	Employee Rate by Gender Parliamentary Elections Rate [a]
Natural and Living Environment (2 CSV files)	Green Spaces Rate Drinking Water Access Rate
Auxiliary Dimensions (2 CSV files)	Net Average Wage Resident Population

[a] Sets of data downloaded from the portal of the Permanent Electoral Authority of Romania

A. Data Currency Issue

Data currency or timeliness is an indicator which measures the quality of data which reflects the degree of their timeliness in relation to the nature of the activity for which the date is being used [7]. Although the API of the INSSE includes an entry regarding the last date of update of the data sets, this date is available only for the data sets as entities, and not for the records from the data sets. This feature does not allow to identify whether the data set has been modified due to adding new records or whether the existing records have been modified.

B. Data Source Inconsistency

For the analyzed data sets, the data model is divided into categories having only 4 common columns: the economic development area, the reporting year, the measurement unit and the actual value. This discrepancy of the data sets implies the application of separate rules for each data category. Another relevant aspect of the way data is stored – the use of the Comma Separated Values (CSV) files, which implies storing data on columns in a text file, columns separated only by a comma or another specific separator. Therefore, storing data in text format restricts the user in terms of types of data related to the stored values, which urge the user to identify the data types based on the columns' description and of the existing values before using these data.

C. Data Inconsistency

The data inconsistency can be seen as the state of the data of not being consistent, that is of not having the format and the value in conformity with the chosen data model [17] or of having discontinuities of data.

TABLE II. ENTRIES STATISTICS

Dimension Name	Expected Input [a]	Missing Values	Inconsistency Rate (%)
Material and Living Condition	400	16	4.00
Productive or Main Activity	320	8	2.43
Health	1,440	0	0.00
Education	480	81	16.88
Leisure and Social Interactions	240	0	0.00
Economic and Physical Safety	640	64	10.00
Governance and Basic Rights	240	8	3.33
Natural and Living Environment	160	8	5.00
Auxiliary Dimensions	142	16	11.27
TOTAL	**3,182**	**201**	**6.32**

[a] The total number of entries that should exist for the data set to be complete

For the analyzed data sets, the data inconsistency is determined by the value of the missing record, as shown in Table II, considering that due to the periodical method of organization of the parliamentary election, the values of the missing years have been corrected with the one of the last years when parliamentary election has been organized in Romania. For example, for the years 2008, 2009, 2010 and 2011, for each year it has been considered the value related to year 2008, year when parliamentary elections have been undergone, proceeding the same manner for the following periods.

As an exception to the previous calculation mode of the results of the turn-out, lacking the statistical data regarding the turn-out for the parliamentary elections from 2004, the value for the year 2007 has been calculated applying (1), realizing the arithmetic mean of the values relative to year 2008-2016.

To decrease the negative effect of the missing records during the process of calculating the QoLI, we have proceeded, taking in consideration that: i) the value fluctuation from one year to the other is linear; ii) by using (1) to calculate the average of the series, the magnitude of the majority of the series is low under 50% than the average.

$$avg = \frac{\sum_{i=start}^{end} data_i}{n} \quad (1)$$

start = beginning year
end = end year
data = the values related to the analyzed column
n = the number of the years for which data are available

Another aspect important to be mentioned regarding the data inconsistency is represented by the absence from certain data sets of the records classified for each county; this shortage restricts to an analysis on economic development areas, not including a detailed analysis on counties.

VI. THE FRAMEWORK ARCHITECTURE

Considering the complex character of the calculation of the Quality of Life Index, the present case of study, at the same time, aims at presenting the way the framework [18] has been conceived for the calculation of this economical-social indicator. Thus, who is interested in realizing the analysis referring to the state of living of the population is absolved from implementing the formulas of calculation of the QoLI, the only tasks that must be done being the supply of the input data and the interpretation of the obtained results.

Figure 1 presents the diagram of the processes of realizing the QoLI framework, the first step being the analysis of the downloaded data sets in order to identify the common elements and the types of data for each individual column. After that, based on the formulated findings, the data model will be created for each analyzed data category, and for the missing records, the average of the respective period will be calculated using (1), so that the impact of the data set inconsistency will have an influence as light as possible when calculating the QoLI.

The second stage implies the actual calculation of the values of the 8 QoLI main topics as they have been described and of the following complementary indicators:

a) the average number of resident persons;
b) the average net salary,

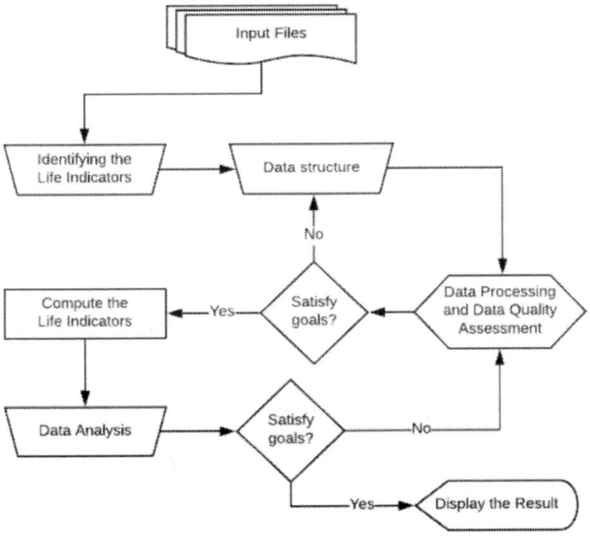

Figure 1. The framework architecture.

values calculated according to the reporting year and to the chosen economic development area. These indicators are used in determining the complementary statistic data, such as the share of the overall income of a household in relation to the average net earnings for the specific area; the share of the education establishments related to 1,000 resident persons, the number of square meters of green space for each inhabitant, and so on.

The intermediate stage to presenting the QoLI result is represented by the analysis of the data, which aims at identifying errors and discrepancies in the calculation process of the indicators. For example, the school drop-out rate, the rate of persons involved in accidents, etc., they are all elements which negatively influence the calculation of the indicators they belong to, which implies that in the final formula their reverse must be considered, that is, to determine the proportions of population that is not affected.

With the identification of the correction that must be made on the data so that they can reflect the real-life situation, the flow of operations come back to the sub-stage "Data Processing and Data Quality Assessment" for applying the mentioned modifications, a cycle that will be repeated until obtaining the expected results. In the end, the user will have the possibility of extracting the final result of the Quality of Life Index calculation classified on reporting years and on economic development area calculated using (2).

$$QoLI = \sqrt[8]{\begin{aligned} &conditions * activity * health * edu \\ &* interactions * safety * law * env \end{aligned}} \qquad (2)$$

conditions = Material and Living Conditions Indicator
activity = Productive or Main Activity Indicator
health = Health Indicator
edu = Education Indicator
interactions = Leisure and Social Interactions Indicator
safety = Safety Indicator
law = Governance and Basic Rights Indicator
env = Natural and Living Environment Indicator

Using the geometric mean for the calculation of the QoLI is imposed by the asymmetric character of the indicators which compose the eight dimensions so that the linear compensation of the reduced values of one dimension with the higher values of another dimension will be avoided [19]. Thus, using the geometric mean for calculating the QoLI, will allow that a reduction of 1% of one dimension to register the same impact as a reduction of 1% of any other dimension.

VII. Data Usage

The result of the current analysis can be used both by governmental factors which have at their disposal the legal measures for combating poverty and increasing the living standard of the population and to other actors of the society interested in following the evolution of the economic and social development level in time. The analysis uses a series of statistic data broken down on reporting years and economic development area, which facilitates both the identification of the area which met a considerable advantage, and to those which present an index of the quality of life lower than the other areas.

TABLE III. Foreign Direct Investment in Romania by Years and Regions (millions of Euro)

Region / **Year**	**2007**	**2008**	**2009**	**2010**	**2011**	**2012**	**2013**	**2014**	**2015**	**2016**
Bucharest-Ilfov	27,516	30,594	31,699	32,720	34,021	35,859	36,808	35,665	38,243	42,021
Center	3,541	4,146	3,703	3,909	4,215	4,625	5,179	5,833	5,831	6,379
North-East	672	2,108	975	1,244	1,627	1,767	1,685	1,624	1,662	1,606
North-West	1,907	1,226	1,940	2,232	2,454	2,814	2,665	3,384	3,783	4,108
South-East	2,448	3,551	2,938	3,290	2,970	3,253	2,529	2,898	2,869	3,477
South-Muntenia	2,942	3,411	3,576	3,816	4,059	4,230	4,599	4,194	4,626	4,837
South-West Oltenia	1,379	1,226	2,058	1,928	1,806	2,068	1,912	1,954	2,172	2,080
West	2,365	2,626	3,095	3,446	3,987	4,510	4,581	4,646	5,237	5,605

The result of the calculation of the QoLI is presented using the histograms from Figure 2 and Figure 3, where it can be observed the evolution of the indicators in time, according to the economic development regions. Thus, it can be noted that, as expected, the Bucharest-Ilfov Region, the one which comprises the Romanian capital, is the most developed, being followed by the North-Western Region, the Western Region and the Central Region, and on the other side, the most underdeveloped region being the North-Eastern one, being followed by the South-Western Oltenia Region, the South-Muntenia Region and the South-Eastern Region.

The growth trend of the Quality of Life Index from the central-western region of Romania may be considered as being the result of the consolidation of the industrial poles as Cluj-Napoca, Timisoara and Brasov [20], evolution that can be noticed even from the statistical data regarding the foreign direct investment rate which the National Bank of Romania supplied [21] as it is in Table III. As the statistical data are presented, the Bucharest-Ilfov Region and the Central Region remain on the entire analyzed period on the top of the regions with the height's foreign investment capital in Romania, and the North-Eastern Region and the South-Western Oltenia Region being classified as the most unattractive regions from the point of view of foreign capital attraction.

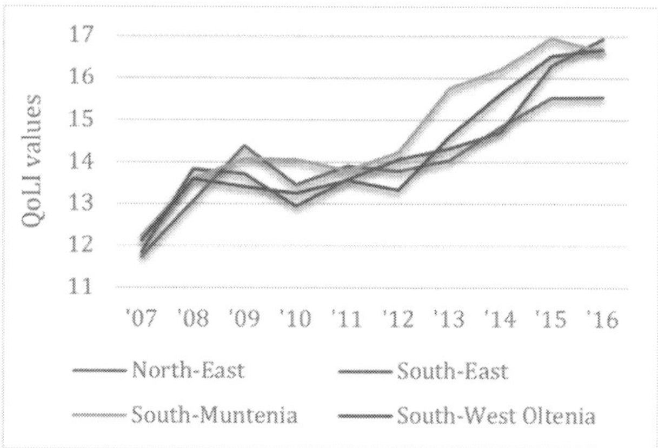

Figure 2. Lowest evolution of QoLI.

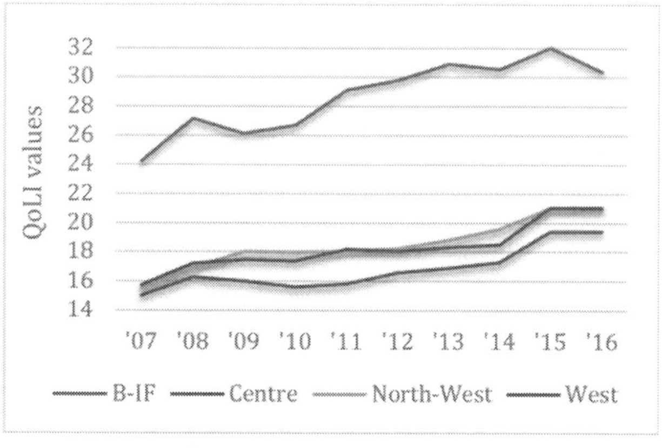

Figure 3. Heist evolution of QoLI.

The importance of foreign capital attraction occurs due to the relation which has in the increase of the state of living of the population. If the financial value of the investments is inconstant, alongside the advantage of attracting the capital for the development of the private area, at the same time, the investors may realize technological and knowledge transfers with the host country, may integrate both highly-qualified employees and unqualified employees, investing, thus in human resources, they may bring new management concepts, may influence the local market structure determining the sector in which they activate to be more productive and, of course, may contribute to the local and national budget by paying taxes, which can materialize in the increase of the level of public investments done in the interest of the citizen [22] .

Another important component which has a major impact on the increase of the state of living of the population is represented by the correct financial remuneration of the work, because, alongside the financial factor needed to each person for leaving, individuals can feel more appreciated if they are remunerated accordingly to the performed work [10]. Therefore, the increase of the self-esteem influences not only the individual satisfaction but also his/her productivity, which translates by the increase of the value of the company they work for, a value which can attract financial investments and can create new workplaces for the resident population.

By analyzing the data relative to the value of the monthly income on household for year 2016 [12], presented in Table IV, it can be noted that in the four regions which register a higher QoLI indicator, the level of the income reaching almost 700 euro; in the Bucharest-Ilfov Region the income is reaching to 911 euro. On the other hand, the level of income on household relative to the other economic development regions do not even reach the level of 600 euro, in the North-Eastern Region, the one which presents the lowest QoLI indicator, the level of income barely reaching 525 euro.

VIII. CONCLUSION

The analysis of the population's living standard is a complex process which is considered the determining of the level of economic development and the degree of satisfaction which a group of individuals has in the society. From this point of view, for calculating the Quality of Life Index, analysts must take into account the use not only of economic indicators which reflect the financial situation but also of the social indicators which reveal the level of satisfaction of individuals, both on personal and professional level.

Analyzing the statistical data previously presented, except for the Bucharest-Ilfov Region, it can be noted a considerable discrepancy between the most developed and the less developed economical region from Romania, for which the level of monthly income per household differs with up to 28%, and the value of foreign investments attracted in the North-Eastern Region represents only 25% of the value of the investments from the Central Region. Thus, the existence of these discrepancies between the economic development regions from Romania may represent an alarm

TABLE IV. MONTHLY AVERAGE OF TOTAL INCOME PER HOUSEHOLD BY YEARS AND REGIONS (EURO) [a]

Region / Year	2007	2008	2009	2010	2011	2012	2013	2014	2015	2016
Bucharest-Ilfov	x	714	746	709	723	703	742	763	812	911
Center	x	535	542	537	574	565	611	563	644	673
North-East	x	480	505	478	504	510	514	474	481	525
North-West	x	551	537	539	582	570	582	589	640	694
South-East	x	483	494	474	504	490	492	477	524	584
South-Muntenia	x	517	532	553	541	548	542	545	545	594
South-West Oltenia	x	492	489	498	500	509	527	510	541	580
West	x	548	574	547	588	617	602	577	618	689

[a] The monthly average of total income per household has been converted from RON to EUR accordingly to the exchange rate provided by The National Bank of Romania [23]

signal for the authorities, enforcing the realization and application of the public politics which should advantage the less developed regions for reducing the existent discrepancy and the increase of the level of the population state residing in less developed regions.

Thus, extending dimensions proposed by Eurostat, QoLI Framework allows for a more complex analysis of the level of quality of life in a region by including factors, such as the degree of school and health infrastructure development, the number of square meters of green spaces per inhabitant, the share of the number of researchers per thousand inhabitants, etc., factors that have a significant influence on the social life of individuals. At the same time, the utility of the framework can be easily extended to any level of administrative detailing by including, in the constant lists, the name of the administrative unit which is desired to be analyzed, regardless of the fact that it is a city, a county, a region, a country or any other administrative form.

The utility of this indicator is incontestable for any part involved in society, from government which need accurate data to identify and apply the best measures for combating poverty, to nongovernmental organizations which supervise the application of the measure on social welfare and regional development, up to individuals who, on the basis of the data supplied by the state institutions or by specialized organizations, can take decisions upon migration towards a more developed area.

If the state institutions authorized to make forecasts and analysis regarding the living standard of the population have access to the data, natural or legal persons are strictly limited to the public data offered by the state institutions, which, unfortunately, cannot be used before processing them. Therefore, it is mandatory to make an analysis in order to ensure the quality of the data by identifying errors and applying specific technics for adjusting them, so that the identified errors will have an impact as light as possible on the calculation.

REFERENCES

[1] E. Neumayer, "The Human Development Index and sustainability - a constructive proposal", Ecological Economics, vol. 39, pp. 101-114, Oct. 2001, doi:10.1016/S0921-8009(01)00201-4;

[2] United Nations Development Programme, Human Development Reports. Human Development Index. [Online]. Available from http://hdr.undp.org/en/content/human-development-index-hdi [retrieved: January, 2019];

[3] The WHOQL Group. "The World Health Organization Quality of Life assessment (WHOQL): position paper from the World Health Organization", Social Science & Medicine, vol. 41, pp. 1403-1409, Nov. 1995, doi:10.1016/0277-9536(95)00112-K;

[4] Eurostat. Quality of life indicators. [Online]. Available from https://ec.europa.eu/eurostat/statistics-explained/index.php/Quality_of_life_indicators [retrieved: January, 2019];

[5] Y. Wand and R. Y. Wang, "Anchoring data quality dimensions in ontological foundations", Communications of the ACM, Nov. 1996, pp. 86-95, doi:10.1145/240455.240479;

[6] W. Fan, "Data quality: From theory to practice", ACM SIGMOD Record, Sep. 2015, pp. 7-18, doi:10.1145/2854006.2854008;

[7] L.L. Pipino, Y. W. Lee, and R. Y. Wang, "Data quality assessment", Communications of the ACM - Supporting community and building social capital, Apr. 2002, pp. 211-218, doi:10.1145/505248.506010;

[8] V. Berenger and A. Verdier-Chouchane, "Multidimensional measures of well-being: standard of living and quality of life across counteries", World Development, vol. 35, pp. 1259-1276, Jul. 2007, doi:10.1016/j.worlddev.2006.10.011;

[9] E. Diener and E. Suh, "Meaasuring quality of life: economic, social and subjective indicators", Social Indicators Research, vol. 40, pp. 189-216, Jan. 1997, doi:10.1023/A:1006859511756;

[10] R. M. de Bustillo Llorente, and E. F. Macías, "Job satisfaction as an indicator of the quality of work", Journal of Socio-Economics, vol. 34, pp. 656-673, Oct. 2005, doi:10.1016/j.socec.2005.07.027;

[11] Kitchin R., "The Data Revolution: Big Data, Open Data, data infrastructures and their consequences", SAGE Publications Ltd, pp. 48-67, 2014, ISBN: 978 1 4462 8748 4;

[12] National Institute of Statistics of Romania. Tempo Online. [Online]. Available from http://statistici.insse.ro:8077/tempo-online/ [retrieved: January, 2019];

[13] Permanent Electoral Authority of Romania. Historical Electoral Romania. [Online]. Available from http://www.roaep.ro/istoric/ [retrieved: January, 2019];

[14] R. Y. Wang and D. M. Strong, "Beyound accuracy: what data quality means to data consumers", Journal of Mangement Information Systems, vol. 12 (4), Spring 1996, pp. 5-33, doi:10.1080/07421222.1996.11518099;

[15] D. M. Strong, Y. W. Lee, and R. Y. Wang, "Data quality in context", Communications of the ACM, May 1997, pp. 103-110, doi:10.1145/253769.253804;

[16] D. P. Ballau and H. R. Pazer, "Modeling data and process quality in multi-input information systems", Management Science, vol. 31, pp. 150-162, Feb. 1985, doi:10.1287/mnsc.31.2.150;

[17] B. Behkamal, M. Kahani, E. Bagheri, and Z. Jemeric, "A metrics-driven approach for quality assessment of linked open data", Journal of Theoretical and Applied Electronic Commerce Research, vol. 9, pp. 64-79, May 2014, doi:10.4067/S0718-18762014000200006;

[18] Quality of Life Index Framework. [Online]. Available from https://github.com/iliedorobat/QoLI-Framework [retrieved: January, 2019];

[19] United Nations Development Programme, Human Development Reports. Why is the geometric mean used for the HDI rather than the arithmetic mean? Available from http://hdr.undp.org/en/content/why-geometric-mean-used-hdi-rather-arithmetic-mean [retrieved: January, 2019].

[20] C. Iacoboaea, O. Luca, and A-M. Nica, "Industry growth poles of Romania", Urbanism. Architecture. Constructions. [Urbanism. Arhitectura. Constructii Journal], vol. 6, Mar. 2015, pp. 57-70;

[21] The National Bank of Romania, "Foreign direct investment in Romania". [Online]. Available from: http://www.bnr.ro/PublicationDocuments.aspx?icid=14364 [retrieved: January, 2019];

[22] J-W. Lee, J. de Gregorio, and E. Borensztein, "How Does Foreign Direct Investment Affect Economic Growth", Journal of International Economics, vol. 45 (1), pp. 115-135, Jun. 1998, doi: 10.1016/S0022-1996(97)00033-0;

[23] The National Bank of Romania, "Exchange Rate List in XML Format". [Online]. Available from: http://www.bnr.ro/Exchange-rate-list-in-XML-format-7512.aspx [retrieved: January, 2019];

Implementing Factors of Information Security in Governmental Organizations of Jordan

Ibrahim Obeidat
Prince Al-Hussein Bin Abdullah II Faculty of Information Technology
Hashemite University
Zarqa, Jordan
imsobeidat@hu.edu.jo

Ala Mughaid
Prince Al-Hussein Bin Abdullah II Faculty of Information Technology
Hashemite University
Zarqa, Jordan
Ala.mughaid@hu.edu.jo

***Abstract*— To maintain the integrity of information technology in governmental organizations, efficacious success factors in information security must be applied. Upon broad assessment and screening on the factors that influence information security, no permutation to successful assessment was reached. In addition, the influence of such factors has yet to be evaluated across the stages of assessment. This research's objective is the discovery of successful implementation of information security factors.**

Keywords- Information security; Success factors; Governmental Organizations.

I. INTRODUCTION

Today's society is data-driven. Collecting data from people, actions, algorithms, and the web has resulted in large data stores, and accommodating all this data has become a major challenge. 'Big data' tends to grow exponentially each year [14]. How secure is confidential information when people are not actually in their offices using a desktop computer, or when they are using a laptop computer on a network set up by a network administrator, When people take advantage of networking to use cloud computing services or to access e-mail on their own documents, they may accidentally risk the loss and/or disclosure of sensitive data and confidential client information. Organizations must pay more attention to data security and use protection tools to help secure their sensitive data and the confidential client information. Weak security systems used by the organizations may lead to data breaches and theft, resulting in major data losses and loss of customer's confidence in their service provider. The hierarchal structure of current organizations has placed more of emphasis on reinforcing possible breaches on an individual level due to the fact that Organizations depend more and more on computers and that computing control has been brought down to the individual desktop. Hence, realizing the importance of the type of environment people work in. More employees are interacting with technology to commence their daily tasks, and employees have established a greater threat because they have direct access to an organization's assets [5]. Also, information that is generated and stored on their individual desktop must remain confidential to the concerning party, this is because insufficient protection of confidential information may result in destruction, delay or disclosure to an illegal party [15]. Conventional computer systems may be desirable, but conventional security mechanisms are not sufficient against unauthorized access in cloud systems [7]. Network systems have provided many advantages to organizations, essentially providing a means of access to facilities and resources from any computer, anytime, anywhere, bringing about a technological revolution. However, organizations need to give more attention and consideration to their system security and need to guarantee that unauthorized individuals cannot access their information. A standout amongst the most undesirable circumstances to happen in systems is the unapproved access. This sort of access might be cultivated by an organization's official, or an unofficial intruder, or both. Such access may significantly harm the organization's notoriety by taking its imperative information, which favors adversely the organization's business dealings and diminishes its client's trust.

A number of risks and threats exist in the operational environment of computers and networks, particularly where they can become exposed to security breaches. There could be various reasons for the vulnerability, including an incorrect installation of systems, incorrect usage or malicious software.

In general, information shared among two or more computers over a network, may be exposed to the risk of intrusion. There are four ways of intrusion that can negatively affect the system [24]:

- Interception: An unwanted entity between the transmitter and the receiver steals the information.
- Interruption: Any unwanted entity between the conversations of two nodes stops the message and prevents it from being passed to the destination.
- Modification: An unwanted entity at the middle of a conversation of two nodes changes the sender's

messages, modifying their information before forwarding them to the receiver.
- Fabrication: A type of lie; here, one party is fabricated, and the other participants on the network are unaware that the messages are not from a valid participant.

Computer networks make it easier for organizations to distribute their business worldwide at a low cost. The Internet in particular increases the trading operations where organizations are targeting billions of customers. The open nature of the Internet makes it easy for people to access services from all over the world by using their own devices. Companies have developed and implemented easy access applications to provide their services over the Internet.

II. LITERATUE REVIEW

Studies on the factors affecting risk assessment practice and information security are light and there is a lack of experimental research in the area of security risk management [1]. Therefore, a need to consult a literature on factors affecting information security which helps us to identify a set of factors that may potentially affect the successful undertaking of information security risk assessment practices in organizations. These are listed in Table 1[4].

TABLE 1 SECURITY FACTORS

Critical Success Factors	Reference Discipline
Management support	Risk assessment Risk management Information security
User security awareness	Risk assessment Risk management Information security
Technical experts	Risk assessment Risk management Information security
Alignment with organization's objectives	Risk assessment Risk management Information security
Funding	Risk assessment Risk management Information security

"Information security relates to an array of actions designed to protect information and information systems" [4]. However, in statistics protection does not consist of only the information itself but also the entire infrastructure that enables its use, it covers hardware, software programs, threats, physical protection, and human factors, where each of these components has its own features. Consequently, information security plays a major role in the internet age of technology. Given that the number of organization security breaches is increasing daily, and the more available the information, the greater the dangers, it is expected that security will need to be tightened [17].

Because of the quantity of personnel, packages, and structures increases in the organizations, the control of the groups information becomes more difficult and therefore vulnerability potential propagates. Considering preferable practice of hardware and software program, notwithstanding, encouraging and empowering worker conduct, the organizations must make utilization of records and protection regulations. Data security coverage is a mixture of principles, rules, methodologies, strategies, and equipment installed to protect the business enterprise from threats. These guidelines also help agencies to become aware of its facts property and define the company mindset to these statistics belongings [16].

The authors of [3][10][19][26] agree that established standards, together with the worldwide widespread ISO 27002, are an excellent starting point for shaping the statistics safety policy to improve statistics safety in a company/business. ISO 27002 provides some recommendations associated with successful implementation of facts protection and is particularly supposed to help management to make decisions and then pass the important actions to those in management positions. ISO 27002 deals with:

- Security policy, objectives, and activities that properly reflect business objectives,
- Clear management commitment and support,
- Proper distribution and guidance on security policy to all employees and contractors,
- Effective 'marketing' of security to employees (including managers),
- Provision of adequate education and training,
- A sound understanding of security risk analysis, risk management, and security requirements,
- An approach to security implementation which is consistent with the organization's own culture,
- A balanced and comprehensive measurement system to evaluate the performance of information security,
- Management and feedback suggestions for improvement.

The authors of [2][16][20][21] quantify the causes and consequences of threats to information tackled by organizations. The following threats have been acknowledged by their researches:

1. Outside threats: computer viruses; herbal catastrophe; junk emails and hacking incidents.
2. Internal threats: set up or use of unauthorized hardware, peripherals; abuse of computer to get admission to controls; physical robbery of hardware or software program; human mistake; damage with the aid of an aggravated worker; use of employer resources for prohibited communications or sports

(porn browsing, electronic mail harassment) and installation or use of unauthorized software programs.

III. METHODOLOGY

The aim of this research is to evaluate the effect of the different information security factors implementation on governmental organizations. This research used the exploratory method by using a semi-structured qualitative method for collecting data and the grounded theory to get the results. The Data was categorized by defining patterns or topics and organizing them to derive meaning. This research was conducted in Jordan, for several governmental organizations. The research will depend on table 1 on designing the interview. There are more than 60 governmental organizations in Jordan , we used the semi-structured method to interview the selected samples , the samples consists of a mixture of Information technology and Information Security experts, in which they representing most of the governmental organizations in Jordan, we spent from forty minutes to one hour interviewing the population of the research, most of the expert samples were highly educated in IT, and most of them have more than three years' experience in their work, the semi-structures questioner was chosen in such a way to encourage the Population to explore their experience in their job as an Information Security Experts to grasp the success factors and the actions taken to secure the information. The selected sample is related to the in-depth nature of the qualitative approach used by author [30]. Reliability was addressed by a clear visualization of the research variables by means of multiple coders and case study procedure [22]. The questioners were clearly defined and have a summary of all the factors before given to the interviewees. The interview was conducted at the interviewee's convenient time.

IV. RESEARCH DISCUSSION AND FINDINGS

The success of the information security factors derived from the results are discussed below:

A. *User Security Awarness and Training*

The majority of the interviewees conceded to the organizations security. They imagined that the security can be accomplished by expanding the awareness and training. Some even admitted that awareness was next to nothing in their organization, and that the employees thought that the sole measure of security to maintain integrity was by using the username and password. Thus expanding, the awareness can be implemented through training employees in order to establish a sense of information security amongst them. The interviewees have requested the need of proceedings with preparations and plans to achieve execution of data security approaches. Author [8] Claims that organizations need to have continuing education and training plans to accomplish the essential outcome from the implementation of information security policies.

The 2002 security awareness index report mentioned by author [12] concluded that organizations all over the world are failing to make their employees aware of the security problems and concerns. The interviewees concluded that the majority of the security incidents in their organizations came out from their own employees identified as insider threat damage, this approves what author [23] finds, that employees are the biggest threat to information security. Other interviewees said that the outsider attacks come only from viruses and spam. Besides which, the interviewees do not face any real attack, but the viruses came from their employees when the employees themselves opened spam email or attached files. "The human side of computer security is easily exploited and constantly overlooked. Companies spend millions of dollars on firewalls, encryption, and secure access devices, and it is money a waste, because none of these measures address the weakest link in the security chain", where humans are the weakest link in the security chain [25]. So, if the security fails, that will weaken any organization. The interviewees also commented on some of the employee behavior claiming that some of them leave their computers on, other employees write the username and password on a small sheet near the computer and this will break the confidential to unauthorized people. That's why the research recommend doing a continuous course in training and awareness to all levels in the organization.

B. *Management Support*

Management commitment was essential in implementing the factors of information security, it was reflecting in assigning IT managers in the organizations' department to identify the importance of security in their organizations. A successful implementation of information security factors need very qualified staff. The Management tends not to start any procedure to guarantee the security of organizations because naturally they feel that the IT department is responsible for selecting the correct technologies, installing the essential software tools, keeping the technology in the organization and protect the organization's information [29]. That is what our interviewees confirmed; they said our management does not know everything we have to explain and convince them about the importance of the security of the organization and keep the IT department updated to keep the organization information secure. One of the interviewees said we cannot do anything without their permission; they have to give us support in implementing the security factors. Another expert said if the management does not understand our need to information security, whatever we do to prevent attacks and keep our information safe will fail. Hone et al. [18] clarify that the performance and the behavior of employees towards information security will be more coherent with secure behavior if the top management shows concern about the organization security. Thus it is recommended that the security procedures is set by the attitudes of those at the topmost of the organization [27]. Management will not support the information security except if they can see that it supports the organization's important business purpose [28]. Hereafter they must be persuaded of the importance of information security before they will run enough budget, and act to apply the information security policy [9].

C. Funding

All expert interviewees agreed upon that the budget is the major concern that affects the successful implementation of information security; the budget is needed to buy the software tools for identifying the vulnerabilities and recommended controls, so funding must be sufficient because without enough money organizations cannot be secured. Hinde [27] defines budget as the financial facility which firstly wisely estimates the costs and secondly measures the access required to the resources to reach a successful implementation of information security. Budgets generally depend on the manner in which individuals' investments translate to outcomes, but the impact of security investment often depends not only on the investor's own decisions but also on the decisions of others [26]. One of the experts said that the vendors of security tools do not mention that after a while these tools must be updated to meet the new threats and attacks so without sufficient money our system organization will be vulnerable to the new attacks. It was, therefore, suggested that if the Organizations does not have the appropriate software tools or hardware that will lead to difficulties in control some security concerns like access control tools, assisting the employees to apply some security principles such as changing the password regularly or logoff after finishing their work. Another interviewee said that if they do not have the proper resources that may lead to lack of implantation of information security factors.

D. Alignment With the Organization's Objectives and Polices

Information security policy is a set of arrangements set by organizations' to guarantee that all data innovation clients' inside the space of the organization or its subsystem comply with rules and plans related to the security of digital information at any point inside the organizations' of the specialist. Each organization should ensure and control its information, moreover, it ought to be conveyed both inside and outside the organization's boundaries. This may cruel that data may need to be scrambled, authorized through a third party or an establishment and may have confinement set on its dissemination with reference to a classification framework laid out within the data security approach. The information security policy may be a plan identifying the organization's crucial resources with detail explanation with what is worthy, unsatisfactory and sensible behavior for the employee to ensure the security of data [13]. There is no question that the selection of good information security policy is the introductory degree that must be in place to play down the threat unsatisfactory utilize any of the organizations' data assets.

The interviewees said if we have a good information policy, compelling execution of this policy, acknowledgment from the employees, adhere to our rules and not try to control them, then that will positively affect the organization's performance and security. The participators mentioned that the organization's policy ought to be clear, understood by the employees, and it should be updated regularly.

IV. FINDINGS

Organizations ordinary do nothing in terms of security as long as nothing goes off-base but when things do go off-base they all of a sudden pay consideration and part of action is required to recover from the attack or the threat they face, indeed in spite of the fact some of the full-time recovery is inconceivable [11]. The observational findings developed from the interviewees affirm the significance of key basic information security factors mentioned in Table 1. Another new factor was found to be important which is using a suitable software tool. The important part of the management plays a recognized role in finding the suitable resources and managing the necessary policies and strategies, the management should provide essential funds and the right resources to guarantee that the controls are implemented, and this finding is balanced with author [6] which says that the management commitment in all levels is vital to guarantee the implementation of information security factors.

V. CONCLUSION AND FUTURE WORK

In this research a set of factors were illustrated that applies a great influence on different phases of the organizations' security. In spite of the fact that these factors are used in the existing literature. But their pertinence in the association of organization security has not been observationally discussed. Also, a new factor which is utilizing appropriate software tools was recognized, in order to facilitate information security in the governmental organizations. The foremost commitment to this paper, is fortifying the informative ability factors drawn from the existing literature, to satisfactory describe the success factors affecting the governmental organization in Jordan.

The findings were of great importance to the governmental organization in Jordan as well as in the organizations in the world, to realize compelling information security, achieve security in the organizations and to decrease the attacks and breaches. The paper recommended to follow-up studies, utilizing different distinctive strategies or diverse instruments. Finally this study is not without shortcoming, first, only five organizations were investigated and hence future work, must focus on multiple organizations. Second, we believe that the findings ought to be compared with non-governmental organizations, in order to study the influence of these factors on the information security of these non-governmental organizations.

References

[1] A. Kotulic, and J. Clark, "Why there aren't more information security research studies" Vol.41,No.5,pp 597-607 ,2004.

[2] B. Lampson, " Computer Security in the Real World, Principles of Computer Systems" IEEE Computer Society,Vol. 1, pp. 37-48,2004.

[3] C. Pfleeger, and S. Pfleeger, " Security in computing" Prentice Hall, N.J., 2017.

[4] C. Richard, " AusCert Australian computer crime & security survey , Sustaining operational resiliency A process improvement approach to security management" Software Engineering Institute, Carnegie Mellon University, 2006.

[5] E. Madigan et al. " The cost of Non-Compliance-When Policies Fail" Proceedings of the32nd annual ACM SIGUCCS conference on User services, pp. 47 – 51, USA,2004.

[6] F. Katz, "The Effect of a University Information Security Survey on Instruction Methods in Information Security"ACM, USA , 2005.

[7] F. Bjorck, " Implementing Information Security Management Systems " Eigth Annual Working Conference on Information Security Management & Small Systems Security, USA ,2001.

[8] G. Dhillon, "Managing and Controlling Computer Misuse", Vol. 7, No. 4, pp. 171- 175,1999.

[9] GAO, "Information security risk assessment:Practices of leading organizations",USA, 1999.

[10] H. Saini and A. Saini , "Security Mechanismsat different Levels in Cloud Infrastructure", International Journal of Computer Applications (0975-8887)Volume 108 No. 2 December 2014.

[11] H. Smith, et al. " Risk management in information systems:problems and potential" Communications of AIS (7) 2001.

[12] International Standards Organisation, ISO/IEC 27002," 2013.

[13] Information Systems Audit and Control Association, "Critical elements of information security program success"2005.

[14] J. Manyika, et al. " Big Data: The Next Frontier for Innovation, Competition, and Productivity" McKinsey Global Institute,2011.

[15] J. McCumber, " Assessing and managing security risk in IT systems: A structured methodology" Auerbach Publications, 2004.

[16] J. McKay, " Pitching the Policy: implementing IT Security Policy through Awareness" SANS Institute,

Management & Computer Security, Vol. 8, No. 1, pp. 31-41,2003.

[17] J. Brown, and S. Duguid, "The Social Life of Information" Boston, Harvard Business School Press,2002.

[18] K. Hone and J. Eloff , "What makes an Effective Information Security Policy", Network Security, Vol. 20, No. 6, pp. 14-16, 2002.

[19] L. Gordon and M. Loep, "Budgeting Process for Information Security Expenditures" Communications of the ACM, Vol. 49, No. 1, pp.121-125,2006.

[20] M. Ernst and L. Young, "Global Information Security Survey " UK , 2013

[21] M. Al-Awadi, K. Renaud , " Success Factors In Information Security Implantation In Organization" IADIS International Conference e- Society,2007.

[22] M. Miles, and A. Huberman, " Qualitative Data Analysis" Sage Publications, Inc., 1994.

[23] N. Doherty and H. Fulford, "Do Information Security Policies Reduce the Incidence of Security Breaches: An Exploratory Analysis",Information Resources Management Journal, Vol. 18, No. 2, pp. 21-39, 2005.

[24] P. Fung and E. Jordan "Implementation of Information Security: A Knowledge-based Approach" The 6th Pacific Asia Conference on Information Systems,Japan, 2002.

[25] R. Anderson, and T. Moore, "The Economics of Information Security" Science USA, Vol. 314, No. 5799, pp. 610-613,2006.

[26] S. Canavan, " An Information Security Policy Development Guide for Large Companies"SANS Institute , Journal of Advanced Nursing, Uk ,Vol. 20, pp.716-721,2004.

[27] S. Hinde,"Security Surveys Spring Crop. Computers and Security", Vol. 21, No. 4, pp. 310-321,2002.

[28] S. Mikko "Information Management & Computer Security" A Conceptual Foundation for Organizational Information Security Awareness". Vol. 8, No. 8, pp. 31-44,2000.

[29] T. Tryfonas, et al. " Embedding Security Practices in Contemporary Information systems Development Approaches" Information Management & Computer Security, Vol. 9, No. 4, pp. 183-197. Siponen, M.T. 2001.

[30] T. Carr , " The Strengths and Weaknesses of Quantitative and Qualitative Research :What Method forNursing" Journal of Advanced Nursing, Vol.20,pp.716-721, 1994.

Classifying Vehicles' Behaviors using Global Positioning Systems Information

Alessandro Silacci*, Julien Tscherrig*, Elena Mugellini* and Omar Abou Khaled*
Emails: alessandro.silacci@hes-so.ch, julien.tscherrig@hes-so.ch,
elena.mugellini@hes-so.ch and omar.aboukhaled@hes-so.ch
*HES-SO, University of Applied Sciences and Arts Western Switzerland

Abstract—**This study presents a solution to enhance the cities' traffic control by classifying particular vehicles' behaviors. A Support Vector Machine (SVM) approach is presented, enabling the system to classify cars that are looking to park and those that are simply transiting through a city. Through this paper, we also propose a new way of managing the high density of traffic data using a grid. The results show that the system is able to distinguish the two different behaviors with an accuracy averaging 80%.**

***Keywords*–Machine learning; Intelligent Traffic System; Feature Selection; Global Positioning System**

I. Introduction

Today's big cities are getting submerged by the traffic growth. It started to become critical as the traffic grew and the cities are now facing problems like traffic congestion and others, although a desperate try to mitigate them. Thus, Intelligent Transportation Systems (ITS) and research in that sense, are also getting more attention. Most cities struggle to counteract such issues due to the lack of flexibility in their architecture. The use of ITS solutions is therefore helpful when a city tries to understand the possible bottlenecks or other particular behaviors observable in its streets. Through these identification capabilities the cities are trying to solve the problems linked to their architecture.

We based our research on [1] data, which provides the Global Positioning System (GPS) location of many smartphones at a given interval in the city of Aracaju (Brazil). The dataset is composed of either people simply walking, taking a bus or a car. Using such location technology has been motivated by the wide amount of device capable of using it, considering the growth of the smartphone market.

The following study is oriented towards enriching a city's knowledge of its traffic by differentiating the parking patterns of the transiting patterns by extracting it from the Global Positioning System's data of a moving vehicle. The Section III show details about the dataset and the features that we selected or created, our system is explained in the Section III-C, its results and a final discussion are presented in Section IV and Section V respectively.

II. Related Work

Behavior detection or classification is a field where many research projects are trying to respond the best they can, it is even defined as the field having the least research by [2]. In the agricultural domain, farmers are trying to understand how their cattle behave during a certain period of time. Therefore, they use specific sensors but also couple them with the GPS information they get [3]- [5].

Researchers identified that the raw GPS points cannot be used very efficiently. Therefore, information like the speed, direction or distance was inferred from the GPS records and the time of the capture [6]. Most of the reviewed papers would rather focus their models on determining the users' actual activity across the time. This means that they were first trying to determine if the participant was moving, if so what the transportation mode he was using. [7] proposed a system based on fuzzy logic to identify if a person was walking, taking some sort of transportation method or simply staying. Their model is capable of determining the three situations according to the angle between the points and the speed computed from it. Based on few features, the model is capable of giving the probability of the actual segment to pertain to one of the three sets.

A machine learning approach was used in an article from [8] which labelled multiple segments of a GPS trace. Labelled segments were checked for errors using some fuzzy logic rules, ending in a multi-staged technique to provide the corresponding label to a segment. The usage of SVM was helpful in classifying the mode of transportation used, since the model was capable of identifying four types of vehicle types (car, bus, train or tram). [9] also proposed a multilayered classification model, composed of a decision tree and a Hidden Markov Model (HMM). Using their pipeline, they were able to categorise transportation modes like running, walking, biking, stationary position and motorised transport (no distinction).

The work from researchers in [10] are exposing different ways of training an Artificial Neural Network for pattern recognition, and the results tend to demonstrate that this depends on the amount of data available. [11] developed a neural network, based on a multi-layer perceptron model that is capable of identifying the mode of transportation used by a person. They offer, through a mobile application called *TRACIT*, the capabilities to determine when a trip began and finished and how the person travelled in order to enhance surveys' processes and ease their use. They also note the importance of certain features in determining the type of transportation, like the acceleration and the total distance of the trip. The previously presented systems were beaten by *TrajectoryNet*, a Recurrent Neural Network (RNN) model proposed by [12]. It was able to classify GPS trajectories in four categories; bike, car, walk and bus, with the precision of 98% which is beating at least by 4% the results of [8]. Similarly, [13] presented two different approaches of managing the raw GPS tracking points. They used fuzzy logic rules and a random forest model in order to recognise indoor and in-vehicle travels and mentioned some problems to determine if a pedestrian was walking or not.

Researchers like [14] also tried to predict potential accidents or traffic congestion based on data inferred from the GPS location of vehicles. They segmented roads using various points along them and then computed different variables relatively to them. [15] were able to extract and classify three traffic congestion levels using a Decision Tree algorithm with a high accuracy. In order to assess highway traffic conditions, [16] have demonstrated that the SVM and information inferred from vehicles' positions could provide results above 75%.

III. METHODS

A. Data Generation

UCI's dataset is composed of GPS points series that describe the movements of people using their mobile phone GPS antenna. This statement induces that the data had to be filtered while being labelled. The GPS series were displayed and labelled visually, meaning that we relied on the actual position of paths' segments in order to attribute a specific label to them. Going through such process also helped to identify paths that were done by people walking and not using a vehicle.

The second step in the process was to create an appropriate tracks' dataset. Therefore, we decided to create a grid around the city center. Each of the cell is covering a parcel of a hundred meters squared and the total coverage of the city was ten thousand meters squared. We then computed for each grid cell the number of unique tracks going through it. This count helped us understand and filter the useless parts of the grid, reducing the total matrix. Tracks were then processed to produce the dataset which contains four different features. We decided to keep the track_id (which was unique for each record), the "from_win_id" which is the origin's cell id of a track, the "to_win_id" which is the destination cell id, and finally "delta_t" the time delta between the origin to the destination in seconds. An example of the grid with a path is given in the Figure 1 and its matching Table I.

All the records were labelled using two different classes: "transit" meaning the vehicle is transiting through the city and "parking" identifying a car looking for a parking. A path could be segmented with both transiting and parking segments. We additionally created a dataset filtering the paths containing at least two different classes ("parking" or "transit").

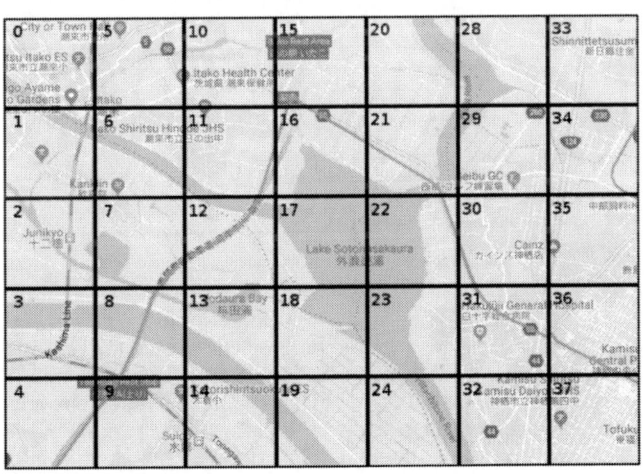

Figure 1. A path (turquoise) going through the grid.

B. Data Analysis

The dataset generated includes a few features, but to assess their variance and to ensure a good usage of them during the training and testing phase we decided to run multiple feature selection techniques. We first tried to understand the variance ratio of each feature and so understand their importance in the

TABLE I. SAMPLE OF THE GENERATED DATASET FOR A PATH.

Track_id	*From*	*To*	*Delta_t*
1	4	9	37
1	9	8	60
1	8	12	200
1	12	11	85
1	11	15	40
1	15	21	172
1	21	22	29
1	22	30	14
1	30	31	56
1	31	36	193
1	36	37	230

future model usage. We therefore used a Principal Component Analysis (PCA) to get a clear observation of the ratios, as demonstrated in Figure 2. Obviously, the track_id revealed to

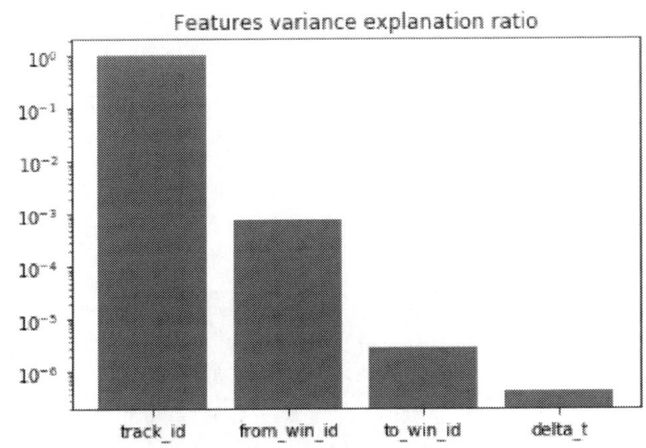

Figure 2. Principal Component Analysis of the dataset in a log scale.

be the most important feature, but we will not use it as it may skew the results by relying too much on this value which may be dynamic in future usage. Another observation from Figure 2 is that the delta between the cell movement has a lot of same values, but this is understandable since the vehicles could take the same time to transit through cells. We further explored with two types of feature selection techniques, the filters and the wrappers. Filters are based upon statistical measure results and provide a score for each feature, while wrappers are using machine learning models in order to determine a feature ranking depending on the score obtained by the classifier using a particular set of them.

We started with the filters and therefore selected the ANOVA-F measure as demonstrated in Figure 3 and the χ^2 which is observable through Figure 4. The results provided

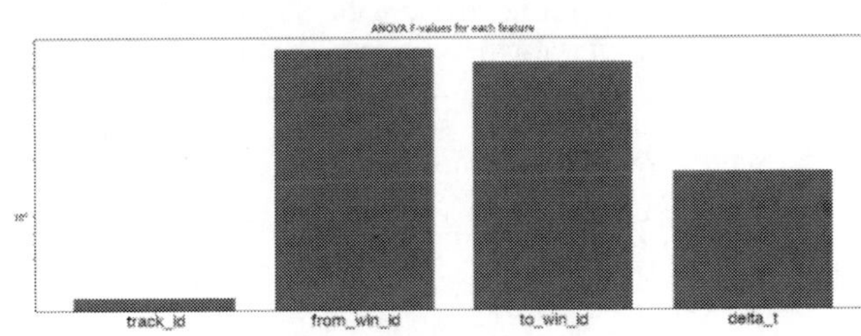

Figure 3. The ANOVA-F feature selection scores.

by the two measures are slightly different, especially looking at the track_id and delta_t features which are interpreted differently. This is due to their specific characteristics, where

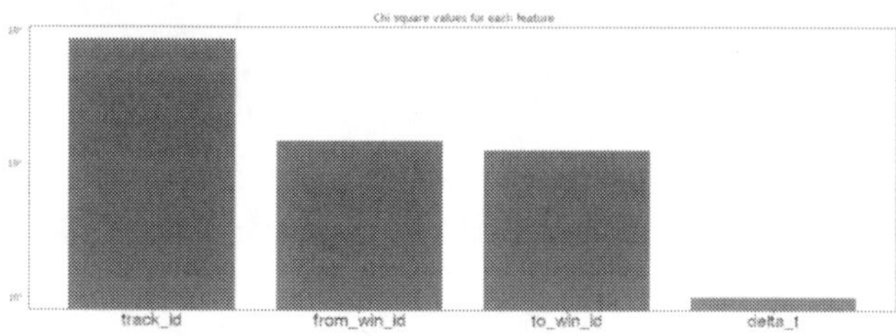

Figure 4. The χ^2 feature selection scores.

the χ^2 is a measure taking more the number of times the same observations is made between a feature value and the class and ANOVA-F is scoring features by analysing the variance of Fisher's test values.

As for the wrappers, we used a Decision Tree where we selected the two best features. The model and approach is based on the scikit-learn python library [17]. Using the model, we obtained a new histogram for the Decision Tree as shown in and Figure 5. By omitting the track_id feature from Figure 2, Figure 3, Figure 4 and Figure 5, one can still make the observation that the origin cell is determinant in the dataset generated.

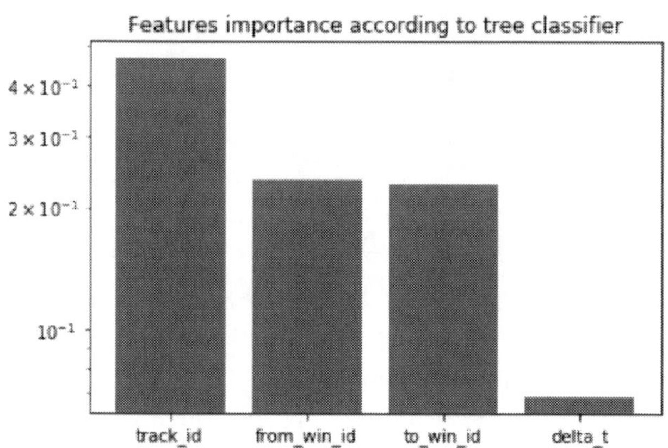

Figure 5. Decision Tree feature selection results.

C. Model Selection

We ran the whole dataset in a pipeline composed of multiple classifiers. We dedicated 70% of the dataset to be the training set and used it to make a 5-fold cross-validation. Results of the classifications were then compared as in Figure 6. We observed the standard deviation of the results and the accuracy for each classifier and came to the conclusion that the SVM was the promising model to use.

We decided to further explore the SVM classifier and made the fine-tuning of its hyper-parameters using a grid searching approach. The algorithm was given four different parameters range configurations and used a 3-fold cross-validation. The best scores were obtained using the following parameters:

- Kernel: Radial Basis Function (RBF)
- C: 1.0
- Tolerance: 0.001

IV. Results

We ran each dataset through the feature selection techniques described earlier and compared the results. At each step, the resulting dataset containing only the selected features were used to classify the 30% test set that has never been used during the previous steps.

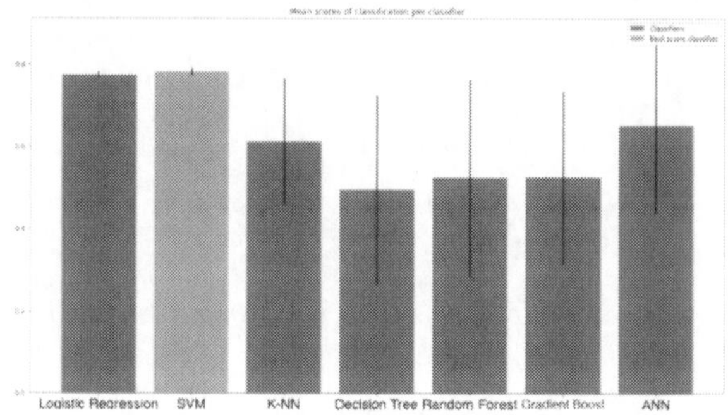

Figure 6. The accuracy results of all the tested classifiers and their standard deviation.

By comparing the two confusion matrices in Figure 7a and Figure 7b resulting from the classification using the whole set of features, we observed that the filtered paths' classification was harder. The model is providing 3.56% of false positive for the transit class while for the whole dataset it represented only 0.06%. We observed an inverted tendency on the false positives of the parking class with this error representing 16.35% and 13.91% respectively for the non-filtered and the filtered dataset. This is certainly due to an unbalance between the number of transit records and the parking ones.

By running the results of each feature selection subsets we observed that the best-performing one was the whole dataset. This is demonstrated by Table II, which summarizes different scores of three different measures. Reducing the features did not enhance the results, even if the results are still good. As the paths were entirely present in either the training or testing set, using all the features was not skewing the algorithm. The results also demonstrate that our model is capable of providing a classification precision of 86%.

TABLE II. Comparison of the results obtained by running all the different subsets of each dataset.

Dataset	*Precision*	*Recall*	*F1-score*
all features, all paths	86	0.84	0.81
all features, filtered paths	80	0.81	0.79
2 best tree features, all paths	83	0.81	0.78
2 best tree features, filtered paths	75	0.75	0.71
2 best ANOVA-F features, all paths	77	0.79	0.78
2 best ANOVA-F features, filtered paths	75	0.72	0.63
2 best χ^2 features, all paths	78	0.81	0.77
2 best χ^2 features, filtered paths	77	0.78	0.75

V. Conclusion

To conclude our study, we demonstrated a new approach attempting to answer the problematic linked to one of the least researched domains in Intelligent Transportation Systems. We were able to obtain significantly good results in detecting whether a car was looking for a parking place or simply transiting through the city. We compared results of many different subsets, using techniques normally used for dimensionality reduction. Unfortunately, these subsets did not provide better results, but at least we identified that a key factor in the decision-making was the origin of the vehicle, if we ignore the path's id.

Results might even be further enhanced by a better annotation technique, and a better data collection quality as the

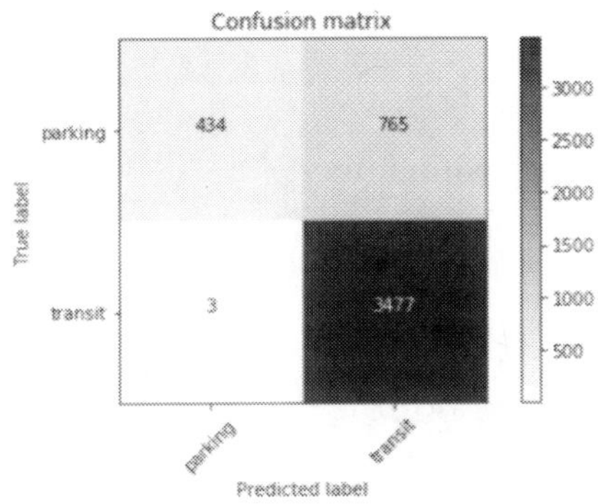

(a) Using the whole dataset.

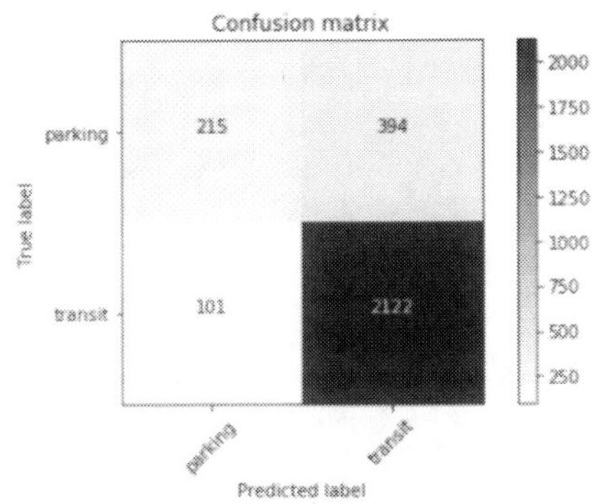

(b) Using the filtered dataset.

Figure 7. Comparison of the confusion matrices.

UCI dataset was based on people's smartphone location system and not directly from cars. This will be the subject of a future work as this study is part of an HES-SO directed project named Mobicam, specifically meant to solve the data collection and data treatment problematic.

Further work could also investigate more classes for behaviors like stopping to get somebody, waiting for somebody or traffic congestion.

ACKNOWLEDGMENT

The research program Mobicam is part of the large-scale thematic research programs of the University of Applied Sciences and Arts of Western Switzerland (HES-SO). The authors gratefully acknowledge funding from HES-SO.

REFERENCES

[1] M. O. Cruz, H. T. Macedo, R. Barreto, and A. P. Guimarães, "UCI gps trajectories data set," 2018. [Online]. Available: https://archive.ics.uci.edu/ml/datasets/GPS+Trajectories

[2] S. Sivaraman and M. M. Trivedi, "Looking at Vehicles on the Road: A Survey of Vision-Based Vehicle Detection, Tracking, and Behavior Analysis," IEEE Transactions on Intelligent Transportation Systems, vol. 14, no. 4, Dec. 2013, pp. 1773–1795.

[3] E. D. e. a. Ungar, "Inference of Animal Activity From GPS Collar Data on Free-Ranging Cattle," Rangeland Ecology & Management, vol. 58, no. 3, May 2005, pp. 256–266. [Online]. Available: http://www.sciencedirect.com/science/article/pii/S1550742405500344

[4] S. e. a. Grünewälder, "Movement Activity Based Classification of Animal Behaviour with an Application to Data from Cheetah (Acinonyx jubatus)," PLOS ONE, vol. 7, no. 11, Nov. 2012, p. e49120. [Online]. Available: http://journals.plos.org/plosone/article?id=10.1371/journal.pone.0049120

[5] M. Schwager, D. M. Anderson, Z. Butler, and D. Rus, "Robust classification of animal tracking data," Computers and Electronics in Agriculture, vol. 56, no. 1, Mar. 2007, pp. 46–59. [Online]. Available: http://www.sciencedirect.com/science/article/pii/S0168169907000026

[6] M. Boukhechba, A. Bouzouane, B. Bouchard, C. Gouin-Vallerand, and S. Giroux, "Online Recognition of People's Activities from Raw GPS Data: Semantic Trajectory Data Analysis," in Proceedings of the 8th ACM International Conference on PErvasive Technologies Related to Assistive Environments, ser. PETRA '15. New York, NY, USA: ACM, 2015, pp. 40:1–40:8. [Online]. Available: http://doi.acm.org/10.1145/2769493.2769498

[7] N. Wan and G. Lin, "Classifying Human Activity Patterns from Smartphone Collected GPS data: A Fuzzy Classification and Aggregation Approach," Transactions in GIS, vol. 20, no. 6, Dec. 2016, pp. 869–886. [Online]. Available: https://onlinelibrary.wiley.com/doi/abs/10.1111/tgis.12181

[8] L. Zhang, S. Dalyot, D. Eggert, and M. Sester, "Multi-stage approach to travel-mode segmentation and classification of gps traces," International Archives of the Photogrammetry, Remote Sensing and Spatial Information Sciences: [Geospatial Data Infrastructure: From Data Acquisition And Updating To Smarter Services] 38-4 (2011), Nr. W25, vol. 38-4, no. W25, 2011, pp. 87–93. [Online]. Available: https://www.repo.uni-hannover.de:443/handle/123456789/1167

[9] S. e. a. Reddy, "Using Mobile Phones to Determine Transportation Modes," ACM Trans. Sen. Netw., vol. 6, no. 2, Mar. 2010, pp. 13:1–13:27. [Online]. Available: http://doi.acm.org/10.1145/1689239.1689243

[10] G. Ou and Y. L. Murphey, "Multi-class pattern classification using neural networks," Pattern Recognition, vol. 40, no. 1, Jan. 2007, pp. 4–18. [Online]. Available: http://www.sciencedirect.com/science/article/pii/S0031320306002081

[11] P. e. a. Gonzalez, "Automating Mode Detection Using Neural Networks And Assisted GPS Data Collected Using GPS-Enabled Mobile Phones," New York, p. 12.

[12] X. e. a. Jiang, "TrajectoryNet: An Embedded GPS Trajectory Representation for Point-based Classification Using Recurrent Neural Networks," arXiv:1705.02636 [cs], May 2017, arXiv: 1705.02636. [Online]. Available: http://arxiv.org/abs/1705.02636

[13] J. Wu, C. Jiang, D. Houston, D. Baker, and R. Delfino, "Automated time activity classification based on global positioning system (GPS) tracking data," Environmental Health, vol. 10, no. 1, Nov. 2011, p. 101. [Online]. Available: https://doi.org/10.1186/1476-069X-10-101

[14] S. Kamran and O. Haas, "A Multilevel Traffic Incidents Detection Approach: Identifying Traffic Patterns and Vehicle Behaviours using real-time GPS data," in 2007 IEEE Intelligent Vehicles Symposium. Istanbul, Turkey: IEEE, Jun. 2007, pp. 912–917. [Online]. Available: http://ieeexplore.ieee.org/document/4290233/

[15] T. Thianniwet and S. Phosaard, "Classification of Road Traffic Congestion Levels from GPS Data using a Decision Tree Algorithm and Sliding Windows," 2009, p. 5.

[16] Y. Ma, M. Chowdhury, A. Sadek, and M. Jeihani, "Real-Time Highway Traffic Condition Assessment Framework Using Vehicle–Infrastructure Integration (VII) With Artificial Intelligence (AI)," IEEE Transactions on Intelligent Transportation Systems, vol. 10, no. 4, Dec. 2009, pp. 615–627.

[17] F. e. a. Pedregosa, "Scikit-learn: Machine learning in Python," Journal of Machine Learning Research, vol. 12, 2011, pp. 2825–2830.

Implementation of AP Selection System in a Heterogeneous Wireless Network

Yuya Chikasawa and Norihiko Shinomiya

Graduate School of Engineering
Soka University
1-236 Tangi, Hachioji, Tokyo, Japan
Email: shinomi@soka.ac.jp

Abstract—**In recent years, the increasing amount of data arisen from mobile terminals has deteriorated the response speed felt by users especially in a crowded place. Our previous studies have proposed a method of identifying an application being used by each terminal and selecting the optimum access point. However, there are some considerations in an actualizing the system. In order to compose a more realistic environment, this research developed a prototype system with an Android application on each mobile terminal and a control server. Some network performances are evaluated from the perspective of assignment status and computation time.**

Keywords–Wi-Fi service, Round-Trip Time, assignment problem, Android.

I. INTRODUCTION

While the Long Term Evolution (LTE) has been in widespread use and the line speed for data communications has also been improved, the exploding data traffic that evolving applications require lead to increase the utilization factor of public WiFi services from now on. However, the response speed that users feel might become longer due to throughput degradation on a public WiFi station because of increasing network load in a crowded place such as a railroad station and a classroom in an academic campus. Particularly, Japanese train stations are congested during commuting rush hours.

One of the above causes is considered that there are some mismatches between users and Access Points (APs). Therefore, it is essential to associate with an appropriate AP to improve the Quality of Experience (QoE). A problem to lead a user to an appropriate AP is named an AP selection problem. The current association policies are mostly based on a selfish user's behavior maximizing its own throughput [1][2]. However, it should be realized that different users have different needs since running applications have their particular Quality of Service (QoS) requirements [3]. Our previous studies [4] have proposed a method of identifying an application being used by each terminal and selecting the optimum AP.

II. PREVIOUS RESEARCH

A. System Model

Our proposed system includes a control server, plural APs, and mobile terminals in Figure 1. Each AP is constantly associated with a Measuring Terminal (MT) that is dedicated to measuring the response speed. MTs regularly obtain RTT and throughput by using ping and PathQuick, and send the information to the control server. PathQuick is a systematic approach to estimate the throughput in brief time [5].

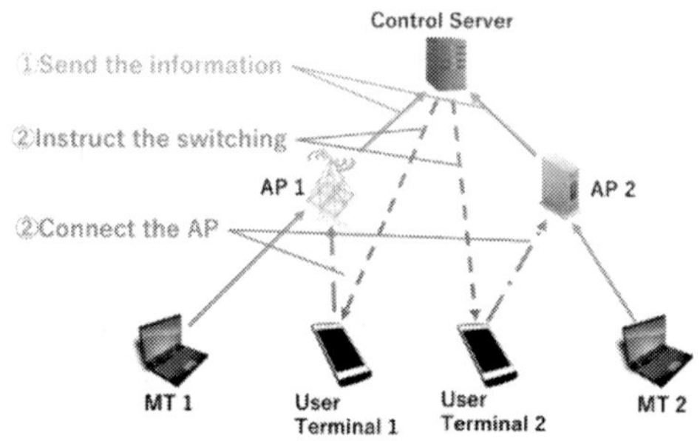

Figure 1. System Model

The control server solves an assignment problem by the Hungarian method to find the optimum AP for each user based on the information acquired from the MTs and the running applications on user terminals. Then, the server sends the suitable AP information to terminals.

Finally, according to the information sent from the control server, all user terminals switchover to the optimal AP.

B. Problem Formulation

There are some real-time applications, which require more strict RTT between a user terminal and a destination server, and others which might strongly demand throughput. The former applications belong to a group G_{RTT} and the latter ones belong to a group G_{TP}. Therefore, the needed RTT (RTT_{need}) and throughput (TP_{need}) are defined by four different types of applications shown in TABLE I.

TABLE I. $RTT_{need} \cdot TP_{need}$

Application	*Group*	RTT_{need}	TP_{need}
Call Application	G_{RTT}	200ms	-
Browser	G_{TP}	-	6Mbps
Video Application	G_{TP}	-	2Mbps
Others	-	-	-

$$S_i = \begin{cases} \frac{RTT_{need}}{RTT_{link}} & (APP_i \in G_{RTT}) \\ \frac{TP_{link}}{TP_{need}} & (APP_i \in G_{TP}) \end{cases} \tag{1}$$

Equation (1) expresses a satisfaction degree S_i of each mobile user. APP_i indicates an application running on terminal i. RTT_{link} and TP_{link} indicate RTT and throughput provided when connecting to the AP i. The objective is to maximize the harmonic mean for all S_i.

C. Research Tasks

In the previous research, the system was evaluated by simulating only an assignment algorithm in a control server. However, it is needed to consider the detailed communication contexts and a practical network environment to develop an implementation plan for a real case. This paper explains a system with actual devices, such as user terminals and a control server, and evaluates the validity of the assignment results and computing time by constructing the system.

III. Development and Implementation

The software on a user device includes the five main functions, "Obtain the available AP informations.", "Switch the connection automatically.", "Measure the response speeds.", "Identify the running application.", and "Communicate with the control server.". The system used an Android application which is relatively easy for implementation.

The software on a control server includes the four main functions, "Communicate with the user device.", "Decide the needed response speed.", "Calculate the assignment problem.", and "Store the virtual terminal informations.". Also, because of fairness, the control server must be located on a different network, and be able to access the Internet.

IV. Simulations and Evaluations

A. Definition of Satisfaction Degree

TABLE II. RTT_{need}

Application	RTT_{need}
Call Application	200ms
Browser	85ms
Video Application	256ms
Others	-

In this paper, the response speed considered is only RTT at this stage, for that reason the applications included in G_{TP} need to be redefined. The redefined RTT_{need} is shown in TABLE II. Instead of using (1), the satisfaction degree RTT_{gap} is derived by subtracting RTT_{need} from RTT_{link}. If the RTT_{gap} is a negative value, it is set to 0. The objective in this paper is to minimize the total amount of the RTT_{gap}.

B. Conditions

In the experiment, the number of APs is set to 3, the number of terminals is set to 50 (pattern 1) and 70 (pattern 2), and the terminal capacities of AP are set to 20, 25, 30 in pattern 1 and 30, 40, 50 in pattern 2. The RTT_{link} is set to increase by 3ms or 4ms for each connected terminal. This research also verified the greedy method and the random method. The greedy method prioritizes assignment in order from the terminals with the shortest response speed required, and the random method assigns the terminals in a random manner.

C. Results and Discussions

The results are shown in TABLE IV. The experimental results have demonstrated that the Hungarian method gains the highest satisfaction degree compared with two other methods. The satisfaction degree by the Greedy method does not increase because a terminal judges an appropriate AP according to a transient response speed.

TABLE III. CONDITIONS

Case	RTT_{link} increase(ms)	AP capacity
case1-1	3	20
case1-2	3	25
case1-3	3	30
case2-1	4	20
case2-2	4	25
case2-3	4	30
case3-1	3	30
case3-2	3	40
case3-3	3	50
case4-1	4	30
case4-2	4	40
case4-3	4	50

TABLE IV. RESULT

Case	*Average of* RTT_{gap}(ms)		
	Hungarian	greedy	random
case1-1	0	0	0
case1-2	0	1.36	0
case1-3	0	4.96	0.07
case2-1	0	2.54	0.58
case2-2	0	7.36	1.52
case2-3	0	12.16	1.88
case3-1	0	6.2	1.8
case3-2	0	12.39	1.64
case3-3	0	19.67	1.37
case4-1	1.22	15.2	7.85
case4-2	0	22.1	7.03
case4-3	0	35.47	6.4

This research defines computing time as a processing interval from identifying an application to establishing a connection to an assigned AP. The greedy method and the random method finish the calculation within below 1 second in every case. However, the Hungarian method finishes that within around 12 seconds in the most frequent processes. This processing time leaves room for improvement on the effectiveness.

V. Conclusion

This research implemented the previously proposed system with actual devices and showed the higher satisfaction degree by using Hungarian method. The developed system has to be extended with considering TP in order to improve the effectiveness, since the experiments consider only RTT. The processing time in our proposed system has been found to be longer for users in a certain case. The future tasks include devising a simpler approximate method for rapidity.

References

[1] M. W. E. Aryafar, A. Keshavarz-Haddad and M. Chiang, "Rat selection games in hetnets," in INFOCOM, 2013 Proceedings IEEE, 2013, pp. 998–1006.

[2] S.-p. Y. S. A. M. Gerasimenko, N. Himayat and Y. Koucheryavy, "Characterizing performance of load-aware network selection in multi-radio (wifi/lte heterogeneous networks)," in Globecom Workshops, 2013 IEEE, 2013, pp. 397–402.

[3] S. Y. C. Ceken and H. Arslan, "Interference aware vertical handoff decision algorithm for quality of service support in wireless heterogeneous networks," Computer Networks, vol. 54, no. 5, 2010, pp. 726–740.

[4] Y. T. H. Hideo, E. Kameda and N. Shinomiya, "Towards sustainable heterogeneous wireless networks: A decision strategy for ap selection with dynamic graphs," Computer Networks, vol. 132, 2018, pp. 99–107.

[5] T. Oshiba and K. Nakajima, "Quick end-to-end available bandwidth estimation for qos of real-time multimedia communication," in IEEE Symposium on Computers and Communications (ISCC), 2010, pp. 162–167.

Analytics-Driven Digital Platform for Regional Growth and Development: A Case Study from Norway

Salah Uddin Ahmed, Steinar Aasnass, Fisnik Dalipi, and Knut Hesten
University of South-Eastern Norway
Hønefoss, Norway
e-mail: {salah.ahmed, steinar.aasnass, fisnik.dalipi}@usn.no,
knut.hesten@gmail.com

Abstract—**In this paper, we present the growth barometer (Vekstbarometer in Norwegian), which is a digital platform that provides the development trends in the regional context in a visual and user-friendly way. The platform is developed to use open data from different sources that is presented mainly in five main groups: goals, premises or prerequisites for growth, industries, growth, and expectations. Furthermore, it also helps to improve decision-making and transparency, as well as provide new knowledge for research and society. The platform uses sensitive and non-sensitive open data. In contrast to other similar digital platforms from Norway, where the data is presented as raw data or with basic level of presentations, our platform is advantageous since it provides a range of options for visualization that makes the statistics more comprehensive.**

Keywords- digital platform; growth barometer; regional growth; analytics; visualization.

I. INTRODUCTION

Nowadays, open data plays an indispensable role for governments' strategy to deal with many innovation challenges of the future. Furthermore, open innovation philosophies and approaches are being launched and adopted by public sectors in many different countries [1][2]. In Norway, many governmental agencies have embraced the open data initiative and are making data available for public use. Hence, businesses and citizens can now access and utilize these open data resources to create innovative value-added products and services [3]. When it comes to defining the meaning of open data, we use the definition provided by Open Data Institute, which defines open data as "data that is made available by government, business and individuals for anyone to access, use and share" [4]. The global economic potential value of open data has been estimated to $3 trillion [5]. On the other hand, the potential and advantage of Open Government Data (OGD) for enhancing services in different economic sectors has not been realized to a large extent [6].

In this paper, by using open data provided by *Statistics Norway* [7], *Real Estate Norway* [8] and *the Brønnøysund Register Centre* [9], we present the *Vekstbarometer* digital platform, an analytics-driven web application, which contains regional indicators presented along with research-based knowledge relevant to regions' growth. According to the conceptual model presented in Figure 1, regional growth is associated with growth in Value Creation, Employment, Workplace and Population. A region's growth is often measured by growth in GDP (Gross Domestic Product_. However, the aim of the policy is to contribute to higher welfare and transform the region into better place to live and run business. In order for the Growth Barometer to be able to explain developments and provide relevant information related to political and business decisions, a broader definition of growth is therefore needed. The indicators are based on open data while statistical visualizations can be generated also for purposes other than regional growth. We have focused our study in the region of Ringerike from the southeastern part of Norway, which has recently seen a decline in the number of jobs and weak economic growth. To the best of our knowledge, there is no similar open-data based system previously developed or introduced, which encompasses research-based knowledge on a regional level in Norway. Nationally, there exist different digital platforms, but they are all different because not only they are using different data categories, but they also have different purposes. Several regions have business barometers based on survey data, collected on annual basis and register data. They forecast the national and regional business trends. One example is Konjukturbarometer Østlandet [10], a digital platform that contains, among others, a knowledge-based database on developments in the counties of Hedmark, Oppland, Oslo, and Akershus. The Confederation of Norwegian Enterprise (NHO), which is Norway's largest organization for employers and the leading business lobbyist, is another example of digital platform. Their platform, Økonomibarometeret [11] covers the market situation, operating profit, investments, and employment on a county and national level.

The main intention behind developing our innovative system, which can be accessed at *vekstbarometer.usn.no*, is to provide public sector authorities and local industries a management tool with key indicators related to the region's growth. Apart from having the potential to enhance public's sector transparency and engagement of civil society, our system can also contribute towards improving economic growth through processing and illustrating regional open data in a comprehensive way.

The rest of paper is structured as following: Section 2 presents related work, Section 3 highlights the need of digital platform for regional development in Ringerike, while Section 4 introduces the *Vekstbarometer* system and the technology used for its development, along with its strength and impact for regional growth. Lastly, Section 5 concludes the paper and provides some insights about potential future work.

II. RELATED WORK

Due to the emergence and pervasiveness of ICT (Information and communication Technologies), many governments across the globe have been undertaking initiatives to transform themselves into e-governments [12], and subsequently are encouraging citizen participation in governments. OGD is one of the main extensions of such e-government initiatives [13]. OGD is making data freely available and accessible to all with the goal to ensure public accountability and transparency [14], to empower innovation in different economic sectors and to enhance efficiency in administration.

Nevertheless, in order for stakeholders to derive the public value out of the open data, it is of paramount importance for the data sets to be re-usable, comprehensive, interpretable, complete, and permit user-friendly interface. Moreover, government authorities should be proactive towards ensuring that the data sets are published according to stipulated norms, such as protecting personal and private information of the users, or prohibiting the release of sensitive data related to national security. In this perspective, the Norwegian government has created a license for open government data and have recommended all data owners in the public sector to apply the license, which contains, inter alia, information on preserving confidential and personal data [15]. When it comes to global status and trends of open data in the context of readiness, implementation and impact, Norway ranks among the top ten best countries in the world [16].

In the literature, there are two categories of OGD research. The first category is mainly based on conceptual frameworks and theoretical proposals [17][18], also including studies discussing the main stages of the OGD life-cycle [19]. The second category, where our work belongs, includes studies that are conducted in different countries by using OGD at the national or local level. Furthermore, this category is characterized by open data exploration and exploitation, where data from multiple sources of government agencies are processed and visualized for further use, such as to conduct various analysis, create mashups, to enhance the interpretability of open data, or even innovate upon the open data.

Over the past years, multiple applications have been developed based upon the open data sets across the world, focusing primarily on larger cities, such as Chicago [20][21], New York [22], Dublin [23], St. Petersburg [24], Singapore [25].

In spite of the interest and the rapid proliferation of open data platforms, many challenges remain with the accessibility and usability of platforms using open data, data quality and completeness, and interpretability of open data. When it comes to enhancing the interpretability of open data, the authors of the research work [20][21] conduct a case study to analyze the open socioeconomic data released by the city of Chicago, where they apply different visualizations tailored for univariate, bivariate and multivariate analysis. This approach helped them to understand that exploring open urban data can lead to more effective data interpretation. Considering the usability for user interface design of open data platforms, a case study scenario involving a transportation challenge in Dublin City identified important patterns for highly usable open data platforms for open data policy, recommending these platforms should adopt user-friendly technology and social media platforms [23]. From architectural point of view, there is a work presented by [25]. Here, the authors developed an open data platform prototype and illustrate the requirements and the architecture of open real time digital platform to serve as a base for programming the city of Singapore, and provide visual data analytics in an urban context.

III. THE NEED FOR A DIGITAL PLATFORM

Several key factors related to growth and welfare points to the wrong direction of development for the region Ringerike. The region has around 43,000 inhabitants while the number of total new employment for the region was only 145 people over the past 10 years [26]. The number of jobs decreased was 321 for the same period. At the same time, value creation for the region's business sector has shown a weaker development compared to other regions that can be naturally compared with Ringerike, i.e., neighboring regions with similar background and assets. If this negative trend is not reversed, the Ringerike community will face the consequences of declining private and public welfare. This will make the region a less good place to live. However, politicians and businesses in the region are optimistic in terms of the future. New high-speed railway from Oslo to Ringerike region, and the new four-lane highway from Oslo to Hønefoss is planned to be completed around 2028. This gives enormous opportunities for the region to reverse the negative trend and create new growth that will ensure future welfare and good living conditions in the region. Nevertheless, in order to achieve this growth, it requires good decisions from the region's public authorities and industry. A growth barometer that monitors the growth in the region and significant conditions for growth could provide a useful management tool for strategic decisions.

The target user group for the barometer will be politicians, municipal administration, business and the community. There are large amounts of statistics and information related to growth and development for municipality regions from different sources. However, there is a need to provide these statistics and information in a customized way targeted for the use in Ringerike region, develop new and better statistics, and break down the statistics at regional and local level. In the preparatory work, we have conducted a simple survey to find similar tools or platforms as growth barometer for other regions in Norway.

We have found a large number of solutions, but none with the approach and objectives that we mentioned here. In this context, we believe that a digital platform like growth barometer could give Ringerike region a significant competitive advantage over other regions that are also working towards regional growth and development.

A. *The logical model of Barometer*

The conceptual model behind the growth barometer is given in the Figure 1 below.

IV. VEKSTBAROMETER - THE DIGITAL PLATFORM TECHNOLOGY

The growth barometer (*Vekstbarometer* in Norwegian) is a digital platform that provides the development trends in the regional context in a visual and user-friendly way. The platform uses data from different sources that is presented mainly in five main groups: goals, premises or prerequisites for growth, industries, growth, and expectations.

Each group contains several categories and each category contains several variables, which actually contain the statistical data. The groups and the categories form the information architecture of the digital platform, which is shown in the Figure 2.

The group goal contains categories: Population, Value Creation, Employment, Jobs, and Welfare. Each of these

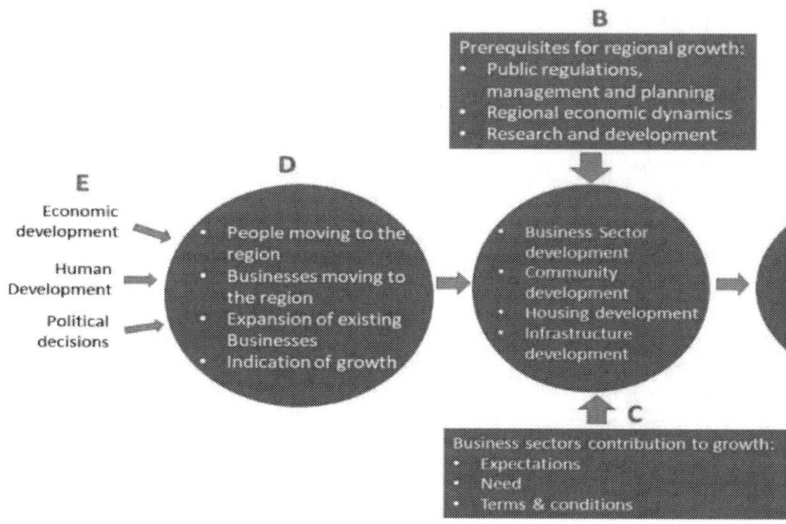

Figure 1. The logical model behind the vekstbarometer

The objective of regional development is given through the points in (A), i.e., higher value creation, employment, jobs and higher populations. Nationally, there will always be a certain amount of people and businesses considering to "relocate". There will be national competition to get these businesses and individuals to establish themselves in our region. Here, conditions for regional growth (B) and local industry's contribution to local growth (C) can serve as lucrative points for capturing a good share of the influx of national movements of persons and businesses. If the conditions (B) and the local business sector's efforts (C) are large, this portion will be large. The result will be a major influx of businesses and individuals. We assume that growth targets mentioned in (A) could be achieved together with regional economic dynamics linked to business development, housing construction, etc.

categories contain a number of variables that are not shown in the figure. These variables represent the data analyses and the visual representations in the form of charts, graphs, and diagrams. For example, the population category contains ten variables, some of which are: total inhabitants, age-wise population, population change trends, net population change etc. Each variable is represented by a number, for example total inhabitants (1), age-wise population (25). The numbers are not assigned in any order; rather they were assigned when the statistics of the variable were being added in the system.

The variable number can be seen from the URL; when browsing a certain statistics from the navigation menu the URL gets changed with the variable number.

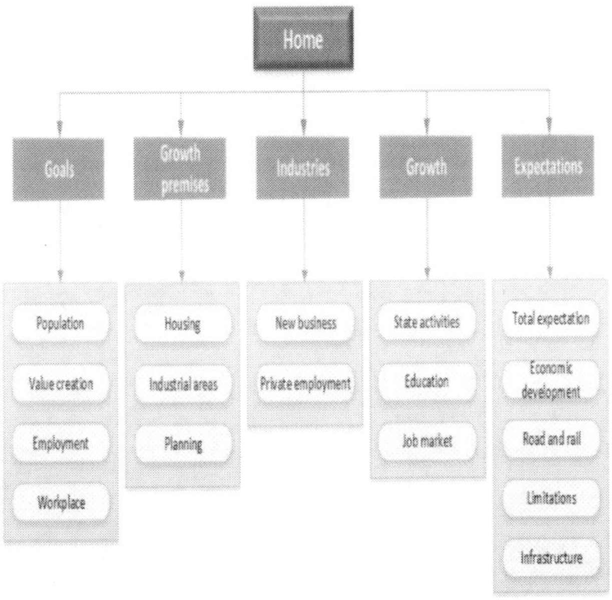

Figure 2. Information architecture of the application

Thus, the statistic variable 25 can be accessed from the navigation menu, as well as from the url by appending the variable number after the URL given at [27].

Apart from presenting the open data, *Vekstbarometer* also presents survey data from the local industries that reflects the expectations and assumptions of the local entrepreneurs and business owners. The application consists of mainly three parts: backend, presentation and database. The schematic architecture of the growth barometer application is given in Figure 3.

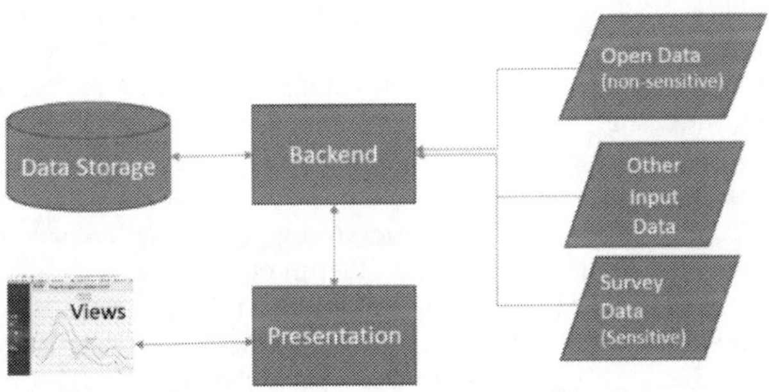

Figure 3. *Vekstbarometer* system architecture

Back-end's main feature is to process requests from the presentation layer. Based on the requests, it retrieves raw data from the database, sort the data and send them to the presentation. Backend retrieves data from external data storage such as open data that are provided by others through APIs (Application Programming Interface). It also processes other input data to the system and survey data. Data from external sources are retrieved in the desired formats and are saved in the database for storage. External data sources are fetched periodically to keep the main database updated. Presentation takes care of conversion of data transmitted from backend, transformation of these and display on-screen to end-user. This is the main part of the application that the user sees and interacts.

The database holds the persistent and transient data that are critical for running the application. We have used *MySQL* databases for the persistent storage and *Angular 2* for presentation and frontend, and *PHP* for Backend.

A. *Data*

Vekstbarometer is a data visualization platform. It includes several kinds of data. Some data are sensitive and some are not sensitive. Data that are already presented as open data by other outlets, such as *Statistics Norway* are non-sensitive. Since these data are already available and open for public, we do not have any restrictions on showing them in raw format or in modified format. Apart from non-sensitive data, there are data or part of data that contains some sensitive information about people or businesses that should not be made publicly available, e.g. a person's personal number (social security number) or a business's sales and marketing plans, confidential customer or supplier information, etc. These data contain privileged or proprietary information that only certain people are allowed to see. In our system, we present data collected through surveys from the companies in the region, which contain sensitive information. However, these data are not represented in a way that are trackable to individual response level. Rather, the data in the system are presented only as aggregated data. We make sure that data does not contain any attributes that can directly identify a person's response. Identifiers, business names, or organization numbers are removed from the data set and the results are published only as aggregates.

Besides, we follow the GDPR (General Data Protection Rules) rules when collecting data from local businesses. Most of the data are collected from other sources by some operations such as filtering or making queries in order to fit our local needs that are represented by the statistics variables in our system. However, the barometer also shows some newly created data that are not available in any other data sources.

B. *Visualizations*

Data is presented using different kinds of charts and diagrams. The diagrams include line charts, bar charts, stacked columns, stacked percentage column, column with drill down, pie charts etc. For visualizations, we have used a javascript library called *Highcharts*. With *Highcharts* is it is possible to create charts in many shapes, like heat maps, waterfall series and more. Additionally, the charts are highly configurable, customizable, and interactive.

By configurable and customizable, we mean that values can be added and removed on the charts on the fly. As an example, the Figure 4 below presenting variable 25, which shows age-wise population comparisons in different regions, we can choose the age groups that will be presented in the graph. The graph shows not only the percentage of an age group, but also the absolute value of that group in a tooltip text when mouse is hovered over that group. Besides the customization features, the regions in the x-axis are linked to a detailed view of the age wise population chart for only that region (Figure 5), thus making the visualization configurable and interactive at the same time.

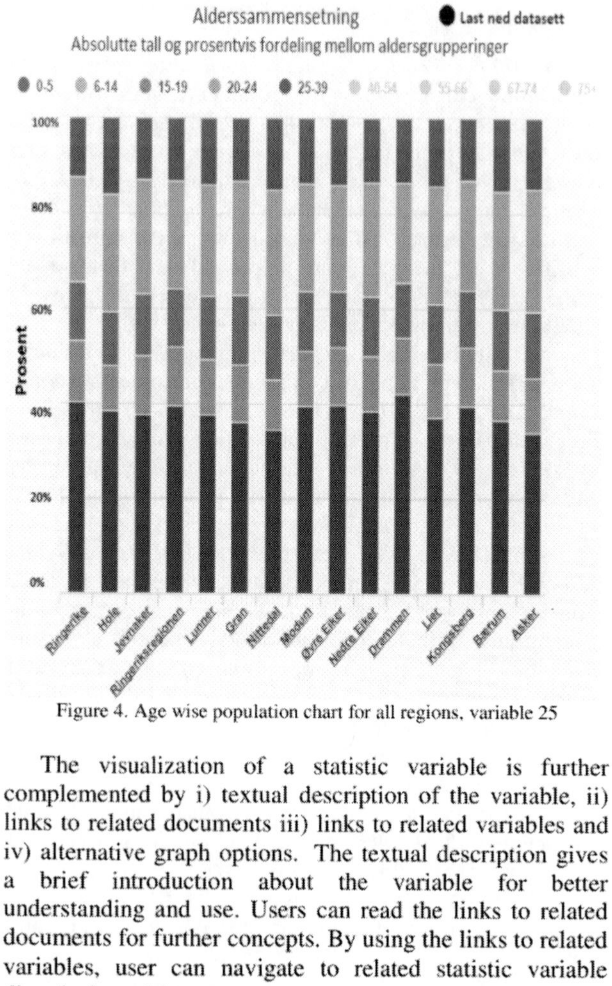

Figure 4. Age wise population chart for all regions, variable 25

The visualization of a statistic variable is further complemented by i) textual description of the variable, ii) links to related documents iii) links to related variables and iv) alternative graph options. The textual description gives a brief introduction about the variable for better understanding and use. Users can read the links to related documents for further concepts. By using the links to related variables, user can navigate to related statistic variable directly from this page.

Alternative graph option lists a number of options, and by selection one from those options, the user can view the same statistical variable in a different form of presentation, for example linear chart, bar chart, pie chart etc.

C. *The Strength and Impact of the platform*

The digital platform shows data in an easy, comprehensible and meaningful way. Although some data already exist in other data outlets, our platform adds value by making a better presentation of the data.

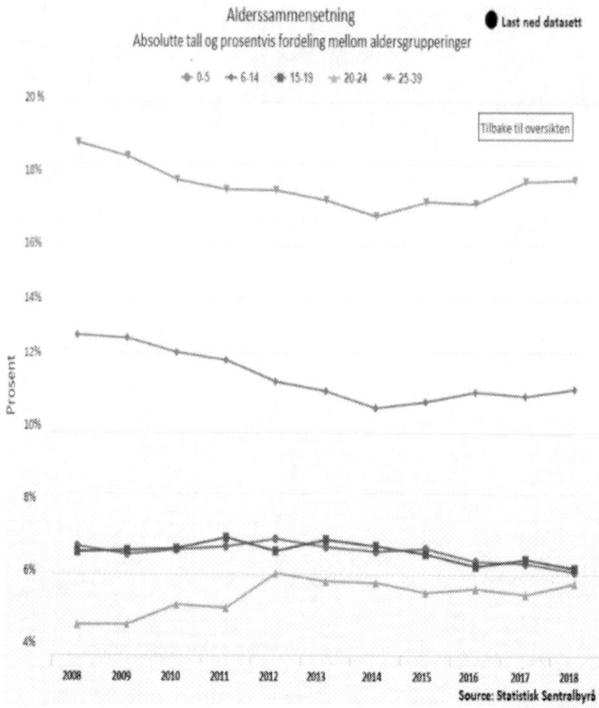

Figure 5. Age wise population chart for a specific region, variable 25

Furthermore, in contrast to other platforms, such as [28]-[32], where the data is presented as raw data or with basic level of presentations, our platform is advantageous since it provides a range of options for visualization that makes the statistics more comprehensive. Even in case where the platform is showing existing data from other sources, still we add value on it.

In addition to showing already existing data, the platform shows some new data. The new data can be of two types: i) newly formed data, ii) newly created data. Newly formed data is created by combining and filtering data from multiple sources where the data were partly available but the in the form that is presented here.

On the other hand, newly created data is the case where we create, collect or gather very new data that were not available or presented in any other platform. As an example of newly formed data we can mention "future population growth" which is represented in our platform as statistical variable 56 (see Figure 6). Here, the future expected population growth is taken from three different sources: *Statistics Norway* assumptions, political assumption and housing building assumption. This new variable shows the lack or surplus of housing capacities with political assumptions or the *Statistics Norway* assumption and gives a good indication if they are feasible or not compared to the housing capacities that are planned for the region. When it comes to the possibility of downloading data and images, besides showing the statistics in visual form, the platform also provides the option to download data in multiple formats, such as csv, pdf, xls, png and jpeg image, svg vector image, etc. It also provides the option of printing the chart and view the data of the chart in tabular forms. These options increase the usability of the tool and facilitates multiple use cases for the users of the system. Other users can use customized graphs and charts from our platform and include them in presentations or documents.

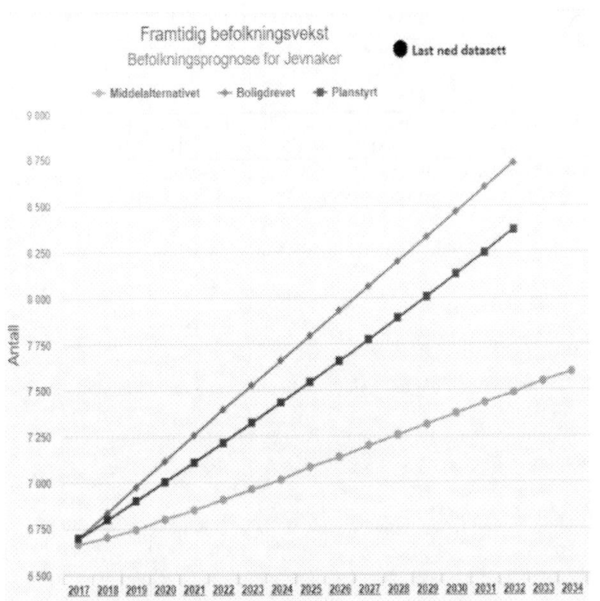

Figure 6. Future population growth, variable 56

The *vekstbarometer* platform is a constituent part of the five years long Growth Barometer project, which is managed by the Regional Development Group at the University of South-Eastern Norway (usn.no). Since the initiation of the project, a status report is issued continuously presenting the current regional growth. The Ringerike region also has a business policy strategy that sets the premises for how business policy is to be pursued to create growth in the region's business community. The strategy is created based on *Vekstbarometer* platform and presents the annual results of the regional growth according to the growth objectives given at Figure 1. Moreover, the municipality authorities can rely on vekstbarometer data in order to define their priorities and make better decisions.

V. Conclusion and Future Work

In this paper, inspired by the recent developments in the field of open data initiatives, we have presented the *Vekstbarometer* digital platform. We developed the platform to combine multiple open data sources to generate various visualizations. This gives insights into the regional growth and development, and demonstrates the usefulness of open data in regional context. Furthermore, it also helps to improve decision-making and transparency, as well as provide new knowledge for research and society. The platform uses sensitive and non-sensitive open data.

As a future work, we intend to expand the functionality of the platform by expanding the dataset and focus on converting the digital platform into a fully-fledged and mobile-friendly application.

Acknowledgment

The authors greatly acknowledge the grant from Sparebank1 Ringerike Hadeland, which kindly supported this project, and the important contribution given by Emil Kalstø, who performed some programming tasks.

References

[1] T. Nam, "Suggesting frameworks of citizen-sourcing via Government 2.0", Government Information Quarterly, vol. 29, pp. 12-20, 2012.

[2] S.M. Lee, T. Hwang, D. Choi, "Open innovation in the public sector of leading countries", Management Decision, vol. 50, pp. 147-162, 2012.

[3] https://www.difi.no/fagomrader-og-tjenester/digitalisering-og-samordning/apne-data [Accessed, 8 Jan 2019]

[4] The Open Data Institute [Online]. *Open Data Roadmap for the UK.* Available from: https://theodi.org/article/open-data-roadmap-for-the-uk-2015/

[5] J. Manyika, M. Chui, P. Groves, D. Farrell, S. V. Kuiken, and E. A. Doshi, 2013. "Open data: Unlocking innovation and performance with liquid information." Technical report, McKinsey & Company (2013).

[6] M. Janssen, Y. Charalabidis, and A. Zuiderwijk, "Benefits, adoption barriers and myths of open data and open government". Inf. Syst. Manag vol. 29, no. 4 , 258–268, 2012.

[7] https://www.ssb.no/en/ [Accessed 4.1.2019]

[8] http://eiendomnorge.no/en/boligprisstatistikken/ [Accessed 7.1.2019]

[9] https://www.brreg.no/home/ [Accessed 4.1.2019]

[10] https://konjunkturbarometer1.no/ [Accessed 4.1.2019]

[11] http://okonomibarometer.nho.no/ [Accessed 4.1.2019]

[12] M. Mpinganjira, "Use of e-government services: the role of trust", International Journal of Emerging Markets, Vol. 10 No. 4, pp. 622-633.

[13] T. Jetzek, M. Avital, and N. Bjørn-Andersen, "Generating sustainable value from open data in a sharing society", in Bergvall-Ka° reborn, B. and Nielsen, P. (Eds), Creating Value for All Through IT, IFIP Advances in Information and Communication Technology, Springer, Berlin Heidelberg, 2014.

[14] R.E. Sieber, and P.A. Johnson, "Civic open data at a crossroads: dominant models and current challenges", Government Information Quarterly, Vol. 32 No. 3, pp. 308-315.

[15] https://data.norge.no/nlod/en/1.0 [Accessed 3.1.2019]

[16] F. Esmeralda Ramos, "Open Data Development of Countries: Global Status and Trends", 2017 ITU Kaleidoscope: Challenges for a Data-Driven Society (ITU K), 27-29 Nov 2017, Nanjing, China. DOI: 10.23919/ITU-WT.2017.8246984

[17] B.W. Wirtz and S. Birkmeyer, "Open government: origin, development, and conceptual perspectives", International Journal of Public Administration, Vol. 38 No. 5, pp. 381-396.

[18] P. McDermott, "Building open government", Government Information Quarterly, Vol. 27 No. 4, pp. 401-413.

[19] J. Attard, F. Orlandi, S. Scerri, and S. Auer, "A systematic review of open government data initiatives", Government Information Quarterly, Vol. 32 No. 4, pp. 399-418.

[20] R. Barcellos, J. Viterbo, L. Miranda, F. Bernardini, C. Maciel and D. Trevisan. "Transparency in practice: using visualization to enhance the interpretability of open data". In Proceedings of The 18th Annual International Conference on Digital Government Research, Staten Island, NY, USA, June 07-09,2017.

[21] M. Kassen, "A promising phenomenon of open data: a case study of the Chicago open data project", Government Information Quarterly, Vol. 30 No. 4, pp. 508-513.

[22] M. Sutherland, M. Cook, "Data-Driven Smart cities: A closer look at organizational, technical and data complexities". In Proceedings of The 18th Annual International Conference on Digital Government Research, Staten Island, NY, USA, June 07-09,2017.

[23] E. Osagie, M. Waqar, S. Adebayo, A. Stasiewicz, L. Porwol, A. Ojo, "Usability Evaluation of an Open Data Platform". In Proceedings of 18th Annual International Conference on Digital Government Research, Staten Island, NY, USA, June 2017.

[24] S.S. D Dawes, L. Vidiasova, and O. Parkhimovich, "Planning and designing open government data programs: an ecosystem approach", Government Information Quarterly, Vol. 33 No. 1, pp. 15-2

[25] K. Kloeckl, O. Senn & C. Ratti, "Enabling the Real-Time City: LIVE Singapore", Journal of Urban Technology, 19:2, 89-112, DOI: 10.1080/10630732.2012.698068

[26] https://vekstbarometer.usn.no/assets/documents/2018.pdf [Accessed 4.1.2019]

[27] https://vekstbarometer.usn.no/statistic/25 [Accessed 9.1.2019]

[28] http://www.telemarksbarometeret.no/ [Accessed 4.1.2019]

[29] http://www.naringsbarometeret.no/ [Accessed 4.1.2019]

[30] https://legacyweb.nho.no/oppsiden/ny/html/files/VA-rapport_2016-31_NHOs_KommuneNM_2016.pdf [Accessed 4.1.2019]

[31] http://www.innovasjonnorge.no/no/regionalomstilling/verktoy/naringsvennlig-kommune/ [Accessed 9.1.2019]

[32] https://www.nho.no/Politikk-og-analyse/Offentlig-sektor-og-naringslivet/kommunenm/ [Accessed 5.1.2019]

A New Security Approach for the Spectrum Access in Vehicular Networks

Ayoub Alsarhan
Dept. of Computer Information System
Hashemite University
Zarqa, Jordan
e-mail: ayoubm@hu.edu.jo

Ahmed Al-Dubai
School of Computing
Edinburgh Napier University
Edinburgh, UK
e-mail: a.al-dubai@napier.ac.uk

Yousef Kilani
Dept. of Computer Information System
Hashemite University
Zarqa, Jordan
e-mail: ymkilani@hu.edu.jo

Muhsen Alkhalidy
Dept. of Computer Science and Applications
Hashemite University
Zarqa, Jordan
e-mail: muhsen@hu.edu.jo

Abstract— **Vehicular ad hoc networks (VANETs) have been instrumental in intelligent transportation systems that enhances road safety and road management significantly. This technology enables communication among vehicles where drivers can share road information conditions. However, users can threaten spectrum access caused by launching passive and active attacks that prevent nodes to access spectrum efficiently. Securing spectrum access has become critical issue in VANET to ensure reliability and trustworthiness. In this paper, a novel collaborative approach during the spectrum access process is proposed. In our approach, vehicles are divided into clusters and Road Side Unit (RSU) is used to manage spectrum access for each cluster. RSU monitors the traffic for each node and identifies the malicious and misbehaving nodes. The proposed approach measures the node's data reliability using a decision function. The scheme is applicable to a wide range of VANET applications, such as traffic safety, commercial applications, and Internet access.**

Keywords— Resource management; VANETs; trust management; security; misbehavior detection.

I. INTRODUCTION

Recently, VANETs are adopted to enhance road safety and to improve efficiency of traffic management. In VANET, vehicles cooperate to relay warning messages and road condition which improve safety significantly [1]-[3]. Each node in VANET (i.e., vehicles and RSUs) are equipped with different environmental sensors, processing, and wireless communication devices. VANETs support various applications that have been developed to innovate solutions to real life problems [1]-[3]. These applications include life safety, commercial applications, and Internet access. VANETs' applications can be classified based on communication model into the following categories: Vehicle to Infrastructure (V2I), Vehicle to Vehicle (V2V) and the hybrid communication.

In order to enhance road safety, vehicles should monitor the nearby vehicles to avoid accidents. Traffic status might be stored at RSU where collected data from vehicles can be processed and then RSU disseminates road status to other vehicles. Because vehicles move at high speeds, the likelihood of VANET disconnection increases. Thus, sufficient number of road side units should be installed to maintain connectivity in VANET. Some of VANETs' applications, i.e., safety applications, require timely and accurate data. However, VANETs are vulnerable to numerous security threats and attacks that may make VANETs unavailable to the users. These attacks have several impacts on the VANET performance and users. For instance, the following are attacks that VANET may face [4]:

- Attacker may send false messages about the road status. The attacker may send wrong information in VANETs to vehicles for exchanging this information.
- The misbehaved vehicle may change the context of messages over VANET.
- The malicious vehicle sends a high volume of messages to overwhelm nodes, reserve VANETs' bandwidth, and consume nodes' resources.
- The eavesdropper vehicle injects some malicious codes to crash the control system in vehicle.

In safety application, any vehicle in VANET detects an accident, emergency or sudden changes in speed or direction should report new road status to RSU [1]-[3]. RSU disseminates traffic alerts to all vehicles in the cluster. Warning messages should be delivered very fast in a high reliable manner to prevent accidents. However, if the reported data to RSU is faulty or malicious, then a traffic jam can take place, thus, result in life-threatening [4]. Hence, it is necessary to secure data communication in VANETs. The rest of this article is organized as follows. First, related work and our contributions to the paper are introduced in Section II. Next, VANET is presented in Section III. We describe the proposed security scheme in Section IV. Then, we present some of the performed tests and show the performance of the VAET under different conditions with our scheme in Section V. Finally, the article is concluded in Section VI.

II. BACKROUND

Recently, there has been growing research interest and a great deal of emphasis placed in VANET security. In [5], authors proposed a new security scheme where public key infrastructure is used for message authentication and integrity. Large number of anonymous public/private key pairs and the corresponding public key certificates are stored in each vehicle. A public/private key pair are used by each vehicle to avoid movement tracking. However, each node would require very high storage capacity to save many key pairs and corresponding certificates. Furthermore, each node should store all anonymous certificates of vehicles. Hence, message verification incurs high cost using this scheme.

In [6], authors proposed CARAVAN scheme where vehicles are divided into groups and the leader for each group acts as a proxy on behalf of all group members. Authors in [7] proposed new Cooperative Neighbor Position Verification (CNPV) security scheme. CNPV uses several heuristics for messages verification. These heuristics include direct verification, crosschecking, and multipoint location verification. CNPV detects any node announcing false positions and this node is prevented from relaying any message in the network. CNPV considers only nodes that advertise correct information about their positions to forward critical information. It adopts support vector machine (SVM) classifier to determine the authenticity of the messages. SVM uses vehicle attributes and message content for detecting untrustworthy nodes.

In [8], the proposed scheme determines the false messages by monitoring the behavior of nodes after receiving the road status reports. It computes the "degree of belief" for each primary information by correlating secondary information observed by more than one node. Authors proposed new filter in [9] to specify spurious messages. Messages should pass through two-layer filter for classification purposes. In the first layer, some features for the message are used for rapid filtration. These features include digital signature verification, time validation, geographic location validation, and support from RSU. In the second phase, alert message is evaluated accurately. The filter uses incremental back propagation neural network (BPNN) and the support from neighbors to recognize the behavior the node. Authors in [10] proposed a new scheme for intrusion detection that combines BPNN and support victor machine for spurious messages.

Some security schemes adopt node reputation for detecting untrustworthy nodes. Reputation is approximation of node behavior based on collective opinion about a node [11]. It represents node's behavioral history which is used to predict node behavior in future. In [11], authors proposed new reputation management approaches. To detect hackers/liars, they suggested new service reputation and

Figure 1. Architecture of VANET

feedback reputations. The proposed scheme integrates trust management model with a pseudonym technique to preserve privacy. Reputation model is used to resist the tactical attacks. In order to recognize false messages, information entropy and majority rule are integrated to reputation algorithm. In [12], distributed trust model (DTM) is proposed for motivating selfish nodes to cooperate more. For each node, the cost for sending data is computed based on the node's behavior, so that malicious nodes pay more for communication. Most of the existing security schemes for VANET focus only on assessing the trustworthiness of nodes by analyzing the history of the nodes. However, these schemes have omitted the evaluation of the trustworthiness of the data shared among these nodes in VANET. In contrast, our scheme detects malicious nodes based on reported data. These nodes are evicted form VANET by RSU. Thus, multiple attacks can be avoided by focusing on nodes' data instead of focusing on the attacks. In order to improve the accuracy of trust function, the trust level for each node is calculated considering the trustworthiness of data. Moreover, the trust model makes a decision more scientifically, dynamically, and adaptively where trust level for each node is calculated and changed with the number of communication interactions.

III. NETWORK OVERVIEW

Each road is divided into K segments. We assume that the existence of RSU manages the traffic at each segment (cluster). Each node is equipped with a single IEEE 802.11b based transceiver. The spectrum is partitioned into non-overlapping channels (16 channels for each RSU with 5 MHZ spacing with transmission and power mask restrictions similar to the ISM band), which is the basic unit of allocation.

Our system model for VANET is depicted in Figure 1 where both communications model are allowed (i.e., V2I, and V2V). Each vehicle is outfitted with radio communication gear that acts as a relay point for other nodes as well as an RSU. In our work, all vehicles are equipped with assistance of on-board sensors. These sensors include an GPS receiver, speedometer, accelerometer, and digital map to help a vehicle to gather road data. Each node in the cluster senses the road status and reports the data to RSU. Each vehicle is considered within the range of ith RSU if:

$$S_{j,i} \geq T \quad (1)$$

where $S_{j,i}$ is the signal power received at i^{th} RSU from j^{th} node, and T is the threshold for signal power. Signal power is computed as follows:

$$S_{j,i} = S_0(\frac{d}{d_0})^{-n} \quad (2)$$

where d_0 is the close-in reference distance, n is the path loss exponent, and S_0 is the signal power at distance d_0.

IV. Proposed Aproach

Each vehicle in VANET gets a value called a trust level (T_l), which describes the level of reliability of the node. Trust level for a node is computed as follows:

$$T_l = \frac{F_m}{T_m} \tag{3}$$

where F_m is the number of false messages that a node sent, and T_m is the total number of messages that were sent by a node. Trust level (T_l) is the key parameter in our scheme to secure VANET by monitoring the nodes' activities and detect the misbehaving nodes. Our scheme handles four different behavior categories (ways) that may threaten VANET and degrades its security and performance. The following threat model is considered in this paper:

(i) Selfish behavior where a node does not follow VANET's protocol. An attacker does not cooperate with nodes in VANET and rejects to forward data packets.
(ii) A node behaves in a malicious, misbehaving, and cheating way where it emulates RSU and sends false status of road to other nodes in VANET.
(iii) A node behaves in a malicious, a node launches denial of service (DoS) attack one or more VANT's resources (i.e., medium, and RSU) to prevent other nodes from accessing VANET for their data transmission.
(iv) One or multiple adversary nodes may launch objective function attack to change communication parameters such as signal power, center frequency, encryption type, and public-key cryptography and the symmetric key cryptography.

The main objectives of our scheme are threefold, namely *high data rate*, *secure communication* and *maximizing VANET utilization*. To make the communication in VANET secure, the public-key cryptography and the symmetric key cryptography are generated and used for communication between nodes. Firstly, public-key cryptography is used in VANET to ensure data security until a symmetric key is shared between RSU, and the node. The symmetric key is generated and assigned to new node in the class during the node's authentication process. It is worth indicating that the key is used for encrypting and decrypting all messages in VANET.

A symmetric key is used to encode the messages. The receiver decodes the data using the same key. Nodes exchange certificates, IDs, and symmetric key. RSU keeps track of all nodes in its cluster. After gathering road data, all nodes send their data to RSU. The data gathered by node j are represented by vector Xj. For node j, RSU compares the node's j data with other nodes and if they match, RSU decides that node j is a trustworthy node; otherwise it is untrustworthy node. The dissimilarity between node's j data and node i is computed as follows:

$$d_s(i,j) = \max_f \left| X_i(f) - X_j(f) \right| \tag{4}$$

where $X_i(f)$ is the fth dimension for j^{th} node. Each dimension of the vector X_i corresponds to an attribute of a vehicle. Each node constructs more than one vectors which contain information about vehicles in the road. The vector includes the speed of each vehicle on the cluster, and the position for the vehicle. Each node gathers information and sends the data periodically to RSU through beacon messages. Upon the reception of the different data reports from the cluster nodes, RSU analyzes these reports to extract the road status and decides the reliability of the reported nodes. A decision functions a bout j^{th} node can be described using the following function:

$$Q_j = \begin{Bmatrix} 1, d_s(i,j) \geq \gamma, \forall j \in G \\ 0, d_s(i,j) \prec \gamma, \forall j \in G \end{Bmatrix} \tag{5}$$

where G is the set of nodes in VANET, and γ is the dissimilarity threshold. Q_j is a decision function that is executed by a RSU to decide whether j^{th} node is trustworthy or not. RSU decides whether the jth node is untrustworthy if the dissimilarity between node's j data and node i is greater than threshold γ. RSU selects node based on the trust level. RSU does not receive data from untrustworthy nodes. It informs other nodes in VANET to discard any message from these nodes. Therefore, spectrum utilization is increased significantly.

V. Performance Evaluation

We simulate the proposed scheme to specify the adversary nodes in VANET which degrade the performance of the network. Table I shows the network simulated with values used for the parameters required. Results are analyzed to clarify the importance and the effectiveness of our scheme to secure data over VANET by monitoring nodes behavior and analyzing nodes' data. The key performance measures of interest in the simulations are:

(1) Throughput, which is the average rate of successful message delivery over a communication channel.
(2) Utilization, the average amount of time the spectrum is kept busy. The utilization is calculated as follows:

$$U = \frac{B_t}{S_t} \tag{6}$$

where B_t is the amount of time in which the spectrum is kept busy, and S_t is the simulation time. The results are averaged over enough independent runs so that the confidence level is 95% and the relative errors do not exceed 5%. We examine the performance under different parameter settings.

TABLE I. SIMULATION PARAMETERS

Parameter		Value
Number of nodes		200
Number of channels per RSU		40
Number of messages per node		Random
Type of interface per node		802.11 b
MAC layer		IEEE 802.11 b
Transmission power		0.1 watt
Packet size		512
Max Vehicle Speed		80 km/h
Number of malicious nodes		10,20,30,40, 50
Simulation Device	Intel i5 Core	2.50GHz
	Process cores	2 x 2.50GHz
	RAM	6 GB
	OS	Windows 7 64 bit

Figure 2 illustrates the simulation results in terms of throughput for VANET using our security scheme (secure VANETs, (SV)) and VANET without security mechanism (NSV). It is apparent that from the figure that the throughput shifts into higher level when the number of malicious nodes decreases to the lowest possible number. Sometimes, malicious nodes reject forwarding packets. Furthermore, the attacker might keep sending RSU false reports to gain exclusive access to the spectrum and to prevent other nodes from utilizing unused spectrum. Hence, the number of dropped packets increases significantly, which lowers throughput. Packet drop ratio is plotted under various number of malicious nodes as shown in Figure 3. It can be observed that the drop ratio increases as the number of malicious nodes is increased. Our scheme excludes malicious nodes in VANET. Thus, drop ratio is decreased when attack is detected and attackers are prevented from forwarding packets.

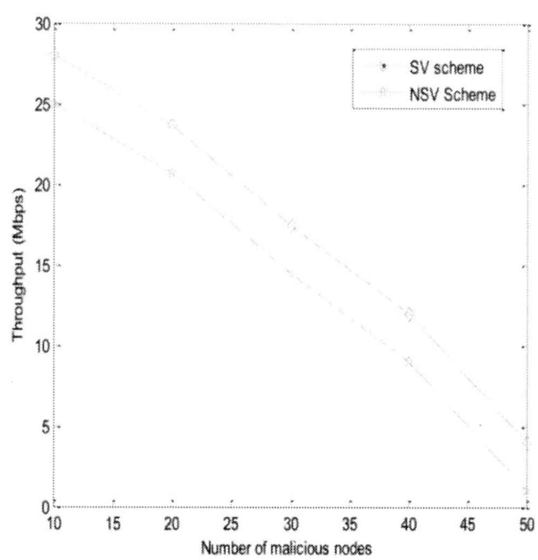

Figure 2. Throughput comparison for the two schemes

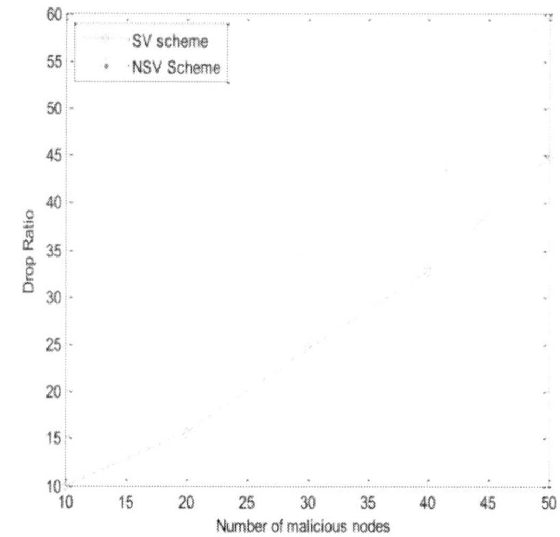

Figure 3. Packet drop ration comparison for the two schemes

For fixed arrival rate, the utilization for VANET's resources is plotted under various number of malicious nodes in Fig. 4. It can be observed that system utilization decreases as the number of malicious nodes is increased. Dummy messages are sent by attackers to jam channels and reserve VANETs' resources. Hence, VANET will not be available to licensed users. The results in Fig. 4 show the ability of our scheme to enhance the utilization of the network's resources. In our scheme, RSU does not receive reports from untrusted nodes. Furthermore, it informs trustworthy to neglect untrusted nodes' messages. Thus, untrusted nodes are prevented from forwarding messages and they won't be able to generate false messages to RSU.

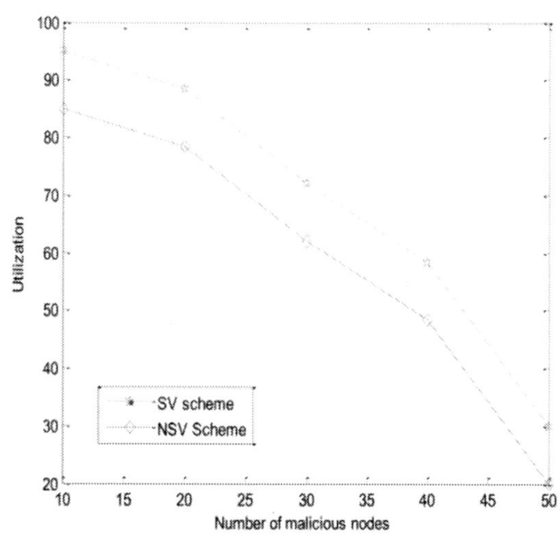

Figure 4. Utilization comparison for the two schemes

VI. CONCLUSION AND FUTURE WORK

Securing VANET communication is very important to save lives by guiding drivers to spotting hazards and improving road safety and traffic conditions. Different attacks might be launched by adversary nodes. These attacks degrade the performance and reliability of VANET significantly. Thus, this paper has presented a security scheme that monitors nodes behavior in VANET to identify and to exclude adversary nodes. In this paper, the trustworthiness of data is evaluated for each node to extract the set of untrustworthy nodes. To validate the proposed scheme, we conducted simulation experiments. The experimental results stress the ability of our scheme to improve the performance of VANET by eliminating malicious nodes. As future directions, several criteria will be used to assist the node trust, including, functional trust and recommendation trust from other nodes. In addition, different operating scenarios and conductions will be considered.

REFERENCES

[1] S. K. Bhoi and P. M. Khilar, "Vehicular Communication - A Survey," *IET Networks*, vol. 3, no. 3, pp. 204-217, 2014.

[2] S. Bitam, A. Mellouk and S. Zeadally, "VANET-Cloud: A Generic Cloud Computing Model for Vehicular Ad Hoc Networks," *IEEE Wireless Communications*, vol. 22, no. 1, pp. 96-102, February, 2015.

[3] T. W. Chim, S. M. Yiu, L. C. K. Hui and V. O. K. Li, "VSPN VANETBased Secure and Privacy-Preserving Navigation," *IEEE Trans. On Computers*, vol. 63, no. 2, pp. 510-524, February, 2014.

[4] Hasrouny, H., Samhat, A.E., Bassil, C. and Laouiti, A., VANet security challenges and solutions: A survey, *Vehicular Communications*, 7, pp.7-20., 2017

[5] M. Raya and J. P. Hubaux, "Securing vehicular ad hoc networks," *Journal of Computer Security – Special Issue Security Ad Hoc Sensor Networks*, vol. 15, no. 1, pp. 39-68, 2007.

[6] K. Sampigethaya, L. Huang, M. Li, R. Poovendran, K. Matsuura and K. Sezaki, CARAVAN: providing location privacy for VANET, in: *Proceedings of the Workshop on Embedded Security in Cars (escar) '05*, 2005.

[7] M. Fogue *et al.*, "Securing Warning Message Dissemination in VANETs Using Cooperative Neighbor Position Verification," in *IEEE Transactions on Vehicular Technology*, vol. 64, no. 6, pp. 2538-2550, June 2015.

[8] A. Vulimiri, A, Gupta, Pramit Roy, S Muthaiah and A. Kherani "Application of secondary information for misbehavior detection in VANETs," in Proc. NETWORKING 2010, Chennai, India, pp. 385-396, 2010.

[9] J. Zhang, L. Huang, H. Xu, M. Xiao and W. Guo, "An Incremental BP Neural Network Based Spurious Message Filter for VANET," *2012 International Conference on Cyber-Enabled Distributed Computing and Knowledge Discovery*, Sanya, pp. 360-367, 2012.

[10] Y. Liu, Y. Shi, H Feng, and L. Wang, "Intrusion detection scheme based on neural network in vehicle network," *J. Communs.*, vol. 35, no. Z2, pp. 32-239, Nov. 2014.

[11] J. Wang, Y. Zhang, Y. Wang, and X. Gu, "RPRep: A robust and privacy-preserving reputation management scheme for pseudonym-enabled VANETs," *Int. Journal Distributed. Sensor Network*, vol. 2016 , Art. no. 6138251, 2016

[12] N. Haddadou, A. Rachedi, and Y. Ghamri-Doudane, "A job market signaling scheme for incentive and trust management in vehicular ad hoc networks," *IEEE Trans. Vehicular Technology*, vol. 64, no. 8, pp. 3657-3674, Aug. 2015.

Unkown Territories

The strategy of social media usage by law enforcement agencies

Azi Lev-On
School of Communication
Ariel University
Israel
e-mail: Azilevon@gmail.com

Gal Yavetz
Department of Information Science
Bar-Ilan University
Ramat-Gan, Israel
e-mail: Gal.javetz@gmail.com

Abstract— **The article explores the perceptions of senior police officers concerning the place of social media in the current media ecology, and the desired mode of operation of the police within them. The study demonstrates that the different forms of social media are perceived as significant arenas in the contemporary media landscape, which are "here to stay" and the police has a "duty of presence" in them. Still, this presence should focus primarily on information-providing and image-enhancing activities, avoiding "confrontations" about contested issues.**

Keywords- Social Media; Police; Public Administration.

I. Introduction

New media, especially social media, enable government agencies to communicate with citizens and disseminate information fast and directly, recruit people and organize collective actions. Such uses may have implications for the character of relationships between citizens and governments, as well as for how citizens perceive government agencies' image.

One of the public institutions that are constantly in contact with citizens is the police. The main research question in this paper is how senior police officers perceive the use and impact of online social media. For this purpose, 15 semi-structured interviews were conducted with police officers in the rank of Major General and above, who finished their service in the Israeli police from 2006 onwards.

The Findings demonstrate that the interviewees recognize online social media as a centerpiece of the contemporary media landscape, with significant possibility to impact the image of the police. According to the interviewees, the police digital strategy should focus primarily on information-providing and image-enhancing activities, while avoiding confrontations on contested issues.

Section II of the paper presents the theoretical background and research literature on the adoption and use of social media by public agencies, especially law enforcement agencies such as police, and the advantages and implications of using such environments. Section III presents the main research goals and questions. Section IV presents the method. Section V reviews the preliminary findings. Sections VI concludes the paper.

II. Literature Review

Social media are becoming important intermediaries between public institutions and citizens [1]. The usage of social media by public institutions may enable them to disseminate and receive information quickly and efficiently, recruit people for various purposes, interact more closely with the public, and possibly improve decision-making and problem-solving processes [2]. Still, public institutions are often known for their rigid hierarchical structures and bureaucratic red tape, and less for their excellence in service provision and adaptation to new technologies [3]. Hence, no wonder they are considered late and limited adopters of new and, particularly, social media.

The use of social media *by the police*, like its usage by other public institutions, can have many advantages. Information can be sent quickly to many people without mediation, such as information on missing persons [4]. Information can also be efficiently received from people and organizations, including complaints against the police or against private individuals, or information on crimes and suspects [4][5]. Social media can also assist in mobilizing the public and enable public participation in planning processes. These uses can significantly improve the work of the police, improve its contact with the public, and also contribute to its image [6]. But while significant literature addresses the usage of social media by the police, there are very few studies that address the perceptions of decision-makers in the police about the place of social media in the current media ecology, and the desired mode of their operation.

III. Research Questions

1. How do senior police officers perceive social media? Is it a passing phenomenon or a permanent component of the current media ecology?

2. According to the senior officials' perception, what should the goals of the police activity on social media be?

IV. Methodolgy

In order to answer the research questions, semi-structured interviews were conducted with policemen from the rank of Major General and above, who finished their service in the police from 2006 onwards. This study only deals with senior police officers, due to their broader and more in-depth perspective on the organization's needs and the factors influencing the police-citizen relationship. The officers were selected based on their year of retirement. Since Facebook (the main social platform in Israel) has only been open to the public since 2006, only the policemen who served in the police this year onwards dealt with the question of relations between the police, social media and citizens.

15 senior police officers were interviewed. Most of the interviews were conducted in person, in a location chosen by the interviewees. In only a few cases where there were technical difficulties or unwillingness of the interviewees to hold a face-to-face meeting, telephone interviews were conducted. The interviews were semi-structured, consisting of 15 questions and lasting between 40 minutes and 2 hours. Interviews were used to present the phenomenon through the participants' perceptions and their own words [7]. The interviews were recorded and transcribed. A thematic categorical division of these transcriptions was performed, in order to identify, evaluate and report prominent themes [8].

V. Preliminary Findings

Many of the interviewees made it clear that in their opinion, social media activity should be an important and strategic goal for the organization, and that more resources should be invested in it. Interviewee I-1 declared that social media are significant tools for building public trust:

"Improving service to the citizenry is critical for your ability to generate trust, and we should definitely use the new media platform [for this purpose]"

Interviewee I-6 described social media as important sources of information for the police to convey to citizens:

"The police is disseminating all kinds of messages on Facebook, and we have to do this systematically and correctly. Both extract information and disseminate information..."

This kind of two-way communication and information streams require investment and proper resources, as interviewee I-6 said:

"It cannot be that there is a social conversation on social media and the police are not involved, the organization has to invest in it. Investing means getting more people, teams, standards and enacting new policies."

Despite the statements about the importance of police activity on social media, most respondents expressed reservations about bi-directional and dialogical behavior, and believed that the activity should mainly be with an emphasis on providing information and positions [9] rather than conducting conversations with the public. They argue that brief and practical responses are sufficient without waiting for a response from the public or addressing such responses further.

Interviewee I-5 argues that it is desirable for the police to respond to such public concerns but only briefly and only in its page:

"You cannot run after anyone who posts something in any Facebook group about you. Maybe in some exceptional cases an official police representative, needs to intervene in the discussion, and provide a link and tell everyone, 'Guys, come on read the facts'".

However, most of the interviewees did not see even such a minimal response as useful. For example, Interviewee I-9 does not see the need to participate in any discussion with the public about police matters:

"I would present the position of the police in a very solid and precise manner and let time do its work. I would not participate in the conversation itself.... This discourse will exhaust itself sooner or later, and the fact that we react and participate in this discourse, that is the fuel for the fire."

VI. Conclusions

The paper studies perceptions of senior police officers about the place and usage of online social media, in the contemporary media ecology. Findings show that the interviewees recognize online social media as a centerpiece of the contemporary media landscape, with significant consequences in terms of the abilities to send and receive information, which can impact the image of the police. At the same time, there is a clear concern about the possible fallbacks of entering long conversation with citizens, where officers prefer a minimal response approach in such cases.

Future studies can examine the perceptions of senior decision-makers in other public organizations regarding online social media, and also investigate the 'customers' side: What are the citizens' perceptions of this activity, and how exposure to it influences opinions and attitudes towards the police.

References

[1] R. Sandoval-Almazan and J. R. Gil-Garcia, 'Are government internet portals evolving towards more interaction, participation, and collaboration? Revisiting the rhetoric of e-government among municipalities', Gov. Inf. Q., vol. 29, pp. S72–S81, Jan. 2012.

[2] G. F. Khan, B. Swar, and S. K. Lee, 'Social Media Risks and Benefits: A Public Sector Perspective', Soc. Sci. Comput. Rev., vol. 32, no. 5, pp. 606–627, Oct. 2014.

[3] O. Serrat, 'Social Media and the Public Sector', in Knowledge Solutions, Singapore: Springer Singapore, 2017, pp. 925–935.

[4] Ministry of Public Security, 'Social Media and an Interactive Police Force – Police 2.0', 2012.

[5] A. Meijer and M. Thaens, 'Social media strategies: Understanding the differences between North American police departments', Gov. Inf. Q., vol. 30, no. 4, pp. 343–350, Oct. 2013.

[6] J. Crump, 'What Are the Police Doing on Twitter? Social Media, the Police and the Public', Policy Internet, vol. 3, no. 4, pp. 1–27, Jan. 2011.

[7] A. Shkedi, Words that try to touch: Qualitative research theory and practice. Tel-Aviv: Ramot, 2003.

[8] V. Braun and V. Clarke, 'Using thematic analysis in psychology', Qual. Res. Psychol., vol. 3, no. 2, pp. 77–101, 2006.

[9] I. Mergel, 'Social media adoption and resulting tactics in the U.S. federal government', Gov. Inf. Q., vol. 30, no. 2, pp. 123–130, Apr. 2013.

Cloud Computing in eGovernment:

Benefits and Challenges

Frank Danielsen
Department of Information Systems
University of Agder
Kristiansand, Norway
frank.danielsen@uia.no

Leif Skiftenes Flak
Department of Information Systems
University of Agder
Kristiansand, Norway
leif.flak@uia.no

Alexander Ronzhyn
Institute for IS Research, University of Koblenz-Landau
Koblenz, Germany
ronzhyn@uni-koblenz.de

***Abstract*—Over the past years, implementation of and research on cloud computing in the eGovernment context have increased substantially. A wide range of benefits and challenges is suggested in the literature. However, these suggestions appear fragmented and disconnected and do not offer a clear overview of the main challenges and benefits. Therefore, there is a need for clarification about both benefits and challenges of cloud computing, especially in the eGovernment context. To address this need, the literature on cloud computing and eGovernment is reviewed in this paper. The findings show that despite the extensive number of benefits and challenges, some stand out from the rest. This paper presents an overview of these, explains them in detail, and suggests avenues for further research.**

Keywords-cloud computing; eGovernment; benefits; challenges.

I. INTRODUCTION

Governments and public organizations in both developed and developing countries are increasingly adopting eGovernment solutions throughout their service portfolios [1][2]. Most often, eGovernment services are provided through the Internet [3][4]. While eGovernment services show substantial potential related to increased efficiency and effectiveness, there are also considerable challenges in transitioning to digital services. The challenges discussed in the eGovernment context are often related to investment and development costs [1], insufficient Information Technology (IT) skills [5], the lack of compatibility and shared standards [3], and the lack of compatible infrastructure [3]. These obstacles are especially challenging for developing countries [6][7]. A proposed solution to several of these challenges is to adopt cloud computing to support eGovernment [4][8]-[10].

Today, the existing literature outlines a plethora of possible benefits and challenges in relation to cloud computing and eGovernment. However, the literature does not present an accessible overview of what the main benefits are and how challenging the adoption of cloud solutions can be.

This paper's objectives are to identify 1) the benefits and 2) the challenges, both associated with cloud computing in the eGovernment context.

To address the objectives, the following research questions are formulated:

1. What are the main benefits of cloud computing in eGovernment?
2. What are the main challenges of cloud computing in eGovernment?

These questions are addressed by performing a systematic review of peer-reviewed scientific literature on the use of cloud computing in eGovernment.

The rest of this paper is structured as follows: Section II describes the use of cloud computing in the eGovernment domain and explores possible implications for its use in public service provision. Section III presents the methodology for the literature analysis. Section IV explains the results of the analysis. Section V discusses the findings, providing answers to the two research questions. Finally, Section VI presents the conclusion and several suggestions for further research.

II. CLOUD AND EGOVERNMENT

As a theme in conjunction with the government, cloud computing emerged in 2009 [11], where the exploration of implementation [12][13] and associated key issues [14] were studied. The potential use of cloud computing technologies in eGovernment was supported by Cellary and Strykowski [15], who recommended cloud infrastructure as the default solution for digital public services generally. Cloud adoption by the government has been studied repeatedly [9][16]. On this basis, Mohammed et al. [17] suggested an eGovernment cloud adoption model that would list the factors contributing to the adoption of the technology in public service.

Cloud computing is perceived as a possible solution to the challenges that governments face regarding the dramatic increase in computational data [13]. The Internet of Things (IoT) devices collect significant amounts of data, especially in the smart city context. Sensors collect environmental data, with the potential to be used for evidence-based decisions, increasing the effectiveness, efficiency, and responsiveness of public services [18]. E-participation platforms, crowdsourcing, and social media mining also contribute to the increase in the data collected by governments. However, due to its properties (complexity, heterogeneity, and volume), Big Data cannot be efficiently analyzed using traditional methods [19]. Cloud computing can provide the necessary storage and computational capacities [18][20] to store and analyze very large volumes of data. In this regard, cloud computing is considered one of the crucial components of the realization of smart cities, usually viewed in combination with IoT [21]-[23], providing the necessary capacities and aiding in automated decision making [24].

In Gartner's latest overview of the top trend hype cycle for digital government [25], cloud computing is identified as a growing hype. The European Union (EU) explicitly mentions cloud computing in Agenda 2020, underlining its importance and estimating that the European cloud market would reach €44.8 bn by 2020 [26]. Following the recommendations of the European Commission's Cloud Strategy 2012 [27], many EU countries have developed their own national cloud strategies [28]. However, only a few countries have backed up these strategies with the development of their government cloud infrastructure to support public administration, with several notable exceptions, such as the UK, Spain, and Denmark [29][30].

III. METHODOLOGY

Any literature review relies on systematic, rigorous, and well-established methods to help avoid cherry picking, biases, and a poor selection of relevant literature. Otherwise, the sample would likely not contain an accurate overview of existing knowledge and would therefore be of limited scientific value [31]. This review is based on Okoli [32] and Webster and Watson [33] methods, whose goal is to identify and analyze relevant literature to answer this present study's research questions.

To explore the research questions and identify existing knowledge in the literature, the following search queries were used: ("cloud computing") AND ("e-government" OR "eGovernment" OR "electronic government").

Three databases were searched for relevant articles: Scopus, Web of Science, and Digital Government Reference Library (DGRL). The DGRL is a highly regarded EndNote library consisting of over 10,299 references of peer-reviewed publications in the domains of digital government/governance and digital democracy.

Additionally, we applied the following inclusion criteria: 1) contain the search phrases based on the research questions and 2) be peer reviewed and published in journals or conference proceedings. The exclusion criteria required discarding the articles that were 1) irrelevant to the research objectives, 2) not in English, and 3) not offered for download or otherwise inaccessible. This process yielded a literature sample of 51 articles (Figure 1). The articles were published between 2011 and 2018 (Figure 2).

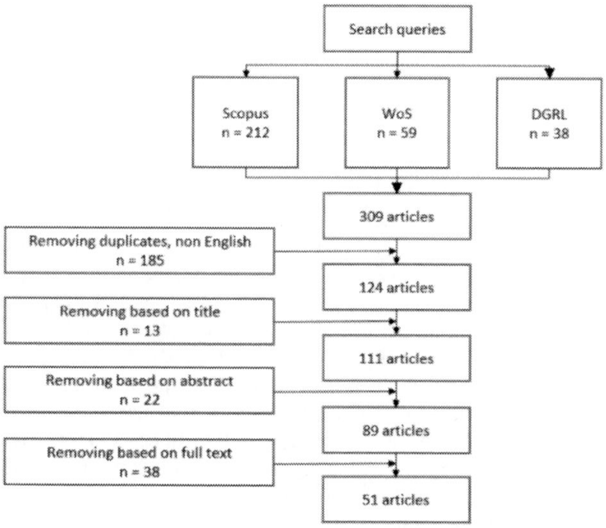

Figure 1. Literature review process.

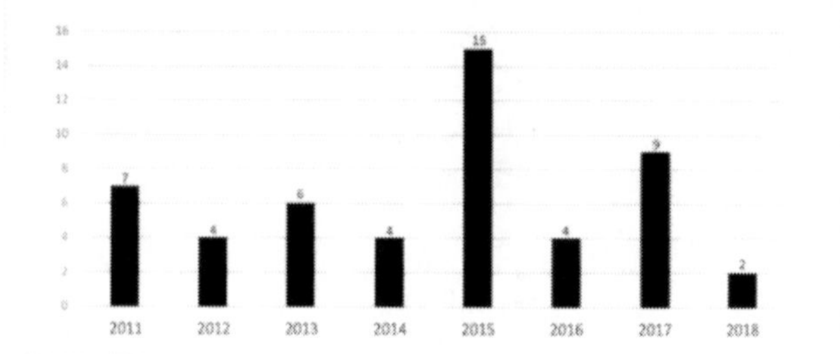

Figure 2. Literature per year.

IV. RESULTS

A. *Benefits of Cloud Computing*

The studies discussing cloud computing in eGovernment settings report a number of benefits. Some benefits are studied in depth, while others are superficially mentioned. Out of the 51 papers, 46 mention benefits to some extent. In total, 49

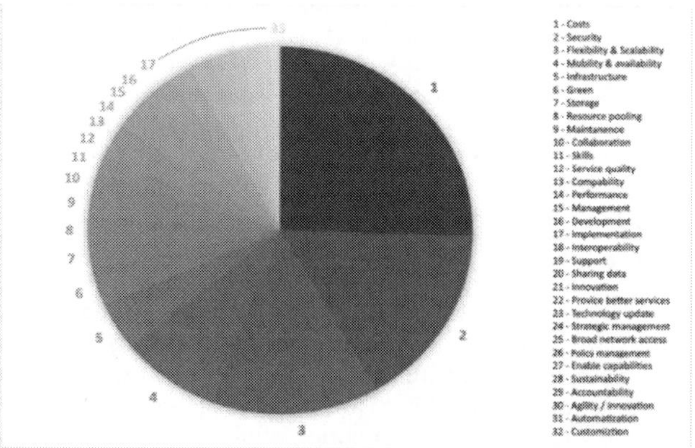

Figure 3. Benefits

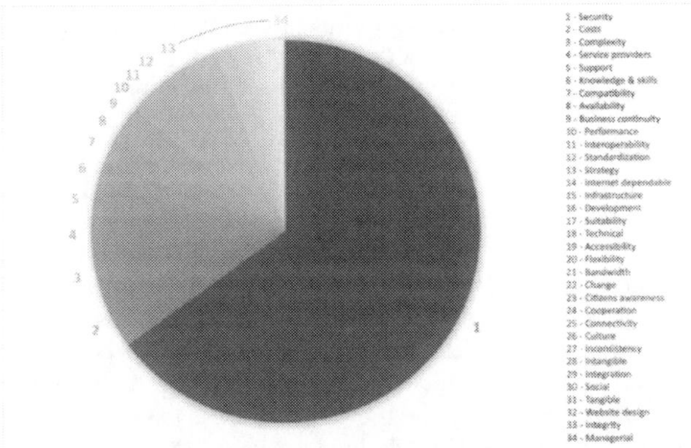

Figure 4. Challenges

benefits are identified in the first round of analysis. In the second iteration, some of the benefits found in the first round are grouped together, resulting in 32 distinct benefits.

A pie chart (Figure 3) illustrates the relative proportions of the papers that focus on each benefit and how focused they are. Table I (Appendix) lists the benefits and the associated literature, where three benefits stand out: cost reduction, security, and flexibility and scalability.

B. *Challenges of Cloud Computing*

Our analysis indicates differences in the extent to which the various challenges are studied. In total, 38 papers include discussions on cloud computing challenges. A total of 54 challenges were identified in the first iteration. A second iteration of the analysis resulted in 34 distinct challenges.

Similar to the benefits, a pie chart (Figure 4) illustrates the relative proportions of the papers that focus on each challenge and how focused they are. Table II (Appendix) lists the challenges and the associated literature. The challenges that stand out are security issues, costs, and complexity.

V. DISCUSSION

In this section, the findings from our analytical efforts are summarized and discussed, focusing on benefits and challenges.

Of the 51 papers reviewed, only seven use theories in their research. This indicates a lack of theoretical development in the eGovernment field in relation to cloud computing.

A. *Benefits of Cloud Computing*

Of the 32 identified benefits, cost reduction, security, and flexibility and scalability are mentioned much more frequently in the literature than the rest. Therefore, these three benefits are further explored.

1) *Cost reduction*

Cost reduction is a key driver for public organizations considering migrating to cloud solutions [1][8][34]. Of the 51 papers, 38 suggest cost reduction as an advantage for public agency use of cloud computing. Costs relating to the purchase and the installation of information and communication technology equipment, software, and infrastructure can be greatly reduced [1][7][11][28][35]. Public organizations can also upgrade or downgrade their capacities as needed and pay only for the resources used (economy of scale) [10][11][36][37]. Several researchers believe that human resource costs can be reduced as well [10][11]. Savings on software licenses can also occur, especially when using open source programs [10][38]. By purchasing large quantities of hardware and software, cloud service providers can offer more economical solutions. Opportunities, such as the creation of server parks near power stations, affordable sites, and so on, can also contribute to lower costs [10]. A study estimates that government agencies would save between 50% and 67% of eGovernment operation costs by moving governmental applications into private or public clouds [28]. For example, the governments of the UK and Spain use cloud computing to reduce costs [28][29].

2) *Security*

Security is regarded as the largest obstacle to public organizations' deployment of cloud computing, but several researchers suggest substantial security benefits. Security can be improved with centralized security management [10][39][40]. Public organizations with one centralized system instead of silo structures can provide security enhancements [10]. Cloud computing can also offer backup solutions (e.g., use cloud storage to upload the backup or the supplier's own backup and disaster recovery solutions), which will likewise satisfy the requirements of off-site storage in different locations [39]. Restoration and recovery can be performed swiftly [39]. Private cloud solutions with stricter security are more appropriate for governments than public cloud solutions [6]. Cloud-based solutions for security have been developed, for instance, "identity in the cloud," which is an authentication service based on cloud technology [41].

3) *Flexibility and scalability*

Flexibility and scalability are benefits of cloud computing in the eGovernment context [1][28][29][35][38]-[40][42]-[44]. The pay-as-you-go pricing model allows an instrument of scaling, depending on user demand [5][28][42], thereby achieving flexibility in the form of rapid elasticity [6][37][43]. This especially allows an increased number of users, user loads, and applications [1][11]. This is possible due to virtualization technologies [45], where nodes can be seamlessly added to the public organizations' resource pools [10]. Public organizations can control these scaling options without interfering with suppliers or humans [2][40]. These options can even be fully automated [10]. Cloud computing also offers access to applications and stored data, anytime and anywhere [39]. Cloud computing has massive storage capabilities [11]. Denmark benefited from cloud computing scalability during the World Climate Conference in 2009, where the expectation of high load peaks made the use of traditional solutions unsustainable [28]. Cloud computing suppliers typically offer flexible contract terms to ensure scalability [39].

4) *Other benefits*

Interestingly, several authors argue that cloud computing offers environmental benefits because of enhanced efficiency of resources and less consumption of power [1][6][11][42].

Payment models (e.g., pay-as-you-go) may offer considerable benefits as the current climate of economic difficulties affects government budgets worldwide [5][7][28][39].

B. *Challenges of Cloud Computing*

Security issues, costs, and complexity are the most frequently mentioned challenges, especially security issues (Figure 4). These three challenges are further explored in the following subsections.

1) Security issues

Many studies highlight security as the main issue or one of the most critical challenges for adopting cloud computing in eGovernment [2][11][28][29][35][38][45]. Security risks associated with cloud computing are prominent in eGovernment systems [28][46]. This situation can create trust issues [38][46] that in turn can lead to adoption barriers [9][43]. This matter is crucial for national security [11]. Public organizations transfer much of the security control to cloud computing suppliers, which leads to the government's reduced ability to control data [4][6][37] and therefore requires complete trust [34]. By using cloud computing, public organizations store their data in the cloud, resulting in the challenge of protecting the data [28]. Data that are not kept in the government's premises and are therefore under less control might lead to concerns about unauthorized access and misuse [2].

Moreover, data privacy law enforcement is not globally uniform [6]. Most governments have data protection regulations that do not allow storage of sensitive data in other countries, where cloud computing suppliers offer international mirrored sites for data storage [1]. It is difficult to check whether the cloud computing suppliers fulfill their promises of protection and storage of sensitive data [2]. High data encryption is therefore recommended [2]. It is also important to implement proper access control, authentication, and authorization [47][48]. There is the need for auditing as well, which is another challenge in cloud computing systems. In countries where cloud computing systems are based on public clouds, shifting to private clouds might help overcome this challenge [28]. Other mentioned challenges are users' use of e-payment systems [38] and cloud-based e-voting [6]. All of the above issues require physical security (data and information stored in a secure location) and logical security (protection from threats, such as hacking, intrusion, and viruses) [2]. Cloud computing suppliers are starting to support governments' security requirements. One example is Fabasoft, a supplier that offers secure authentication, supporting the national eID systems of Austria, Germany, and Switzerland [28].

2) Cost

Several studies highlight cost as a crucial challenge [2][4][9][29][49]. This is somewhat confusing, given that cost reduction is viewed as the main benefit of adopting cloud computing solutions. Alkhwaldi, Kamala and Qahwaji [46] highlights high maintenance and operational costs. High costs may also be related to security solutions. Some studies also cite the higher costs associated with activities aimed at preventing lock-in (being dependent on one cloud supplier, with difficulty in changing the supplier or the solutions) [2][4]. Other challenges for cloud computing can be hiring IT experts, facilitation of network requirements, adoption costs, and government budgets allocated for cloud computing [9].

3) Complexity

Several studies emphasize complexity as a major challenge, which adversely affects the adoption of cloud solutions [8][34], thus hindering the realization of the benefits [39]. Complexity also contributes to user dissatisfaction [39]. The lack of standards for cloud computing often leads to problems surrounding its adoption or difficulties in changing suppliers (of cloud services) [1]. Cloud service providers might also procure their services through a third party and therefore increase the risks of chain failure and interruption of cloud services [2].

4) Other challenges

One notable challenge is the potential lack of the IT experts required to manage cloud computing [9]. This issue is interesting because of the finding that one of the drivers of the migration to cloud computing is reducing the need for IT expertise. It is also interesting that despite the research indicating an expected increase in performance [40], another study reports concerns related to under-performance [4].

VI. CONCLUSION

This study has aimed to explore and understand the phenomenon of cloud computing in the eGovernment context. To this end, we adopted a literature review approach, collecting and analyzing 51 relevant research articles and discussed cloud computing in the digital government domain.

Our analysis identified 32 distinct benefits of cloud computing in eGovernment. Of the 32 benefits, cost reduction, security, and flexibility and scalability are the most prominent. Among the 34 distinct challenges identified, those related to security are by far the most frequently mentioned in the reviewed literature. No consensus has been reached about the cost benefit of moving to cloud solutions as costs are mentioned among both benefits and challenges of the cloud technology.

The limitations of this study include the choice of search terms (some related terms can also be included in the search) and the selection of databases. Some challenges and benefits are possibly better described in the more general computer science literature, while remaining applicable to the eGovernment domain.

Nonetheless, we believe this review offers a useful overview of the use of cloud computing in eGovernment. It can be a starting point for more in-depth research on the applications of this technology for the provision of public services.

ACKNOWLEDGMENTS

The research leading to these results has been developed in the context of the Gov 3.0 Project. It has received partial funding from the Erasmus+ Knowledge Alliance, Project

Reference No. 588306-EPP-1-2017-1-EL-EP. We especially thank Jon Switters for his initial review of cloud computing, which has inspired us to undertake this literature review.

REFERENCES

[1] T. Almarabeh, Y. K. Majdalawi, and H. Mohammad, "Cloud computing of E-government." CN, vol 8, pp. 1-8, 2016.

[2] P. R. Joshi, S. Islam, and S. Islam, "A Framework for Cloud Based E-Government from the Perspective of Developing Countries." Future Internet, vol 9, p. 80, 2017.

[3] M. Alshehri and S. Drew, "Implementation of e-government: advantages and challenges" E-Activity and Leading Technologies 2010 (E-ALT2010) Nov 2010.

[4] E. K. Clemons and Y. Chen, "Making the decision to contract for cloud services: Managing the risk of an extreme form of IT outsourcing" Proceedings of the 44th Hawaii International Conference on System Sciences (HICSS-44 2011) Jan 2011 pp. 1-10

[5] F. Mohammed, O. Ibrahim, M. Nilashi, and E. Alzurqa, "Cloud computing adoption model for e-government implementation." Information Development, vol 33, pp. 303-323, 2017.

[6] E. Abu-Shanab and F. Estatiya, "Utilizing Cloud Computing in public sector cases from the world" International Conference on Applied System Innovation (ICASI 2017) May 2017 pp. 1702-1705

[7] F. Khan, K. Surat, A. W. Tareen, and M. Saeed, "Addressing the Challenges of E-government in Developing Countries through Public-Private Partnership Model Based on Cloud Computing." Journal of Applied and Emerging Sciences, vol 5, pp. 59-65, 2016.

[8] F. Mohammed, A. I. Alzahrani, O. Alfarraj, and O. Ibrahim, "Cloud Computing Fitness for E-Government Implementation: Importance-Performance Analysis." IEEE Access, vol 6, pp. 1236-1248, 2018.

[9] M. A. Wahsh and J. S. Dhillon, "An investigation of factors affecting the adoption of cloud computing for E-government implementation" 3th IEEE Student Conference on Research & Development (SCOReD 2015) Dec 2015 pp. 323-328

[10] D. Zissis and D. Lekkas, "Securing e-Government and e-Voting with an open cloud computing architecture." GIQ, vol 28, pp. 239-251, 2011.

[11] F. Mohammed and O. Ibrahim, "Models of adopting cloud computing in the e-government context: a review." Jurnal Teknologi, vol 73, pp. 51-59, 2015.

[12] D. C. Wyld, Moving to the cloud: An introduction to cloud computing in government. 2009: IBM Center for the Business of Government.

[13] D. C. Wyld, "The cloudy future of government IT: Cloud computing and the public sector around the world." IJWesT, vol 1, pp. 1-20, 2010.

[14] S. Marston, Z. Li, S. Bandyopadhyay, J. Zhang, and A. Ghalsasi, "Cloud computing—The business perspective." Decis Support Syst, vol 51, pp. 176-189, 2011.

[15] W. Cellary and S. Strykowski, "E-government based on cloud computing and service-oriented architecture" 3rd International Conference on Theory and Practice of Electronic Governance (ICEGOV 2009) Nov 2009 pp. 5-10

[16] E. Kuiper, F. Van Dam, A. Reiter, and M. Janssen, "Factors influencing the adoption of and business case for Cloud computing in the public sector" 24th annual eChallenges (e-2014) Oct 2014 pp. 1-10

[17] F. Mohammed, O. Ibrahim, and N. Ithnin, "Factors influencing cloud computing adoption for e-government implementation in developing countries: Instrument development." JSIT, vol 18, pp. 297-327, 2016.

[18] E. Al Nuaimi, H. Al Neyadi, N. Mohamed, and J. Al-Jaroodi, "Applications of big data to smart cities." JISA, vol 6, pp. 25, 2015.

[19] J. Šuh, V. Vujin, D. Barać, Z. Bogdanović, and B. Radenković, "Designing cloud infrastructure for big data in e-government." JUE, vol 4, pp. A26-A38, 2015.

[20] Z. Khan and S. L. Kiani, "A cloud-based architecture for citizen services in smart cities" 5th IEEE/ACM International Conference on Utility and Cloud Computing (UCC 2012) Nov 2012 pp. 315-320

[21] A. Botta, W. De Donato, V. Persico, and A. Pescapé, "Integration of cloud computing and internet of things: a survey." FGCS, vol 56, pp. 684-700, 2016.

[22] N. Mitton, S. Papavassiliou, A. Puliafito, and K. S. Trivedi, "Combining Cloud and sensors in a smart city environment." EURASIP JWCN, vol 2012, pp. 247, 2012.

[23] B. Tang, et al., "A hierarchical distributed fog computing architecture for big data analysis in smart cities" ASE BigData & SocialInformatics (ASE BD&SI 2015) Oct 2015 pp. 28

[24] J. Jin, J. Gubbi, S. Marusic, and M. Palaniswami, "An information framework for creating a smart city through internet of things." IEEE IoT journal, vol 1, pp. 112-121, 2014.

[25] S. Moore. Top Trends from Gartner Hype Cycle for Digital Government Technology, 2018. Available from: https://www.gartner.com/smarterwithgartner/top-trends-from-gartner-hype-cycle-for-digital-government-technology-2018/ Retrieved: Feb 2019

[26] E. commision, "Cloud computing." vol, 2019.

[27] P. Chastanet. European Cloud Strategy 2012. Available from: https://ec.europa.eu/digital-single-market/en/european-cloud-computing-strategy Retrieved: Feb 2019

[28] B. Zwattendorfer, K. Stranacher, A. Tauber, and P. Reichstädter, "Cloud computing in e-government across europe" 2nd Joint International Conference on Electronic Government and the Information Systems Perspective and International Conference on Electronic Democracy (EGOVIS 2013) 2013 pp. 181-195

[29] G. Elena and C. W. Johnson, "Factors influencing risk acceptance of Cloud Computing services in the UK Government." IJCCSA, vol 5, pp. 1-16, 2015.

[30] S. Jones, Z. Irani, U. Sivarajah, and P. E. Love, "Risks and rewards of cloud computing in the UK public sector: A reflection on three Organisational case studies." Inf Syst Front, vol 19, pp. 1-24, 2017.

[31] B. Kitchenham, et al., "Systematic literature reviews in software engineering–a systematic literature review." IST, vol 51, pp. 7-15, 2009.

[32] C. Okoli, "A guide to conducting a standalone systematic literature review." CAIS, vol 37, pp. 879-910, 2015.

[33] J. Webster and R. T. Watson, "Analyzing the past to prepare for the future: Writing a literature review." MISQ, vol 26, pp. xiii-xxiii, 2002.

[34] N. Samsudin, R. Hashim, S. Fuzi, and K. Zakaria, "Crowdsourcing and Cloud Computing: Outsourcing and Backsourcing Alternatives for e-Government Services" Colloquium on Administrative Science and Technology (CoAST 2013) Jan 2015 pp. 349-360

[35] C. J. Stefanou and A. Skouras, "E-government: applications in the labor and social security regulatory area." TGPPP, vol 9, pp. 448-464, 2015.
[36] A. Breil, P. Hitzelberger, P. D. S. Carvalho, and F. Feltz, "Exploring data integration strategies for public sector cloud solutions" Advancing Democracy, Government and Governance (EGOVIS 2012) Sep 2012 pp. 271-278
[37] F. K. Tibenszkyné and S. Gábor, "E-government cloud computing" 4th Annual Conference pf the Europian Decision Science Institute (EDSI 2013) Jun 2013
[38] T. Kotka and I. Liiv, "Concept of Estonian Government cloud and data embassies" 4th International Conference on Electronic Government and the Information Systems Perspective (EGOVIS 2015) Sep 2015 pp. 149-162
[39] O. Ali, J. Soar, H. McClymont, J. Yong, and J. Biswas, "Anticipated benefits of cloud computing adoption in Australian regional municipal governments: an exploratory study" The Pacific Asia Conference on Information Systems (PACIS 2015) Jul 2015 pp. 1-18
[40] J.-W. Lian, "Critical factors for cloud based e-invoice service adoption in Taiwan: An empirical study." IJIM, vol 35, pp. 98-109, 2015.
[41] B. Zwattendorfer, K. Stranacher, and A. Tauber, "Towards a federated identity as a service model" 2nd Joint International Conference on Electronic Government and the Information Systems Perspective and International Conference on Electronic Democracy (EGOVIS 2013) 2013 pp. 43-57
[42] N. N. ALMutairi and S. F. Thuwaini, "Cloud computing uses for e-government in the middle east region opportunities and challenges." IJBM, vol 10, pp. 60, 2015.
[43] R. Hackney, et al., "Cloud Based e-Government Services: a proposal to evaluate user satisfaction" 23rd Americas Conference on Information Systems (AMCIS 2017) Aug 2017
[44] A. B. Sideridis and L. Protopappas, "Recent ICT Advances Applied to Smart e-Government Systems in Life Sciences" 7th International Conference on Information and Communication Technologies in Agriculture, Food and Environment (HAICTA 2015) Sep 2015 pp. 92-106
[45] D. Sreekanth and S. Gladston Raj, "Enhanced e-Government Process Model with Customer Centric Cloud." IJSRCSEIT, vol 2, pp. 848-851, 2017.
[46] A. Alkhwaldi, M. Kamala, and R. Qahwaji, "From e-govemment to cloud-government: Challenges of Jordanian citizens' acceptance for public services" 13th International Conference for Internet Technology and Secured Transactions (ICITST-2018) Dec 2017 pp. 298-304
[47] M. A. Shafique, et al., "Determinants Impacting the Adoption of E-Government Information Systems and Suggesting Cloud Computing Migration Framework." IJACSA, vol 8, pp. 173-182, 2017.
[48] A. B. Sideridis, L. Protopappas, S. Tsiafoulis, and E. Pimenidis, "Smart cross-border e-gov systems and applications" 6th International Conference (eDemocracy 2015) Dec 2015 pp. 151-165
[49] M. Decman and M. Vintar, "A possible solution for digital preservation of e-government: A centralised repository within a cloud computing framework." Aslib Proceedings, vol 65, pp. 406-424, 2013.
[50] M. Al-Ruithe, E. Benkhelifa, and K. Hameed, "Key dimensions for cloud data governance" 4th International Conference on Future Internet of Things and Cloud (FiCloud 2016) Aug 2016 pp. 379-386
[51] F. H. Chanchary and S. Islam, "E-government based on cloud computing with rational inference agent" 8th International Conference on 'High-capacity Optical Networks and Emerging Technologies' 2011 pp. 261-266
[52] T. Clohessy and T. Acton, "Cloud enterprise resource planning (ERP): A viable alternative for Irish e-government" UCC IEEE/ACM 2013 pp. 23-31
[53] S. Dernbecher, "Having the Mind in the Cloud: Organizational Mindfulness and the Successful Use of Desktop as a Service" 47th Hawaii International Conference on System Sciences (HICSS 2014) Jan 2014 pp. 2137-2146
[54] M. A. Hana, "E-government cloud computing proposed model: Egyptian E-Government Cloud Computing" International Conference on Advances in Computing, Communications and Informatics (ICACCI 2013) Aug 2013 pp. 847-852
[55] M. Janssen and A. Joha, "Challenges for adopting cloud-based software as a service (SAAS) in the public sector" European conference on information systems (ECIS 2011) Jun 2011
[56] R. Kurdi, A. Taleb-Bendiab, M. Randles, and M. Taylor, "E-Government information systems and cloud computing (Readiness and analysis)" Development in e-Systems Engineering (DeSE 2011) Dec 2011 pp. 404-409
[57] D. H. Liang, D. S. Liang, and I. J. Wen, "Applications of both cloud computing and e-government in Taiwan." JDCTA, vol 5, pp. 376-386, 2011.
[58] J. Liang, "Government cloud: Enhancing efficiency of E-government and providing better public services" International Joint Conference on Service Sciences (IJCSS 2012) May 2012 pp. 261-265
[59] A. Matus, et al., "On the development of an electronic invoicing solution to integrate SMEs with a tax-collection egovernment-platform" Sixth International Conference on eDemocracy & eGovernment (ICEDEG 2017) Apr 2017 pp. 94-101
[60] F. Mohammed and O. Ibrahim, "Refining E-government Readiness Index by Cloud Computing." Jurnal Teknologi, vol 65, pp. 23-34, 2013.
[61] I. Y. Omar, R. Laborde, A. S. Wazan, F. Barrere, and A. Benzekri, "G-Cloud on Openstack: Adressing access control and regulation requirements" International Symposium on Networks, Computers and Communications (ISNCC 2015) May 2015
[62] K. K. Smitha, T. Thomas, and K. Chitharanjan, Cloud Based E-Governance System : A Survey, in International Conference on Modelling Optimization and Computing, R. Rajesh, K. Ganesh, and S. C. L. Koh, Editors. 2012. pp. 3816-3823.
[63] A. Tripathi and B. Parihar, "E-Governance challenges and cloud benefits" IEEE International Conference on Computer Science and Automation Engineering (CSAE 2011) Jun 2011 pp. 351-354
[64] A. Tsohou, H. Lee, and Z. Irani, "Innovative public governance through cloud computing: Information privacy, business models and performance measurement challenges." TGPPP, vol 8, pp. 251-282, 2014.
[65] M. A. Wahsh and J. S. Dhillon, "A systematic review of factors affecting the adoption of cloud computing for e-Government implementation." ARPN JEAS, vol 10, pp. 17824-17832, 2015.
[66] B. Zwattendorfer and D. Slamanig, "Design strategies for a privacy-friendly Austrian eID system in the public cloud." Computers and Security, vol 52, pp. 178-193, 2015.

[67] B. Zwattendorfer and A. Tauber, "The public cloud for e-government." IJDST, vol 4, pp. 1-14, 2012.
[68] T. Kotka, et al., "Policy and legal environment analysis for E-government services migration to the public cloud" 9th International Conference on Theory and Practice of Electronic Governance (ICEGOV 2016) Mar 2016 pp. 103-108
[69] P. Shynu and K. J. Singh, "A novel temporal access control scheme for outsourced data in cloud with user revocation." EG, vol 13, pp. 274-286, 2017.
[70] Z. Lv, et al., "Government affairs service platform for smart city." Future Gener Comput Syst, vol 81, pp. 443-451, 2018.
[71] B. Alessandro, R. Barbara, and P. Alberto, "E-government and cloud: Security implementation for services" 4th International Conference on eDemocracy & eGovernment (ICEDEG 2017) Apr 2017 pp. 79-85
[72] H. Aljahdali, et al., "Multi-tenancy in cloud computing" 8th International Symposium on Service Oriented System Engineering (SOSE 2014) Apr 2014 pp. 344-351
[73] M. A. Aziz, J. Abawajy, and M. Chowdhury, "Advanced Computer Science Applications and Technologies (ACSAT)" 3rd International Conference on Advanced Computer Science Applications and Technologies (ACSAT 2014) Dec 2014 pp. 470-474

VII. APPENDIX

TABLE I. IDENTIFIED LITERATURE ON BENEFITS.

Identified Benefit	Literature	Identified Benefit	Literature
Cost reduction	[1][5]-[11][29][34]-[44][46][48][50]-[67]	Security	[1][2][6][8][10][28][35][38]-[42][44][46][50][51][53-56][58][59][62][63][68][69]
Flexibility and scalability	[1][2][5][6][9]-[11][28][29][35][37]-[40][42]-[46][50][51][53][56]-[58][60]-[64][66]-[68]	Mobility and availability	[1][2][6][9]-[11][28][29][35][39][40][42][45][50][54][58][59][61][64][67]
Infrastructure	[5]-[8][10][11][29][39][42][45][46][56][61][68]	Green technology	[1][6][10][11][39][42][46][54][56][57][59]
Storage	[1][6][11][39][40][45][46][62]	Resource pooling	[1][6][7][11][40][42][46][60]
Maintenance	[6][11][28][29][39][55][56]	Enabling capabilities	[1][29][39]
Collaboration	[6][10][46][56][58]	Management	[7][46][58][70]
Sharing data	[2][42][70]	Skills	[5][8][11][56]
Compatibility	[5][8][59][63]	Performance	[6][9][40][58]
Innovation	[38][68][70]	Service quality	[10][38][60]
Policy management	[39][51][63]	Broad network access	[1][60]
Implementation	[11][28]	Development	[37][39]
Support	[34][39]	Interoperability	[28][29]
Agility	[29][52]	Accountability	[6][62]
Customization	[6]	Automatization	[6]
Provision of better services	[39]	Technology update	[39]
Strategic management	[10]	Sustainability	[10]

TABLE II. IDENTIFIED LITERATURE ON CHALLENGES.

Identified Challenge	Literature	Identified Challenge	Literature
Security	[1][2][4]-[6][8]-[11][28][29][34][35][37][39]-[44][46][48]-[50][54]-[56][60][61][64]-[69][71][72]	Costs	[2][4][6][9][29][46][49][55][65][67]
Complexity	[5][6][8][9][34][46][65][67]	Service providers	[2][6][34][37][42][49][54][55][64]
Availability	[2][6][29][40][46][73]	Knowledge and skills	[6][39][42][55][65]
Interoperability	[1][11][28][39]	Compatibility	[8][9][65][67]
Internet dependable	[11][35][65]	Technical	[29][39][46]
Support	[6][56][60]	Performance	[4][29][40][55]
Strategy	[2][11][56][60]	Infrastructure	[40][46][73]
Managerial	[6][29][46]	Business continuity	[11][60][68]
Standardization	[29][60][73]	Flexibility	[6][67]
Development	[4][65]	Accessibility	[46][55]
Intangible	[46]	Integration	[6]
Integrity	[6]	Suitability	[2]
Culture	[46]	Inconsistency	[44]
Connectivity	[6]	Cooperation	[8]
Bandwidth	[34]	Social	[39]
Change	[34]	Citizens' awareness	[6]
Tangible	[46]	Website design	[46]

Innovation Policy Analytics for Economic Crisis

Euripidis Loukis
Dept. Information & Communication Systems Engineering
University of Aegean
Karlovassi, Greece
e-mail: eloukis@aegean.gr

Spyros Arvanitis
KOF Swiss Economic Institute
ETH Zürich
Zürich, Switzerland
e-mail: arvanitis@kof.ethz.ch

Charalampos Alexopoulos
Dept. Information & Communication Systems Engineering
University of Aegean
Karlovassi, Greece
e-mail:alexop@aegean.gr

Abstract— **Policy analytics is defined as the exploitation of existing data from government agencies, possibly in combination with data from private sector firms, and using advanced analytical techniques in order to support different stages of public policy making. It constitutes a highly ambitious new generation of electronic (digital) government, aiming to provide substantial support to higher government functions. However, the area of policy analytics is still in its infancy, so extensive further research is required in this area in order to develop effective methodologies for supporting various stages of policy-making in important domains of government intervention. This paper contributes to filling this research gap for a highly important domain of government intervention and policy, the promotion of firms' innovation activity, in difficult times of economic crisis. It presents a methodology for exploiting existing data from Taxation Authorities and Statistical Agencies in combination with data from private sector consulting and business information firms in order to identify characteristics of the firm and its external environment that affect its innovation behaviour (the extent of their product/service innovation reduction) during economic crises. Our methodology exploits findings of previous research in the areas of innovation and economic crises. It can generate valuable insights, which can support substantially the development of innovation policies in times of economic crisis. Furthermore, an application of this methodology is presented, using existing Greek firms' data from the Hellenic Statistical Authority, in combination with data from the business information and consulting firm ICAP, for the economic crisis period 2009 – 2014, which provides interesting insights.**

Keywords - Electronic Government; Digital Government; Policy Analytics; Policy Informatics; Innovation; Economic Crisis.

I. INTRODUCTION

Policy analytics (previously called also as policy informatics) is defined as the exploitation of existing data from government agencies, possibly in combination with data from private sector firms, and using advanced analytical techniques in order to support different stages of public policy making [1]. It constitutes a highly ambitious new generation of electronic (digital) government, aiming to provide substantial support to higher government functions. While the first generation of electronic (digital) government aimed to support government agencies' internal processes as well as their transactions with firms and citizens, and the second generation aimed to support communication and consultation with the society (with a special focus on the exploitation of the social media for this purpose), this new third generation aims to support and enhance the whole cycle of policy-making for addressing serious problems of modern societies [2][3].

Though there has been a long interest in providing support for the design and implementation of important public policies (due to their high importance for and impact on the society and also the large amounts of financial resources they consume), recently this has become much more intensive, leading to an exponential development of policy analytics, mainly for three reasons:

i) The development and success of the data science and business analytics in the private sector, which aims at the exploitation of the large quantities of data collected by firms in order to support decision making, strategy formulation, as well as development of new products and services [4][5].

ii) The increasing availability of data in government agencies, which can provide (after appropriate processing) significant support of policy and decision making. The main sources of these data are: the increasingly complex internal information systems (IS) of government agencies, as well as their electronic transactions and consultations IS; the growing use of social media by government agencies, which generates large quantities of textual data, containing valuable citizens' knowledge, experience, proposals, ideas, opinions and comments; and recently the development of the Internet of Things (IoT), especially in the context of modern cities [6][7].

iii) The increasing complexity and severity of the challenges, problems and needs of modern societies. The 'traditional' social problems that governments face have become more complex and severe, while at the same time new problems have appeared (e.g., due to the globalization of the economy, the climate change, the ageing population, the migration of massive populations from underdeveloped countries or areas facing serious conflicts, warfare or social unrest to the more developed countries) [6][7].

It is widely recognized that the potential of the above massive government data, especially if combined with related private sector data (e.g., from consulting and business information firms), towards the provision of valuable support of highly important public policies, is quite high. This potential can be exploited to a much greater extent if these data undergo advanced processing using various sophisticated analytical techniques from the areas of statistics, data mining, operational research, etc., such as regression analysis, clustering, association analysis, data segmentation, classification analysis, anomaly detection, social network analysis and computer simulation [1]. However, the area of policy analytics is still in its infancy, so extensive further research is required in this area in order to develop effective policy analytics methodologies for supporting various stages of policy-making in important domains of government intervention. Some useful knowledge has already been developed in the area of policy analytics, which includes methodologies for exploiting different sources of data, using advanced basic or more advanced analytical techniques in order to support some of the stages of the policy making cycle in some domains of government intervention, such as the environment [8], the energy provision [9], the justice [10] and the management of emergency crises (both natural disasters, such as earthquakes and hurricanes, and man-made crises, such as terrorism and ethnic violence) [11][12]. However, extensive additional research is required in this area in order to increase our knowledge concerning the exploitation of the large quantities of data available today in government, in combination with data from various private sector firms, and using advanced analytical techniques for supporting all the stages of public policies' development and implementation, in various important domains. It is necessary to experiment with exploiting a variety policy-related public and private sector datasets, using various analytical techniques, from 'traditional' statistical analysis to advanced data mining and artificial intelligent ones, in order to extract from them insights and knowledge that can be useful for policy making.

This paper contributes in this direction towards filling the abovementioned research gaps, dealing with a highly important domain of government intervention and policy: the promotion of firms' innovation. We focus on periods, in which this is more difficult and at the same time more useful for the economy and the society: on periods of economic crisis. It is widely recognized that innovation has become an important element of the modern economy, of critical importance for the competitiveness and growth of firms, sectors and countries [6][7][13]. It involves development of new products and services (or substantial improvement of existing ones) in order to adapt to evolving needs and preferences of customers, development of new markets or market segments, and exploitation of new technologies that have emerged. Governments of various layers (central, regional and municipal governments) of most countries exhibit active interest in promoting innovation, and design and implement policies for this purpose that take the form of financial support through grants, subsidies and tax credits, but also the form of relevant laws and regulations. Government initiatives become much more difficult, but at the same time much more necessary and important in periods of economic crisis, which are an inevitable trait of market-based economies [14][15]. Economic crises are repeatedly occurring with varying intensities and durations in market-based economies, with quite negative consequences for the economy and the society in general. One of the most important (however less observable and debated) negative consequences is the reduction of firms' product/service innovation activities, which has quite negative impact on their medium- and long-term competitiveness. So, during periods of economic crisis it is even more important than in the 'normal' periods to design and implement policies for mitigating this reduction of firms' innovation activities and promoting product/service innovation that can contribute to overcoming the crisis. However, this necessitates a sound evidence-base, which will allow achieving higher levels of effectiveness and maturity of these critical policies.

In this direction this paper presents a methodology for exploiting existing data from Taxation Authorities and Statistical Agencies, in combination with data from private sector consulting and business information firms, in order to identify characteristics of the firm and its external environment that affect its innovation behaviour (the extent of their product/service innovation reduction) during economic crises. Our methodology is based on and leverages findings of previous research in the areas of innovation and economic crises. It can generate valuable insights, as to the types of firms exhibiting higher or lower sensitivity to the crisis with respect to innovation activity, which can support substantially the development of innovation policies in periods of economic crisis. Furthermore, an application of this methodology is presented, using Greek firms' data from the Hellenic Statistical Authority, in combination with data from the business information and consulting firm ICAP, for the economic crisis period 2009 – 2014; it has revealed interesting characteristics of firms and their external environment affecting innovation behaviour during the Greek crisis.

The paper is organized in five sections. The following section II outlines the conceptual background of our study. Section III describes the proposed methodology of innovation policy analytics for economic crisis periods, while Section IV presents the abovementioned application. Finally, Section V summarizes the conclusions and proposes future research directions.

II. BACKGROUND

In this section we briefly present the background of the proposed methodology concerning innovation and economic crise.s

A. *Innovation*

The 'Oslo Manual 2018' [13] defines product/service innovation as 'a new or improved good or service that differs significantly from the firm's previous goods or services and that has been introduced in the market'. Innovation is more than simply a new idea or an invention: it includes implementation, diffusion and active use by other parties, such as individuals, firms or public organisations. It is the wide diffusion of an innovation that can actually generate economic and social positive impact and value. However, beyond the above positive value, innovative products and services might replace some existing ones, and this can cause problems to firms producing the latter (e.g., reduction of sales, profitability and personnel employment), and in general lead to significant disruptions; however, in the long-term innovation leads to economic growth. The main theoretical foundations of innovation have been developed in the beginning of the 20th century by the Austrian economist J. Schumpeter, who created theories on how firms search for new opportunities and competitive advantage over current or potential competitors [16]. He also introduced the concept of "creative destruction" to describe the disruption of existing economic activity that can be caused by innovations creating new ways of producing goods or services, or even entirely new industries.

In the modern economy innovation is highly important for firms' competitiveness, or even survival [6][7]. As new technologies are continuously emerging, firms have to develop new or substantially improved products and services that incorporate and exploit these technologies, acting either as 'first movers' (i.e., before their competitors) - leaders, or as 'late movers' (i.e., after some of their competitors have taken action) – followers. Furthermore, customers' needs and preferences are evolving, and also markets are changing (e.g., new competitors, substitutes or suppliers appear), and firms have to respond by introducing new or substantially improved products and services.

Innovation is a highly knowledge-intensive activity; it requires the use and combination of both internal and external knowledge, which necessitates significant human capital (human competences and skills) as well as organizational capital (appropriate practices and processes). In particular, innovation requires absorbing relevant knowledge from their external environment (e.g., from universities, research centres, suppliers, customers, partners, etc.), combining it with internal knowledge they possess, and then exploiting this combined knowledge for making product/service innovations [17]-[19]. So, modern firms in order to be innovative need to possess high levels of knowledge 'absorptive capacity', which has four main components: a) acquisition capacity (ability to locate, identify, value and acquire external knowledge that is related to firm's products and services); b) assimilation capacity (ability to analyse, process, interpret, understand, internalize and classify the acquired external knowledge); c) transformation capacity (ability to associate and combine the existing knowledge base of the firm with the newly acquired knowledge); d) application or exploitation capacity (ability to incorporate acquired, assimilated and transformed knowledge into new or significantly improved products and services) [18].

Due to the high importance of innovation for firms, sectors and countries considerable research has been conducted for the identification of factors that influence firm's innovation activity, termed as 'innovation determinants'; reviews of this research are provided in [13][20][21][22]. This research has revealed characteristics of the firm and its external environment that affect its innovation activity; the most important of them are size, human capital, adoption of 'organic' non-hierarchical forms of workplace organisation (such as teamwork, decentralisation of decision making and job rotation), technological capabilities, financial resources, creativity and innovation culture, as well as demand prospects and competition, which impact positively firm's innovation activity. A more recent relevant research stream has focused on and revealed the strong positive impact that information and communication technologies (ICT) can have on both the 'process' of innovation (i.e., the design and implementation of it) as well as its 'outcomes' (i.e., the resulting ICT-enabled innovative products and services) [6][7][13][23][24][25][26]. In [25] are identified three main channels through which the use of ICT impacts positively firms' innovation activities. The first channel is the support and improvement of the management of the knowledge (internal or external) required for the innovation process. ICT enables an efficient storage, accessibility and exchange of this knowledge throughout the firm. Internal networks, e-mail systems, and electronic databases all facilitate the transfer of knowledge and the communication between innovation participants. Second, ICT enables a more efficient cooperation for innovation with external partners, which has become even more important in the last twenty years, with the wide adoption of 'open innovation' models [23]. Third, ICT enable new products and services, and also the variety and personalization of existing products and services, which were not operationally and economically feasible before without ICT [24]. Furthermore, some specific kinds of information systems (IS) have been identified, such as enterprise resource planning (ERP), customer relationship management (CRM), business intelligence/analytics (BI/BA) and e-business ones, as well as social media, which can substantially improve firm's absorptive capacity and finally ability for innovation, by enabling the collection and processing of data that can be quite useful for firms' innovation activity [27][28]. Also, the use of cloud computing can provide rapid and low-cost electronic support of product/process innovations, so it can positively impact firms' innovation activity [29][30].

B. *Economic Crises*

One of the most important problems that governments face, and have to address through appropriate policies, are the economic crises of varying intensities and durations that repeatedly occur in market-based economies [14][15]. They can be defined as significant contractions of economic activity, which can be due to 'business cycles' (i.e., the fluctuations that economic activity usually exhibits, with periods of expansion followed by periods of contraction) or other events that happen in the society or economy (such as the oil crisis in the early 1970, or banking crises) [15].

Economic crises have quite negative both short-term as well as medium- and long-term consequences for the economy and the society. The short-term consequences (which are much more 'observable' and widely debated by the society, as they directly affect large number of citizens) include reductions of the demand for many goods and services, resulting in serious decrease of firms' sales, production and profits, leading to reductions in personnel employment and materials' procurement (and through this mechanism the crisis propagates further towards the suppliers, etc.). For the above reasons economic crises increase unemployment, especially among some disadvantaged groups, such as the young people, the low-skilled, the immigrants and the temporary workers [14]. This causes big social problems, increasing the number of citizens living in poverty and social exclusion; furthermore, it increases the required government spending for unemployment benefits, as well as for other types of social welfare and assistance for the unemployed (e.g., further training), while at the same time during these economic crises government income from taxation decreases due to lower firms' profitability and individuals' income.

Another highly important (however much less debated) negative consequence is that during economic crises firms usually reduce investment in fixed assets (e.g., in production equipment, ICT, buildings, etc.) and also in innovations, due to the reduction on one hand of the external demand for products and services, which makes such investment more risky, and on the other hand of the available financial resources for investment [14][15][31][32]. This is called 'pro-cyclical' behaviour' (i.e., investment follows the ups and down of the business cycle), having quite negative impact on firms medium- and long-term competitiveness. Especially the reduction of firms' innovation activities during economic crises decreases the degree of renewal of their products and services, exploitation of emerging new technologies, and adaptation to changing needs and preferences of customers, and results finally in lower competitiveness. However, for some innovation investments has been observed the opposite behaviour by some firms during economic crises: increase, in order to take advantage of lower prices of some required inputs (such as specialized personnel and equipment) [33]; this is called 'anti-cyclical' or 'counter-cyclical' investment behaviour'.

The above negative consequences of the economic crises are not the same for all firms: some firms are more efficient than the others, offer higher value-for-money products and services, so they have weaker negative consequences on their sales revenue, and therefore on employment and investment, including investment in innovation. Therefore, it is important to identify characteristics of the firm and its external environment that affect positively or negatively its sensitivity to economic crises, especially with respect to innovation activity. In this paper we present an innovation policy analytics methodology for this purpose (described in the following section III). This can be quite useful for government agencies in order to develop effective and focused policies for reducing the negative consequences of economic crises on firms' innovation activity. It allows identifying characteristics (with respect to strategy, organization, human resources, use of ICT, external environment) of firms exhibiting lower sensitivity to the crisis with respect to innovation (i.e., lower or even no product/service innovation reduction due to the crisis), and therefore learning from them (which strategies, forms of organization, human resources, kinds of ICT reduce a firm's innovation sensitivity to the crisis). It further allows identifying characteristics of firms exhibiting higher sensitivity to the crisis with respect to innovation (i.e., higher product/service innovation reduction due to the crisis), in order to design effective policies for assisting and supporting them (e.g., financial support of innovation activities, relevant laws and regulations).

III. PROPOSED METHODOLOGY

As mentioned above, the proposed innovation policy analytics methodology aims to identify characteristics of the firm and its external environment that affect its innovation behaviour (the extent of product/service innovation reduction) during economic crises. It exploits findings of previous research in the areas of innovation (concerning innovation determinants, briefly reviewed in the last paragraph of section II.A) and economic crises (see section II.B). In particular, our methodology uses two main data sources:

i) existing public sector data concerning firms' innovation behaviour (i.e., extent of product/service innovation reduction) during economic crises, possessed by Taxation Authorities and Statistical Agencies,

ii) existing public and the private sector data concerning various characteristics of firms (e.g., concerning strategy, organization, human resources, use of ICT) and their external environment, possessed by Statistical Agencies, and also business information firms and consulting firms.

These data are used for the estimation of innovation reduction regression models, having as dependent variables various measures of the reduction of different kinds of firm product/process innovation (e.g., incremental, radical, etc.) due to the economic crisis (INN_RED), and as independent variables various characteristics of the firm and its external environment (fch_k, k = 1,.. ,n):

$$INN\_RED_i = b_0 + b_1 * fch_{1i} + b_2 * fch_{2i} + \ldots + b_n fch_{ni} + b_{n+1} * d\_size_i + b_{n+2} * d\_sector_i , \quad for\ firm\ i \qquad (1)$$

where: d_size are dummy variables for firm size, and d_sector are dummy variables for firm sector affiliation.

These regression models allow the identification of independent variables having statistically significant regression coefficients, which reveal characteristics of the firm and its external environment that affect the extent of innovation reduction due to economic crisis.

In these innovation reduction regression models we can include as independent variables:

a) Firm characteristics that can influence the extent of reduction of sales revenue due to the economic crisis, which is the main determinant of the financial resources available for investments in innovation. For instance, the extent of adopting an export strategy to countries not facing economic crisis can reduce the negative impact of a domestic economic crisis on firm's sales revenue and therefore increase the availability of financial resources for innovation investments.

b) Characteristics of the firm and its external environment that can influence its innovation activity. According to previous research on innovation determinants (briefly reviewed in the last paragraph of section II.A) the most important of them are:

- size (with larger firms in general having more financial

resources for innovation investments, and also more opportunities for bank loans);
- human capital (employing personnel of higher educational levels, competences and skills can increase firms' capacity to perform the extensive and complex knowledge related activities required for making product/service innovations [34] - see third paragraph of section II.A);
- adoption of 'organic' non-hierarchical forms of workplace organisation, such as teamwork, decentralisation of decision making and job rotation (they facilitate the exchange and combination of knowledge of firms' employees from different functions and background, which is of critical importance for innovation [26]);
- financial resources and technological capabilities (for financing projects of product/service innovation, and for producing innovative products/services respectively);
- creativity and innovation culture;
- use of ICT (which as mentioned in II.A can significantly support and enhance both the 'process' and the 'outcome' of innovation [6][7][26], and especially use of some specific kinds of IS that can substantially increase firm's knowledge absorptive capacity and therefore ability for innovation, such as ERP, CRM, BI/BA, e-business, social media and cloud computing [27][28][29][30];

and also some characteristics of firm's external environment that according to previous innovation determinants' research (see section II.A) affect innovation activity, such as:
- demand prospects (larger demand potential increases firm's incentives for fostering product/service innovations);
- competition conditions (higher competitive pressures also increase firm's incentives for product/service innovation).

The above provide useful guidelines for specifying the innovation reduction regression models for the practical application of this methodology.

IV. APPLICATION

The innovation policy analytics methodology described in the previous section III has been applied for the identification of characteristics of Greek firms and their external environment that affect the extent of their product/service innovation reduction due to the long and intensive economic crisis that Greece experienced from 2009 until today. For this purpose, we have used existing Greek firm's data for the period 2009-2014 from two sources: i) the Hellenic Statistical Authority (data concerning the extent of firms' innovation reduction in the period 2009-2014); and ii) ICAP S.A., a well-known business information and consulting firm (data concerning characteristics of firms and their external environment). In particular, we have used data from these two sources for 363 Greek firms, which belong to the most technologically developed manufacturing and services sectors of the Greek economy; 40.2% of them were from manufacturing sectors, 9.4% from constructions, and 50.4% from services sectors; 52.6% of them were small, 36.1% medium and 11.3% large ones. From these data an innovation reduction regression model was estimated.

Our dependent variable is the extent of reduction of firm's product/service innovation due to the crisis, which is assessed in a 5-point Likert scale ("negligible, "small", "moderate", "large", "very large"). In Table 1 we can see the relative frequencies of these values.

TABLE 1. RELATIVE FREQUENCIES FOR EXTENT OF INNOVATION REDUCTION

Negligible	small	moderate	Large	very large
30.5%	21.1%	25.5%	16.4%	6.6%

We can see that more than half (51.6%) of the firms of our sample (coming from the most technologically developed manufacturing and services sectors of the Greek economy, as mentioned above) had negligible or small extent of innovation reduction due to the crisis, while about one quarter (25.5%) had moderate extent of reduction, and less than one quarter of them (23%) had a large or very large extent of innovation reduction.

The independent variables were:
- characteristics of firm: adoption of export strategy (EXP - binary variable); use of 'organic' forms of workplace organization, such as teamwork, decentralization and job rotation (ORG – binary variable); human capital (HC – percentage of firm's employees having tertiary-level education);
- ICT use: extent of use of customer relationship management, business intelligence/analytics and collaboration support systems (CRM, BI/BA, CS – ordinal variables measured on a 5-point Likert scale: "not at all", "to a small extent", "to a moderate extent", "to a large extent", "to a very large extent"); use of social media and cloud computing (SM and CLO – binary variables);
- characteristics of a firm's external environment: decrease of demand in the last three years (DEMDEC – ordinal variable measured in a 5-point Likert scale: "increased strongly", "increased", "remained the same", "decreased", "decreased strongly"); intensity of price competition and intensity of non-price competition (PRCOMP and NPRCOMP - ordinal variables measured in a 5-point Likert scale: "very weak", "weak", "moderate", "strong", "very strong").
- size and sector control variables: two control variables for size: D-L (taking value 1 for large firms having more than 250 employees and 0 for all other firms) and D-M (taking value 1 for medium-size firms having 50 - 250 employees and 0 for all other firms); and one control variable for sector: D-SE (taking value 1 for manufacturing or construction sectors' firms, and 0 for service sectors' firms).

In Table 2 we can see the innovation reduction model we estimated from the above data through ordinal regression estimation (since the dependent variable is a five-level ordinal variable) and using negative log-log link function (as the lower categories of the dependent variable are more probable); the statistically significant coefficients at levels of 1%, 5% and 10% are shown with ***, ** and * respectively.

This model reveals two ICTs that have statistically significant negative effects on the extent of Greek firms' innovation reduction due to the crisis (i.e., reduce the negative effects of the crisis on firms' product/service innovation): the cloud computing and the BI/BA. The use of cloud computing can provide rapid and low-cost electronic support of firm's activities and processes, improving their efficiency, and this can make the firm more resistant to the crisis and reduce the negative impact of economic crisis on its sales revenue. This increases the availability of financial resources for innovation projects. Also, cloud computing can provide rapid and low-cost electronic support of firm's product/service innovations, and this has positive influence on its innovation activity. The use of BI/BA allows extracting useful insights from the data stored in a firm's IS (concerning sales, production, procurement, expenses, etc.), which can lead to efficiency improvements, making the firm more resistant to the crisis, reducing the negative impact of economic crisis on sales revenue, and therefore increasing the availability of financial resources for innovation projects. Furthermore, the use of BI/BA enables gaining valuable insights from firm's sales data, which allow identifying opportunities for making product/service innovations.

TABLE 2. ESTIMATED INNOVATION REDUCTION MODEL

Independent variable	Coefficient	Independent variable	Coefficient
EXP	-0.275**	***CLO***	-0.348**
ORG	-0.073	***DEMDEC***	0.218***
HC	-0.298	***PRCOMP***	0.108
CRM	0.040	***NPRCOMP***	0.084
BI/BA	-0.094*	***D-L***	-0.375
CS	0.033	***D-M***	-0.053
SM	-0.151	***D-SE***	-0.100
Nagelkehre Pseudo $R^2 = 0.125$			

Also, the estimates in Table 2 indicate that the adoption of export strategy has statistically significant negative effect on the extent of Greek firms' innovation reduction due to the crisis (i.e. reduces the negative effects of the crisis on firm's product/service innovation). The adoption of export strategy reduces the reliance of firm's sales revenue on its domestic market. So if there is an economic crisis in the home country of the firm the sales revenue from the domestic market is reduced, but this does not happen with the sales revenue from the markets of the other foreign countries, in which the firm is present (if in these countries there is not economic crisis, or at least it is less severe, which is the case for Greece). Therefore, the negative impact of an economic crisis in a firm's home country on overall firm's sales revenue is finally weaker. This results in higher availability of financial resources that can be used for product/service innovation. Finally, our model indicates that the extent of demand decrease that the firm experienced during the last three years due to the Greek economic crisis has statistically significant positive effect on the extent of innovation reduction due to the crisis (i.e., increases the negative effects of the crisis on firm's product/service innovation). If the firm belongs to a sector that experienced higher demand decrease during the crisis then the decrease of its sale revenue will be stronger, reducing the financial resources for innovation.

Furthermore, interesting and useful insights can be gained also from the independent variables that do not have statistically significant effects on the extent of firm's innovation reduction due to the crisis. They indicate that Greek firms do not exploit their human capital, their organic forms of workplace organization (such as teams, decentralisation of decision making and job rotation) and their collaboration support systems for coping better with the crisis and for promoting product/service innovation. The same holds for their CRM systems and social media. Also, they do not react to competition pressures during the economic pressure with product/service innovation.

Our conclusions indicate that the design and implementation of public policies for promoting and facilitating export activities of Greek firms, and also the use of cloud computing and BI/BA, especially for sectors experiencing higher demand decrease during the economic crisis, would contribute to the reduction of the negative consequences of the economic crisis on their innovation activity, and therefore on their medium- and long-term competitiveness.

V. CONCLUSIONS

In the previous sections has been presented a methodology of innovation policy analytics, for the difficult periods of economic crises that market-based economies repeatedly face. It exploits and combines existing data from Taxation Authorities and Statistical Agencies, and also from private sector consulting and business information firms, and performs advanced processing of them (based on regression modelling), in order to identify characteristics of the firm and its external environment that affect its innovation behaviour (the extent of their product/service innovation reduction) during economic crises. Our methodology is based on and leverages findings of previous research on innovation determinants and economic crises. A first validation of this methodology was made through an application of it in the context of Greece, which provided some first evidence concerning the capabilities and usefulness of it. This application enabled the identification of some characteristics of Greek firms and their external environment that affect their innovation behaviour during economic crisis, which provide a useful base for innovation policy making.

However, our study has some limitations. The proposed methodology is based on the estimation of regression models, so it would be interesting to extend it with estimations of other kinds of models as well, e.g., from the areas of data mining and artificial intelligence (such as various classifiers). Also, the first application of the methodology was based on a cross-sectoral sample of Greek firms, so it would be interesting to proceed to more applications of it, in various other national contexts, and also in specific sectors, for different kinds of firm product/process innovation (e.g., incremental, radical, etc.), and using wider sets of characteristics of firms and their external environments as independent variables.

REFERENCES

[1] J. R. Gil-Garcia, T. A. Pardo, and L. F. Luna-Reyes, "Policy Analytics: Definitions, Components, Methods, and Illustrative Examples", in Policy Analytics, Modelling, and Informatics, ed. by J. R. Gil-Garcia, T. Pardo, L. F. Luna-Reyes. Switzerland: Springer International Publishing AG – Public Administration and Infor-mation Technology, pp. 1–16, 2018.

[2] T. Janowski, "Digital government evolution: From

transformation to contextualization", Government Information Quarterly, 32(3), pp. 221-236, 2015.

[3] Z. Lachana, C. Alexopoulos, E. Loukis, Y. Charalabidis, "Identifying the Different Generations of e-Government – An Analysis Framework" 12th Mediterranean Conference on Information Systems (MCIS 2018), September 28 - 30, 2018, Corfu, Greece.

[4] T. H. Davenport and J. G. Harris, Competing on analytics: the new science of winning", Harvard Business Press, Boston, 2017.

[5] T. H. Davenport, Big Data at Work: Dispelling the Myths, Uncovering the Opportunities, Harvard Business Press, Boston 2014

[6] OECD, "OECD Science, Technology and Innovation Outlook 2016", OECD Publishing, Paris, 2016.

[7] OECD, "OECD Science, Technology and Innovation Outlook 2018", OECD Publishing, Paris, 2018.

[8] J. A. Ekstrom, G. T. Lau and K. H. Law, "Policy Analytics Tools to Identify Gaps in Environmental Governance", in: Policy Analytics, Modeling, and Informatics – Innovative Tools for Solving Complex Social Problems, ed. by J. R. Gil-Garcia, T. Pardo, L. F. Luna-Reyes. Switzerland: Springer International Publishing AG – Public Administration and Information Technology, pp. 289 – 314, 2018.

[9] D. Baer, M. Wimmer, J. Glova, A. Papazafeiropoulou and L. Brooks, "Analysis of Policy Cases in the Field of Energy Policy", in: Policy Practice and Digital Science – Inte-grating Complex Systems, Social Simulation and Public Administration in Policy Research, ed. by M. Janssen, M. Wimmer, A. Deljoo. Switzerland: Springer International Publishing AG – Public Administration and Information Technology, pp. 355 – 378, 2015

[10] S. Vaan den Braak, and S. Choenni, S., "Development and Use of Data-Centric Information Systems to Support Policymakers: Applied to Criminal Justice Systems". In: Policy Analytics, Modeling, and Informatics – Innovative Tools for Solving Complex Social Problems., ed. by J. R. Gil-Garcia, T. Pardo, L. F. Luna-Reyes. Switzerland: Springer International Publishing AG – Public Administration and Information Technology, pp. 99 – 122, 2018.

[11] S. R. Hiltz, P. Diaz, and G. Mark, "Introduction: Social Media and Collaborative Systems for Crisis Management", ACM Transactions on Computer-Human Interaction 18(4), pp. 1-6, 2011.

[12] C. H. Park, and E. W. Johnston, "An Event-Driven Lens for Bridging Formal Organiza-tions and Informal Online Participation: How Policy Informatics Enables Just-in-Time Re-sponses to Crises", in: Policy Analytics, Modeling, and Informatics – Innovative Tools for Solving Complex Social Problems, ed. by J. R. Gil-Garcia, T. Pardo, L. F. Luna-Reyes. Switzerland: Springer International Publishing AG – Public Administration and Information Technology, pp. 343 – 361, 2018

[13] OECD/Eurostat, Oslo Manual 2018: Guidelines for Collecting, Reporting and Using Data on Innovation - 4th Edition, OECD Publishing, Paris/Eurostat, Luxembourg, 2018.

[14] B. Keeley, and P. Love, From Crisis to Recovery – The Causes, Course and Consequences of the Great Recession, OECD Publishing, Paris, 2010.

[15] T. A. Knoop, Recessions and Depressions: Under-standing Business Cycles -2nd edition, Praeger Santa Barbara, California, 2015.

[16] J. Schumpeter, The Theory of Economic Develop-ment: An Inquiry into Profits, Credit, Interest and the Business Cycle, Harvard University Press, Cambridge, MA, 1934.

[17] W. M. Cohen, and D. A. Levinthal, "Absorptive Capacity: A New Perspective on Learning and Innovation", Administrative Science Quarterly, 35(1), pp. 128-152, 1990.

[18] S. A. Zahra, and G. George, "Absorptive Capacity: A Review, Reconceptualization, and Extension". Academy of Management Review, 27(2), pp. 185-203, 2002

[19] C. Camisón, and B. Forés (2010). "Absorptive Capacity: New Insights for Its Conceptualization and Measurement", Journal of Business Research, 63(7), pp. 707-715, 2010.

[20] D. Wan, C. H. Ong, and F. Lee, "Determinants of firm innovation in Singapore", Technovation, 25, pp. 261-268, 2005.

[21] C. Van Beers, A. Kleinknecht, R. Ortt, R. and R. Verburg, Determinants of Innovative Behaviour: A Firm's Internal Practices and its External Environment", Palgrave Macmillan, London, 2008.

[22] M. Buesa, J., Heijs, and T., Baumert, "The determinants of regional innovation in Europe: A combined factorial and regression production function approach", Research Policy, 39, 722-735, 2010.

[23] E. Enkel, O. Gassmann, and H. Chesbrough, "Open R&D and Open Innovation: Exploring the Phenomenon", R&D Management Journal, 39(4), pp. 311-316, 2009.

[24] E. Brynjolfsson, and A. Saunders (2010), Wired for Innovation: How Information Technology Is Reshaping the Economy, MIT Press, Cambridge, Mass., 2010.

[25] L. Kleis, P. Chwelos, R. Ramirez, and I. Cockburn, "Information Technology and Intangible Output: The Impact of IT Investment on Innovation Productivity", Information Systems Research, 23(1), pp. 42-59, 2012.

[26] S. Arvanitis, E. Loukis, and V. Diamantopoulou, "Are ICT, Workplace Organization and Human Capital Relevant for Innovation? A Comparative Study Based on Swiss and Greek Micro Data", International Journal of the Economics of Business, 23(3), pp. 319-349, 2016.

[27] E. Loukis, S. Arvanitis, N. Kyriakou, A. Famelou, M. Chatzianastasiadis, and F. Michailidou, "The Effects of Enterprise Systems on the Absorptive Capacity of Greek Firms", in Proceedings of 10th Mediterranean Conference on Information Systems (MCIS), Paphos, Cyprus, September 2016.

[28] E. Loukis, S. Arvanitis, N. Kyriakou, A. Famelou, M. Chatzianastasiadis, and F. Michailidou, "ERP, e-Commerce, Social Media and Absorptive Capacity of Greek Firms - An Empirical Investigation", in Proceedings of 20th Panhellenic Conference on Informatics (PCI2016), Patra, Greece, November 2016.

[29] S. Marston, Z. Li, S. Brandyopadyay, J. Zhang, and A. Ghalsasi, "Cloud computing – The business perspective)", Decision Support Systems, 51(1), pp. 176–189, 2011.

[30] S. D. Müller, S. R. Holm, and J. Søndergaard, "Benefits of cloud computing: Literature review in a maturity model perspective", Communications of the Association for Information Systems, 37, pp. 851 – 878, 2015.

[31] OECD, OECD Science, Technology and Industry Outlook 2012, OECD Publishing, Paris, 2012.

[32] K. Izsak, P. Markianidou, R. Lukach, R., and A. Wastyn, "The impact of the crisis on research and innovation policies", Study for the European Commission, DG Research by Technopolis Group Belgium and Idea Consult, Brussels, 2013.

[33] S. Arvanitis, Woerter, M., "Firm Characteristics and the Cyclicality of R&D Investments", Industrial and Corporate Change, 23(5), pp. 1141-1169, 2014.

[34] P. Lopez-Garcia, and J. M. Montero, "Spillovers and Absorptive Capacity in the Decision to Innovate of Spanish Firms: The Role of Human Capital", Economics of Innovation and New Technology, 21(7), pp. 589-612, 2012.

Literature Review of Ethical Concerns in the Use of Disruptive Technologies in Government 3.0

Alexander Ronzhyn
University of Koblenz-Landau,
Universitätsstr. 1, 56070 Koblenz, Germany
Nationales E-Government Kompetenzzentrum e.V.,
Schiffbauerdamm 40 – 10117 Berlin, Germany
e-mail: ronzhyn@uni-koblenz.de

Maria A. Wimmer
University of Koblenz-Landau,
Universitätsstr. 1, 56070 Koblenz, Germany
Nationales E-Government Kompetenzzentrum e.V.,
Schiffbauerdamm 40 – 10117 Berlin, Germany
e-mail: wimmer@uni-koblenz.de

Abstract— **'Government 3.0' as the new paradigm brings in new disruptive technologies in the digitization process of the public sector. The massive use of Artificial Intelligence, Machine Learning, Big Data Analytics, Internet of Things and other technologies in public service provisioning that have a potential to significantly influence the life of a large number of citizens demands for a thorough investigation of the ethical concerns. Along a literature review, this paper investigates the ethical issues associated with the implementation of disruptive technologies in the public sector. In the first part of the paper, ten categories of ethical concerns in e-government are identified. Subsequently, these ten categories guide a more detailed review of 74 articles dealing with specific ethical concerns in relation to the implementation of Artificial Intelligence and Big Data in e-government. The literature review revealed important similarities and differences in ethical issues relating to the two technologies.**

Keywords-ethics, government 3.0, e-government, disruptive technologies.

I. Introduction

The discussion of ethics should be an integral part of e-government research, in particular when new disruptive technologies are to be deployed. Often however, ethical considerations are relegated to the "Discussion" or "Future research" sections of the papers. This paper therefore studies existing literature on ethics in e-government. Furthermore, ethical implications of the introduction of new disruptive technologies in e-government are identified.

Ethics has been defined as "*the art of living well*" by Aristotle (cited in [1]) and has been one of the most discussed philosophical concept ever since [2]. Treviño et al. define ethical behavior as "*doing the right thing, showing concern for people and treating people right, being open and communicative, and demonstrating morality in one's personal life*" [3, pp. 131–132]. Ethics in government refers to ethical behavior and to the approach of organizing the processes and rules of governance in a way that shows concern for citizens, is transparent and accountable (cf. good governance principles [4]).

Discussion of ethics in e-government lies on the intersection of the areas of the ethics in government and the Information and Communication Technologies (ICT) ethics. In his paper of 1986, Anderson identified four major ethical issues in ICT: privacy, accuracy, property and accessibility [5]. More than thirty years later these issues are even more important and contentious than at the dawn of the Internet era, for several reasons (particularly in regards to e-government): firstly, the relationship between the government and a citizen is unequal one: citizen is dependent and vulnerable [6]; secondly, ICTs have an effect on public values, and their transformative potential should be also viewed in this dimension [7][8]; thirdly, the landscape of the public sphere is different from the private sphere as the ultimate aims of the organizations involved are very different [9].

This paper studies the subject of ethical implementation of e-government and the ethical introduction and use of the ICTs in public sphere, while we do not discuss questions of ethical decision-making by individual officials in government. The research is a part of the Erasmus+ Gov 3.0 project (https://www.gov30.eu), which aims to establish Government 3.0 as a research domain. The project team defines Government 3.0 as follows:

> *Government 3.0 refers to the use of new disruptive ICTs (such as blockchain, big data and artificial intelligence technologies), in combination with established ICTs (such as distributed technologies for data storage and service delivery) and taking advantage of the wisdom of crowd (crowd/citizen-sourcing and value co-creation), towards data-driven and evidence-based decision and policy making.* [10, p.2]

The Gov 3.0 project identifies and describes new technologies, trends and concepts associated with the Government 3.0 paradigm. Some of these technologies are termed "disruptive" as they are likely to have significant impact on how e-government will be shaped in the future. Along the project, the authors conducted several workshops discussing the Government 3.0 concept and the use of disruptive technologies in public spheres. Ethical issues were one of the most discussed topics along these workshops. Yet despite ethics being one of the biggest concerns of academics along the implementation of new technologies, no systematic review of literature on ethics in e-government has been found. In this paper, we therefore investigate ethics in the implementation of the most significant disruptive technologies, namely Artificial Intelligence (AI) and Big Data.

The structure of the paper is as follows: Section II presents the research methodology of the paper and outlines the research questions, Section III presents results of the literature review of the ethical considerations in e-government, identifying main ethical themes in the research. In Section IV, we present the results of the literature review of the ethical issues concerning AI and Big Data use in Government 3.0. Section V discusses the results of the literature review and concludes with an outlook on future research on ethics in e-government and by reflecting the limitations of the paper.

II. METHODOLOGY

The aim of the paper is to scope the understanding of ethics in e-government and spotting the needs for ethical considerations in Government 3.0, specifically with new disruptive technologies and technological trends. The paper is descriptive and based on a systematic literature review.

Three research questions guide this research:

1. What are the main ethical considerations within the e-government domain?
2. What ethical issues can be identified concerning the implementations of AI and Big Data within e-government?
3. What are the research needs concerning ethical issues of disruptive technologies in e-government?

Following Kitchenham and Charters [11], the articles were collected from the four databases: SpringerLink (http://link.springer.com/), IEEE Xplore (http://ieeexplore.ieee.org/Xplore/), ACM (http://dl.acm.org/) and DGRL (V. 14, only for the first stage). The search was carried out in autumn 2018. Search was restricted to the title and abstract of the papers and was with the search string: "ethics AND ('digital government' OR 'e-government')". This allowed identifying main ethical considerations and themes in e-government, presented in Section III. Reviewing the results of the searches ensured that chosen papers focus on ethical issues, i.e., papers that did not include ethical issues as a main or at least a secondary topic, were not published in a peer-reviewed journal or conference proceeding or were not accessible in full-text were excluded (exclusion criteria).

For the second stage, literature on ethical issues of the specific technologies was searched and reviewed. The search strings "AI | Artificial Intelligence | Big Data AND ('ethical issues' OR 'ethics')" were used, resulting initially in 645 references. After the exclusion criteria were applied, 74 papers were left (27 AI, 47 Big Data papers). First exclusion was made after examining metadata of the articles, while the second exclusion was based on full-text scans of the articles. Out of the remaining papers, we extracted ethical issues applicable to the use of these technologies in e-government.

To analyze ethics aspects specifically related to the disruptive technologies, we used the concept-centric approach suggested by Webster and Watson [12]. For example, the list of broad ethical themes resulting from the first review cycle of ethics was used to codifying the presence or absence of the theme in each paper on ethics in AI and Big Data. The results of this literature review are described in Section IV.

III. ETHICS IN E-GOVERNMENT

Literature review identified 22 articles focusing on ethics in e-government. Table I lists the ten ethical considerations in e-government along with the literature. Subsequently, we summarize the main aspects of these ethical considerations.

TABLE I. ETHICAL CONSIDERATIONS IN E-GOVERNMENT

Ethical considerations in e-government	Articles reviewed
Inclusivity	[6], [7], [9], [13]–[18]
Privacy	[6], [16], [17], [19]–[25]
Data use	[6], [21], [24], [26]
Quality/ Accuracy of information	[9], [23], [25]
Transparency	[7]
Accountability	[19], [27]
Information ownership	[20], [23]
Trust	[6], [7], [9], [19], [23], [28]
Alignment of values	[13], [17], [23], [29], [30]
Cost	[6], [16], [25]

Inclusivity refers to the concern about the inability of some groups of citizens to make use of the digital government services. It is discussed in the context of the digital divide either within a society or between countries. Most common factors causing digital divide are disparity in access to technology, wealth, education or age-related differences [14]. Inclusivity is a significant concern as in some cases e-government services are replacing the traditional ways to interact with the government, so citizens who are unable to use the new services are put in significant disadvantage.

Privacy is the concern about the unauthorized or inappropriate use of individual information by the government or other actors. Privacy is the most discussed ICT-related ethical issue, especially after the advent of social media and large-scale personal data collection [31].

Data use refers to the concern about inappropriate use of collected data. This includes for example the aggregation of data from different sources to infer new information or to de-anonymize individual citizens. This is not a new issue [32], however with the increase of the amount of data about any particular person, cross-referencing different databases has become a significant concern, threatening citizens' privacy.

Concerns on *quality and accuracy of information* relate to the imperfect digitalization of certain data in the transition to digital services. Data errors or incomplete information in databases may result in additional costs for a citizen [25].

Transparency is a concern that certain processes in e-government may become black boxes, impossible to understand by individual citizens. Lack of transparency may lead to the inequality of treatment, when certain decisions are made using invisible decision processes based on data only available to the system [24].

Accountability is related to transparency and concerns the responsibility of government toward an individual citizen in case of problems with or misuse of the digital government system. Accountability is necessary to improve citizen trust in e-government [33].

Information ownership is about the possibility of the digital government system's user to change or restrict access to one's own information. It also concerns the re-use of certain information from the e-government systems by the third parties [34][35].

Trust is a general consideration of the effect that the automatization (and associated de-humanization) of the government services may have on an individual citizen. It also encompasses the issues of government control and surveillance [7][31].

Alignment of values refers to the mismatch between the values of the government and the citizens. Sometimes motivation of the government to introduce digital services (e.g. cutting costs, improving efficiency) may not be aligned with the interests of the citizens, who value accountability and inclusivity of the services [6][16]. This concern is connected to the inclusivity and trust concerns. The discussion of values in this context also touches on the differences of attitudes to the free speech versus security dilemma [17][36] and the difference between values across countries, i.e., imposing western values in the developing countries [13].

Cost consideration refers not only to the financial cost of implementing and running the digital government services but also trade-offs for the citizens, associated with the implementation of e-government services: ensuring inclusive access to government services may increase the workload for the civil servants and thus the cost of public services [6].

IV. Ethical issues in Government 3.0

The second stage of the literature review identifies specific ethical issues related to the new disruptive technologies AI and Big Data in e-government. The issues are categorized along the 10 ethical considerations identified in Section III.

A. *Artificial Intelligence*

The use of AI in government is expected to increase as well as the significance of its effects on issues with moral component [37][38]. Literature distinguishes between 'Artificial Intelligence' (AI) and 'Artificial General Intelligence', A(G)I. "AI in e-government" refers to the use of elements of artificial intelligence to facilitate some of the services and processes, while A(G)I relates to autonomous decision-making and AI-supported robots in the society in future [39]. While the latter has implication for government as well [37], it is not part of our current investigations, as we focus on current implementations of AI in e-government.

TABLE II. Ethical considerations of AI in e-government

Ethical consideration in e-government	Supporting literature
Inclusivity	[40]–[45]
Privacy	[45]–[49]
Quality/ Accuracy of information	[46]
Transparency	[37], [47]
Accountability	[37], [45], [47]–[52]
Information ownership	[53]
Trust	[37], [40], [47], [54], [55]
Alignment of values	[37], [42], [44]–[48], [53], [55]–[60]
Cost	[41], [42], [48], [61], [62]

Of the literature reviewed, 27 papers (Table II) are dealing with ethical issues in the application of AI. Most common categories of the ethical concerns mentioned are values (14), accountability (9), privacy (8), inclusivity (6) and cost (6). In most of the cases, the issues relate to the AI-assisted Big Data use for decision making (both autonomous by AI or AI-assisted). The most common ethical issues in each category are described below.

1) *Major issues*

Accountability: The concerns of this category relate to the automated decision-making by AI systems. Who is responsible or liable for AI making a bad decision (ethically, legally or otherwise)? This is a significant concern in private sector (especially relating to the autonomous vehicles), but also a huge issue in government, where decisions can have implications on a very large scale [52]. Thus the question of liability should not be only discussed when implementing the decision-making systems but also be explicitly addressed in laws [50][51].

Value alignment: while the decisions made by the autonomous AI systems should be ideally based on hard data, there is a concern that such decisions might not be objective [48]. What values should be programmed into the AI making complex data-based decisions is an open question [50][59]. For simple decisions, rules may be straightforward. For some other, choosing between two sub-optimal options may amount to the value judgment [55]. Ensuring transparency and providing sufficient discussions of such algorithms may help address such concerns [55][56].

Privacy: Ethical concerns include using AI for surveillance [45], for profiling [46] and the leakage of personal data (especially in sensitive settings like healthcare) [48][49]).

Inclusivity: AI may also increase inequality between those who control AI and other people [44][45]. The effect of AI on the society needs to be studied to ensure inclusive realization with respect to human rights [40][42][43].

Cost: AI can be a costly endeavor, especially in regard to indirect costs: the increase of automation and move towards automated decision-making is forecast to lead to a profound shift in the structure of the labor market [42][48][61]. Brandy argues that changes may affect public services twofold: directly, when some public officials will lose their jobs as services will be automated; and indirectly, when the increase in unemployment will lead to the increasing pressure on the public sector [62].

2) *Minor issues*

Transparency: AI systems need to be able to "explain" why a certain decision has been made [37].

Trust: There is an issue of trust towards autonomous or AI-assisted decisions [40][55], especially in sensitive settings like healthcare [54].

B. *Big Data*

Big Data already plays an important role in many domains, for example: disaster management [63], healthcare [64][65], food security [66], law enforcement [67] and smart cities [68]. In some cases, Big Data is used for automated decision making, sometimes in conjunction with AI [69].

Ethics and ethical issues emerged as one of the important topics in the Big Data literature review by Lu and Liu [70] appearing in 97 of the collected sources. Other major topics included healthcare applications of Big Data and privacy (which was the fourth most prominent topic related to Big Data overall, trailing only behind technology-related keywords).

The review identified 47 papers dealing with ethical issues in Big Data as shown in Table III. Most named ethical concerns are privacy (40), data ownership (10), data accuracy (9), values (9), data use (6) and inclusivity (6). The descriptions of these ethical concerns along Big Data use in e-government follow below.

TABLE III. ETHICAL CONSIDERATIONS OF BIG DATA IN E-GOVERNMENT

Ethical consideration in e-government	Supporting literature
Inclusivity	[67], [69], [71]–[74]
Privacy	[34], [48], [65], [67], [71]–[106]
Data use	[77], [79], [86], [90], [107], [108]
Quality/ Accuracy of information	[65], [77], [95]–[97], [99], [100], [102], [109]
Transparency	[74], [81], [110]
Accountability	[48], [74], [75], [110]
Information ownership	[34], [48], [69], [71], [78], [85], [97], [98], [106], [111]
Trust	[95], [105]
Alignment of values	[34], [48], [77], [81], [91], [94], [102], [107], [109]
Cost	[48], [65], [95], [98], [103]

1) Major issues:

Privacy: The main concern about Big Data is the ever-increasing amount of personal information collected [34][82], often without the subjects being aware of that collection [90]. Even with de-personalised information there is a significant concern about the cross-reference of data between different datasets to identify the anonymised individuals [76][80][112]. Given large amounts of information collected and the improvements in Big Data Analytics and Machine Learning technologies, it is very difficult to guarantee full anonymity of data [78][96]. In the government context, this concern is connected to the worry about the surveillance state, when government "knows everything" [88][104]. The benefits of the use of Big Data for security and surveillance needs to be balanced against personal freedom and privacy, otherwise it may lead to significant erosion of trust towards government [100][101].

Data ownership: Organisations involved in data collection (e.g. social media companies [113]) may accumulate very large amounts of personal data. While the data may include identifiable and potentially sensitive information, it does not actually belong to the person: often individuals do not even know what kind of information is collected about them [90][106]. Ethical concerns regard making use of personal data by organisations for their own benefit (or even for the benefit of society), without explicit consent from individuals [48][85].

Data accuracy: in e-government contexts, the collected data can be used for decision making or provision of personalised e-government services. Inaccurate or incomplete data can lead to erroneous or biased decisions [95][100][102]. These issues are more significant in the public sector, as citizens cannot always opt-out of a service and potential harm from incorrect data can be larger [109].

Data use: data misuse is a concern about the use of citizen data for purposes other than ones, for which an explicit consent has been given [86][90][108] or a legal ground exists. However, in a dynamically evolving field of e-government it may not be easy to predict every possible scenario, in which the data might be used. A balance should be found for ethical use of data, which would still allow creating innovative public services [79][107].

Alignment of values: similar to the issues discussed in AI, the use of Big Data may lead to the conflict between the values of the government and citizens: between individual and public good [81][94]. It is also necessary to consider the implications of the decisions based on the biased Big Data for the societal stability [48][102].

2) Minor issues

Inclusivity: there is a certain risk of the discrimination based on the dataset used. This can lead to stigmatisation [72], wrong identification in criminal cases [67] and increasing digital divide [71].

Transparency and accountability: in public sector it is important to indicate when and how the data is collected and for what purposes is it used [74][92], while the algorithm creators need to be accountable for their product [48][110].

Trust: improper management of data may lead to the issues with citizen trust towards government. Data management becomes an important concern for the agencies dealing with Big Data, requiring skills and effort [95][105].

Costs: there are cost issues related to the storage and processing of Big Data. By definition Big Data requires significant resources that need to be diverted from elsewhere. Implementing Big Data-based decision making systems, it is necessary to assess the possible trade-offs [48][65][98].

V. DISCUSSION AND CONCLUSIONS

Deploying disruptive technologies in public services brings new ethical challenges that need to be addressed by the researchers and practitioners of e-government. From the literature research, we extracted ten ethical considerations that should be carefully reflected along each project aiming at deploying disruptive technologies in e-government. Ensuring that the implementation of new services properly addresses the inclusivity, privacy, data use, data accuracy, accountability, ownership, trust, alignment of values and cost concerns will help to move towards more responsible design and implementation of the new Government 3.0 paradigm.

This research provides a description of ethical issues in AI and Big Data along the ten ethical considerations. Ethical concerns in the use of AI relate mostly to the accountability of autonomous decision-makers (who is accountable for AI making wrong decision?) and value alignment (what will be the basis for AI decisions?). Privacy and inclusivity are other important issues.

In Big Data, the main concern is privacy: what data should be collected and for what purposes? Information ownership and consent are important ethical issues as well. There is a significant worry about the improper use of Big Data for surveillance, there is an apparent need for ethical discussion regarding the limits of data collection and balancing the benefits of Big Data with its drawbacks.

Finally, the need for legal frameworks and regulation of the use of disruptive technologies arises in both, AI and Big Data ethical discussions [37][51][85][95].

Kidder [114] argues that ethical responsibilities increase with the increase of potential harm resulting from an unethical decision. Both AI and Big Data offer significant benefits for public sector, at the same time having considerable potential for misuse. With the widespread use of ICTs by the governments and digital transformation of governance processes, main ethical concerns shift from the individual decision-making by government officials to the discussion of ethical implementation and management of ICTs and tools in public sector.

Therefore, further research is needed to provide adequate frameworks along the introduction of disruptive technologies in e-government, which help to provide answers to the ethical considerations described in Sections III and IV guiding researchers and practitioners in the assessment of ethics. Further empirical and theoretical research is necessary to address the issues arising from the implementation of disruptive technologies and provide a basis for drafting legal framework regulating these technologies.

Future research should also assess ethics in the implementation of other disruptive technologies identified as a part of the Government 3.0 paradigm [115] (e.g., Augmented and Virtual Reality (see [116] for a discussion of ethical challenges), Internet of Things, Blockchain, etc.).

Limitations of the research conducted in this paper may be imposed by the methodology chosen: some relevant papers dealing with ethical issues may have been excluded if they had no "ethics/ ethical issues" in their title or abstract. Likewise, there are some papers that might not be in any of the databases used for the literature review, but still contain valuable information. A more extensive literature review is needed to overcome these limitations. Despite these limitations, we are confident that the literature review presented here is representative enough to provide valuable insights in the ethical issues in e-government and provide useful outline of the future research directions.

ACKNOWLEDGMENT

This research is developed in the context of the Gov 3.0 Project. It was funded by the Erasmus+ Knowledge Alliance, Project Reference No. 588306-EPP-1-2017-1-EL-EPPKA2-KA.

REFERENCES

[1] E. M. Hartman, "Socratic questions and aristotelian answers: A virtue-based approach to business ethics," *J. Bus. Ethics*, vol. 78, no. 3, pp. 313–328, 2008.

[2] D. Guttmann, *Ethics in social work: A context of caring*. Routledge, 2013.

[3] L. K. Treviño, L. P. Hartman, and M. Brown, "Moral Person and Moral Manager: How Executives Develop a Reputation for Ethical Leadership," *Calif. Manage. Rev.*, vol. 42, no. 4, pp. 128–142, 2000.

[4] OECD, OCDE, "The OECD principles of corporate governance," *Contaduria y Adm.*, no. 216, pp. 183–194, 2004.

[5] R. O. Mason, "Four Ethical Issues of the Information Age," *MIS Q.*, vol. 10, no. 1, pp. 5–12, 1986.

[6] J. B. Berger, "Coercive E-Government Policy Imposing Harm: The Need for a Responsible E-Government Ethics," *Proc. 49th Hawaii Int. Conf. Syst. Sci.*, pp. 2830–2839, 2016.

[7] F. Bannister and R. Connolly, "ICT, public values and transformative government: A framework and programme for research," *Gov. Inf. Q.*, vol. 31, no. 1, pp. 119–128, 2014.

[8] L. Royakkers, J. Timmer, L. Kool, and R. van Est, "Societal and ethical issues of digitization," *Ethics Inf. Technol.*, vol. 20, no. 2, pp. 127–142, 2018.

[9] H. Mullen and D. S. Horner, "Ethical Problems for e-Government: An Evaluative Framework," *Electron. J. e-Government*, vol. 2, no. 3, pp. 187–196, 2004.

[10] G. V. Pereira et al., "Scientific foundations training and entrepreneurship activities in the domain of ICT-enabled governance," in *Proc. 19th Annu. Int. Conf. dg.o '18*, pp. 1–2.

[11] B. Kitchenham and S. Charters, "Guidelines for performing Systematic Literature reviews in Software Engineering Version 2.3.," EBSE, UK, 2007.

[12] J. Webster and R. T. Watson, "Analyzing the past to prepare for the future," *MIS Q.*, pp. xiii–xxiii, 2002.

[13] S. Basu, "Digital Divide, Digital Ethics, and E-government," in *ICTs in Developing Countries*, London: Palgrave Macmillan UK, 2016, pp. 161–169.

[14] E. Mordini *et al.*, "Senior citizens and the ethics of e-inclusion," *Ethics Inf. Technol.*, vol. 11(3), pp. 203–220, 2009.

[15] E. Easton-Calabria and W. L. Allen, "Developing ethical approaches to data and civil society: from availability to accessibility," *Innovation*, vol. 28(1), pp. 52–62, 2015.

[16] B. N. Fairweather and S. Rogerson, "Towards morally defensible e-government interactions with citizens," *J. Inf., Commun. Ethics Soc.*, vol. 4(4), pp. 173–180, 2006.

[17] N. Kapucu, "Ethics of Digital Government," in *Encyclopedia of Digital Government*, A.-V. Anttiroiko and M. Malkia, Eds. IGI Global, 2007, pp. 745–748.

[18] J. W. Weiss, G. J. Gulati, D. J. Yates, and L. E. Yates, "Mobile broadband affordability and the global digital divide - An information ethics perspective," *Proc. HICSS*, vol. 2015-March, pp. 2177–2186, 2015.

[19] J. Lodge, "The dark side of the moon: Accountability, ethics and new biometrics," in *Second generation biometrics: The ethical, legal and social context*, Springer, 2012, pp. 305–328.

[20] R. Heersmink, J. van den Hoven, N. J. van Eck, and J. den van Berg, "Bibliometric mapping of computer and information ethics," *Ethics Inf. Technol.*, vol. 13(3), pp. 241–249, 2011.

[21] R. Domanski, E. Estevez, E. Styrin, M. Alfano, and T. M. Harrison, "Toward an ethics of digital government," *Proc. 19th Annu. Int. Conf. dg.o '18*, pp. 1–4, 2018.

[22] I. Büschel, R. Mehdi, A. Cammilleri, Y. Marzouki, and B. Elger, "Protecting Human Health and Security in Digital Europe: How to Deal with the 'Privacy Paradox'?," *Sci. Eng. Ethics*, vol. 20(3), pp. 639–658, 2014.

[23] G. Kaisara and S. Pather, "Relevance of Ethics in e-Government: An Analysis of Developments in the WWW era," in *Proceedings of the 6th International Conference on E-Government*, 2010, pp. 45–53.

[24] P. Henman, "E-Government, Targeting and Data Profiling," *J. E-Government*, vol. 2, no. 1, pp. 79–98, Dec. 2005.

[25] R. E. Anderson, "Ethics and Digital Government," in *Digital*

Government: Principles and Best Practices, 2004.

[26] D. Goroff, J. Polonetsky, and O. Tene, "Privacy Protective Research: Facilitating Ethically Responsible Access to Administrative Data," *Ann. Am. Acad. Pol. Soc. Sci.*, vol. 675(1), pp. 46–66, 2018.

[27] P. Henman, "E-Government, Targeting and Data Profiling," *J. E-Government*, vol. 2(1), pp. 79–98, Dec. 2005.

[28] G. Sharma, X. Bao, and L. Peng, "Public Participation and Ethical Issues on E-governance: A Study Perspective in Nepal," *Electron. J. e-Government*, vol.12(1), pp. 82–96, 2014.

[29] E. Wihlborg, H. Larsson, and K. Hedström, "'The computer says no!' - A case study on automated decision-making in public authorities," *Proc. HICSS*, vol. 2016–March, pp. 2903–2912, 2016.

[30] A. V. Roman, "Framing the Questions of E-Government Ethics: An Organizational Perspective," *Am. Rev. Public Adm.*, vol. 45(2), pp. 216–236, 2015.

[31] F. Belanger and J. S. Hiller, "A framework for e-government: Privacy implications," *Bus. Process Manag. J.*, vol. 12(1 SPEC. ISS.), pp. 48–60, 2006.

[32] R. O. Mason, "Four Ethical Issues of the Information Age," *MIS Q.*, vol. 10(1), pp. 5–12, 1986.

[33] E. W. Welch, C. C. Hinnant, and M. J. Moon, "Linking citizen satisfaction with e-government and trust in government," *Journal of Public Administration Research and Theory*, pp. 371–391. 2005.

[34] L. Voronova and N. Kazantsev, "The Ethics of Big Data: Analytical Survey," in *2015 IEEE 17th Conf. on Business Informatics*, 2015, pp. 57–63.

[35] R. Heersmink, J. van den Hoven, N. J. van Eck, and J. den van Berg, "Bibliometric mapping of computer and information ethics," *Ethics Inf. Technol.*, pp. 241–249, 2011.

[36] G. A. Sandy, "Mandatory ISP filtering for a clean feed to australian internet subscribers," *15th Am. Conf. Inf. Syst. 2009, AMCIS 2009*, vol. 10, pp. 6951–6958, 2009.

[37] A. Dameski, "A Comprehensive Ethical Framework for AI Entities: Foundations," in *Artificial General Intelligence*, M. Iklé, A. Franz, R. Rzepka, and B. Goertzel, Eds. 2018, pp. 42–51.

[38] A. Smith and J. Anderson, "Digital Life in 2025: AI, Robotics and the Future of Jobs," *Pew Res. Cent.*, 6. 2014.

[39] M. Anderson and S. L. Anderson, "Machine ethics," *IEEE Intelligent Systems*, 2006.

[40] M. Brundage, "Artificial Intelligence and Responsible Innovation," in *Fundamental Issues of Artificial Intelligence*, Cham: Springer International Publishing, 2016, pp. 543–554.

[41] F. Kile, "Artificial intelligence and society: a furtive transformation," *AI Soc.*, vol. 28(1), pp. 107–115, 2013.

[42] W. Zhao, "Research on Social Responsibility of Artificial Intelligence Based on ISO 26000," 2019, pp. 130–137.

[43] P. Boddington, "Some Characteristic Pitfalls in Considering the Ethics of AI, and what to do about them," 2017, pp. 85–97.

[44] M. Drev, "Work Task Automation and Artificial Intelligence: Implications for the Role of Government," in *At His Crossroad*, Cham: Springer, 2019, pp. 35–41.

[45] T. Meek, H. Barham, N. Beltaif, A. Kaadoor, and T. Akhter, "Managing the ethical and risk implications of rapid advances in artificial intelligence: A literature review," in *2016 PICMET*, 2016, pp. 682–693.

[46] K. Y. Lee, H. Y. Kwon, and J. I. Lim, "Legal Consideration on the Use of Artificial Intelligence Technology and Self-regulation in Financial Sector: Focused on Robo-Advisors," 2018, pp. 323–335.

[47] K. Shahriari and M. Shahriari, "IEEE standard review — Ethically aligned design: A vision for prioritizing human wellbeing with artificial intelligence and autonomous systems," in *2017 IEEE Canada IHTC*, 2017, pp. 197–201.

[48] B. C. Stahl and D. Wright, "Ethics and Privacy in AI and Big Data: Implementing Responsible Research and Innovation," *IEEE Secur. Priv.*, vol. 16(3), pp. 26–33, 2018.

[49] K. Miller, "Can We Program Ethics into AI? [Reflections]," *IEEE Technol. Soc. Mag.*, vol. 36(2), pp. 29–30, 2017.

[50] A. Etzioni and O. Etzioni, "AI assisted ethics," *Ethics Inf. Technol.*, vol. 18(2), pp. 149–156, 2016.

[51] R. Rault and D. Trentesaux, "Artificial Intelligence, Autonomous Systems and Robotics: Legal Innovations," 2018, pp. 1–9.

[52] Y.-J. Lee and J.-Y. Park, "Identification of future signal based on the quantitative and qualitative text mining: a case study on ethical issues in artificial intelligence," *Qual. Quant.*, vol. 52(2), pp. 653–667, 2018.

[53] D. Helbing *et al.*, "Will Democracy Survive Big Data and Artificial Intelligence?," in *Towards Digital Enlightenment*, Cham: Springer International Publishing, 2019, pp. 73–98.

[54] J. Danaher, "Toward an Ethics of AI Assistants: an Initial Framework," *Philos. Technol.*, vol. 31(4_, pp. 629–653, 2018.

[55] V. Vakkuri and P. Abrahamsson, "The Key Concepts of Ethics of Artificial Intelligence," in *2018 IEEE ICE/ITMC*, 2018, pp. 1–6.

[56] E. Yudkowsky, "Complex Value Systems in Friendly AI," 2011, pp. 388–393.

[57] J. M. Kizza, "New Frontiers for Computer Ethics: Artificial Intelligence, Virtualization, and Cyberspace," 2016, pp. 207–225.

[58] S. D. Baum, "Social choice ethics in artificial intelligence," *AI Soc.*, pp. 1-12, 2017.

[59] A. Giubilini and J. Savulescu, "The Artificial Moral Advisor. The 'Ideal Observer' Meets Artificial Intelligence," *Philos. Technol.*, vol. 31(2), pp. 169–188, 2018.

[60] S. A. Sora, "Artificial intelligence in a value based management system," *Int. J. Value-Based Manag.*, vol. 1(1), pp. 27–33, Feb. 1988.

[61] G. Su, "Unemployment in the AI Age," *AI Matters*, vol. 3(4), pp. 35–43, Feb. 2018.

[62] J. Bandy, "Automation moderation," *AI Matters*, vol. 3(4), pp. 59–62, Feb. 2018.

[63] S. Akter and S. F. Wamba, "Big data and disaster management: a systematic review and agenda for future research," *Annals of Operations Research*, pp.1–21, 2017.

[64] L. Yin, D. Fassi, H. Cheng, H. Han, and S. He, "Health Co-Creation in Social Innovation: Design Service for Health-Empowered Society in China," *Des. J.*, vol. 20(sup1), pp. S2293–S2303, 2017.

[65] A. Stylianou and M. A. Talias, "Big data in healthcare: a discussion on the big challenges," *Health Technol.*, vol. 7(1), pp. 97–107, Mar. 2017.

[66] B. Evans, "Using Big Data to Achieve Food Security," in *Big Data Challenges*, London: Palgrave, 2016, pp. 127–135.

[67] M. Phillips, E. S. Dove, and B. M. Knoppers, "Criminal Prohibition of Wrongful Re-identification: Legal Solution or Minefield for Big Data?," *J. Bioeth. Inq.*, vol. 14(4), pp. 527–539, Dec. 2017.

[68] M. Batty, "Big data, smart cities and city planning," *Dialogues Hum. Geogr.*, vol. 3(13), pp. 274-279, 2013.

[69] S. Monteith and T. Glenn, "Automated Decision-Making and Big Data: Concerns for People With Mental Illness," *Curr. Psychiatry Rep.*, vol. 18(112), p. 1-12, Dec. 2016.

[70] L. Y. Y. Lu and J. S. Liu, "The Major Research Themes of Big Data Literature: From 2001 to 2016," in *2016 IEEE CIT*, 2016, pp. 586–590.

[71] C. F. Breidbach, M. Davern, G. Shanks, and I. Asadi-Someh, "On the Ethical Implications of Big Data in Service Systems," 2019, pp. 661–674.

[72] H. Mamiya, A. Shaban-Nejad, and D. L. Buckeridge, "Online Public Health Intelligence: Ethical Considerations at the Big Data Era," 2017, pp. 129–148.

[73] L. Kammourieh *et al.*, "Group Privacy in the Age of Big Data," in *Group Privacy*, Cham: Springer, 2017, pp. 37–66.

[74] M. Cuquet, A. Fensel, and L. Bigagli, "A European research roadmap for optimizing societal impact of big data on environment and energy efficiency," in *2017 GIoTS*, 2017, pp. 1–6.

[75] A. Zwitter, "The Network Effect on Ethics in the Big Data Age," in *Big Data Challenges*, London: Palgrave, 2016, pp. 23–34.

[76] P. A. Chow-White, M. MacAulay, A. Charters, and P. Chow, "From the bench to the bedside in the big data age: ethics and practices of consent and privacy for clinical genomics and personalized medicine," *Ethics Inf. Technol.*, vol. 17(3), pp. 189–200, Sep. 2015.

[77] J. S. Saltz, "A Framework to Explore Ethical Issues When Using Big Data Analytics on the Future Networked Internet of Things," in *FNSS 2018*, 2018, pp. 49–60.

[78] A. Richterich, "Using Transactional Big Data for Epidemiological Surveillance: Google Flu Trends and Ethical Implications of 'Infodemiology,'" in *The Ethics of Biomedical Big Data*, Cham: Springer, 2016, pp. 41–72.

[79] G. O. Schaefer, M. K. Labude, and H. U. Nasir, "Big Data: Ethical Considerations," in *The Palgrave Handbook of Philosophy and Public Policy*, Springer, 2018, pp. 593–607.

[80] J. N. Gathegi, "Clouding Big Data: Information Privacy Considerations," in *IMCW2018*, 2014, pp. 64–69.

[81] C. Garattini, J. Raffle, D. N. Aisyah, F. Sartain, and Z. Kozlakidis, "Big Data Analytics, Infectious Diseases and Associated Ethical Impacts," *Philos. Technol.*, Aug., pp. 1–17, 2017.

[82] J.-L. Monino, "Data Value, Big Data Analytics, and Decision-Making," *J. Knowl. Econ.*, pp.1–12, Aug. 2016.

[83] D. Nunan and M. Di Domenico, "Big Data: A Normal Accident Waiting to Happen?," *J. Bus. Ethics*, vol. 145(3), pp. 481–491, Oct. 2017.

[84] J. Collmann, K. T. FitzGerald, S. Wu, J. Kupersmith, and S. A. Matei, "Data Management Plans, Institutional Review Boards, and the Ethical Management of Big Data About Human Subjects," in *Ethical Reasoning in Big Data*, Cham: Springer, 2016, pp. 141–184.

[85] K. Pormeister, "The GDPR and Big Data: Leading the Way for Big Genetic Data?," in *Annual Privacy Forum*, 2017, pp. 3–18.

[86] N. Dorasamy and N. Pomazalová, "Social Impact and Social Media Analysis Relating to Big Data," in *Data Science and Big Data Computing*, Cham: Springer, 2016, pp. 293–313.

[87] M. Steinmann *et al.*, "Embedding Privacy and Ethical Values in Big Data Technology," in *Transparency in Social Media*, Cham: Springer, 2015, pp. 277–301.

[88] H. Hijmans, "Internet and Loss of Control in an Era of Big Data and Mass Surveillance," 2016, pp. 77–123.

[89] A. Narayanan, J. Huey, and E. W. Felten, "A Precautionary Approach to Big Data Privacy," 2016, pp. 357–385.

[90] B. van der Sloot, "Is the Human Rights Framework Still Fit for the Big Data Era? A Discussion of the ECtHR's Case Law on Privacy Violations Arising from Surveillance Activities," 2016, pp. 411–436.

[91] B. Mittelstadt, "From Individual to Group Privacy in Big Data Analytics," *Philos. Technol.*, vol. 30(4), pp. 475–494, 2017.

[92] M. Andrejevic, "Surveillance in the Big Data Era," in *PICT*, Dordrecht: Springer, 2014, pp. 55–69.

[93] Y. Wang, "Big Opportunities and Big Concerns of Big Data in Education," *TechTrends*, vol. 60(4), pp. 381–384, Jul. 2016.

[94] M. Fuller, "Some Practical and Ethical Challenges Posed by Big Data," 2016, pp. 119–127.

[95] D. Helbing, "Societal, Economic, Ethical and Legal Challenges of the Digital Revolution: From Big Data to Deep Learning, Artificial Intelligence, and Manipulative Technologies," in *Towards Digital Enlightenment*, Springer, 2019, pp. 47–72.

[96] X. Zhang and S. Xiang, "Data Quality, Analytics, and Privacy in Big Data," 2015, pp. 393–418.

[97] V. Morabito, "Big Data and Analytics for Government Innovation," in *Big Data and Analytics*, 2015, pp. 23–45.

[98] L. Taylor and C. Richter, "Big Data and Urban Governance," in *Geographies of Urban Governance*, Cham: Springer, 2015, pp. 175–191.

[99] Aqeel-ur-Rehman, I. U. Khan, and S. ur Rehman, "A Review on Big Data Security and Privacy in Healthcare Applications," in *Big Data Management*, Cham: Springer, 2017, pp. 71–89.

[100] I. Stanier, "Enhancing Intelligence-Led Policing: Law Enforcement's Big Data Revolution," in *Big Data Challenges*, London: Palgrave, 2016, pp. 97–113.

[101] A. Gerdes, "Big Data—Fighting Organized Crime Threats While Preserving Privacy," in *Using Open Data to Detect Organized Crime Threats*, Cham: Springer International Publishing, 2017, pp. 103–117.

[102] R. Kitchin, "The real-time city? Big data and smart urbanism," *GeoJournal*, vol. 79(1), pp. 1–14, Feb. 2014.

[103] I. Olaronke and O. Oluwaseun, "Big data in healthcare: Prospects, challenges and resolutions," in *2016 FTC*, 2016, pp. 1152–1157.

[104] J. Richards, "Needles in Haystacks: Law, Capability, Ethics, and Proportionality in Big Data Intelligence-Gathering," in *Big Data Challenges*, London: Palgrave, 2016, pp. 73–84.

[105] M. Mulqueen, "Sustainable Innovation: Placing Ethics at the Core of Security in a Big Data Age," in *Big Data Challenges*, London: Palgrave, 2016, pp. 61–71.

[106] M. Alemany Oliver and J.-S. Vayre, "Big data and the future of knowledge production in marketing research: Ethics, digital traces, and abductive reasoning," *J. Mark. Anal.*, vol. 3(1), pp. 5–13, Mar. 2015.

[107] P. Prinsloo and S. Slade, "Big Data, Higher Education and Learning Analytics: Beyond Justice, Towards an Ethics of Care," in *Big Data and Learning Analytics in Higher Education*, Cham: Springer, 2017, pp. 109–124.

[108] R. Finn and A. Donovan, "Big Data, Drone Data: Privacy and Ethical Impacts of the Intersection Between Big Data and Civil Drone Deployments," 2016, pp. 47–67.

[109] W. J. Radermacher, "Official statistics in the era of big data opportunities and threats," *Int. J. Data Sci. Anal.*, vol. 6(3), pp. 225–231, Nov. 2018.

[110] M. Whitman, C. Hsiang, and K. Roark, "Potential for

participatory big data ethics and algorithm design," in *Proceedings of the 15th PDC '18*, 2018, pp. 1–6.
[111]M. Sax, "Big data: Finders keepers, losers weepers?," *Ethics Inf. Technol.*, vol. 18(1), pp. 25–31, Mar. 2016.
[112]V. Narayanan, P. N. Howard, B. Kollanyi, and M. Elswah, "Russian Involvement and Junk News during Brexit," 2017.
[113]L. Sax, S. Gilmartin, and A. Bryant, "Assessing response rates and nonresponse bias in web and paper surveys," *Res. High. Educ.*, vol. 44(4), pp. 409–432, 2003.
[114]R. M. Kidder, "Ethics: A matter of survival," *Futurist*, vol. 26(2), p. 10, 1992.
[115]Z. Lachana, C. Alexopoulos, E. Loukis, and Y. Charalabidis, "Identifying the Different Generations of Egovernment: an Analysis Framework," in *The 12th MCIS 2018*, 2018, pp. 1–13.
[116]C. Botella, A. Garcia-Palacios, R. M. Baños, and S. Quero, "Cybertherapy: Advantages, limitations, and ethical issues," *PsychNology J.*, 2009.

Challenges and Opportunities in e-Government Education

e-Government Programs Curriculum

Demetrios Sarantis
Operating Unit on Policy-Driven Electronic Governance
United Nations University
Guimaraes, Portugal
sarantis@unu.edu

Soumaya Ben Dhaou
Operating Unit on Policy-Driven Electronic Governance
United Nations University
Guimaraes, Portugal
bendhaou@unu.edu

Charalampos Alexopoulos
Department of Information and Communication Systems
Engineering, University of the Aegean
Samos, Greece
alexop@aegean.gr

Euripidis Loukis
Department of Information and Communication Systems
Engineering, University of the Aegean
Samos, Greece
eloukis@aegean.gr

Abstract— **Public administration and information technology university departments worldwide have responded to the explosion in e-Government by offering related programs or courses. In this study, the authors investigated education programs in e-Government by reviewing the curriculum and course descriptions of 70 programs that had web listings of their programs. Findings suggest that 64 institutions, from 32 countries worldwide, offer e-Government related programs. The programs are classified into four types based on their education level. Offered courses have been classified in 15 clusters. The majority of the proposed courses belong to the areas of Information Systems (20,7%), e-Governance (17,8%), Management (12,9%) and Public Administration (8,4%) clusters.**

Keywords-component; e-Government; Education; Training; Program; Course; Digital Transformation.

I. INTRODUCTION

Although e-Government is a relatively young subfield of the public administration discipline, it has gained significant academic and practical popularity during the last decade. This popularity is mainly due to the increasing and ubiquitous use of various information and communication technologies (ICTs) by citizens, businesses and by all types of public institutions.

The relevance of information and communication technology (ICT) in public sector research and education has markedly increased. Thanks to the practical and academic interest in e-Government, its teaching as an academic subject has also attracted some scholarly attention [1]. That is also reflected in public administration and information systems scientific conferences and journals, which pick up the issue more often within distinct tracks and special issues (e.g. ICDS [2], ICEGOV [3], HICSS [4], GIQ [5] etc.). Even though there are master programs with e-Government at their core, it is not clear how universities take up the topic, what is taught, and how the programs can be classified. This question seems highly relevant, considering how multidisciplinary the e-Government research community is [6]. Nevertheless, there are still relatively fewer studies on e-Government teaching compared to other kinds of e-Government research.

The contribution of this article is twofold: First, despite many publications on e-Government theory and practice, few exclusively examine e-Government education. Second, while the state of information systems and public administration education is soundly documented, the relevant literature in e-Government field is limited. Therefore, this article aims to explore the supply-side in e-Government education from an international point of view. At the core is the question, in which type of programs e-Government is addressed in which manner and what are the course types that are provided.

The rest of this paper is organized as follows. Section II describes the background of our study concerning the needs for e-Government education, as well as existing educational activities for fulfilling these needs. Section III describes the research method. Section IV presents the findings. Section V discusses the results and conclusions close the article.

II. DEMAND AND RESPONSE

During the last two decades, there has been a continuous growth of the e-Government initiatives, as government agencies are increasingly using (and relying on) various types of ICTs for supporting innovations in essential internal functions as well as in their transaction and consultation with citizens [7]. This trend is exponentially increasing, as governments are investing significant financial resources in various kinds of innovation promoting digitization projects. According to Ganapati and Reddick [8] in the U.S.A. the annual federal government ICT budget is over $86 billion, while the state and local government ICT market is valued at over $70 billion. A recent study by Grand View Research

(2017) estimated the global government ICT investment in 2015 at 431.15 billion USD, expected to reach USD 654.73 billion by 2025. At the same time, not only the 'quantity' of ICT investment increases in government, but also its 'quality' as well: from digitization of existing internal processes we proceed to overall 'digital transformation' of government agencies, concerning both their internal administrative and policy making processes, and their interaction with citizens; furthermore, e-Government becomes more 'context-specific', i.e., more closely associated with the specific local, country and sectoral contexts it aims to support [7]. These increase the technological and organizational sophistication of e-Government, making its development more difficult, demanding and risky. This critical size and high complexity of government ICT investment, and also the need for an efficient exploitation, operation and support of the existing government ICT infrastructures, necessitate extensive relevant human capital, which generates wide range of needs for e-Government education. Previous management and economic sciences research has revealed the importance of the human capital of organizations for knowledge intensive innovation related activities, as it improves their capacity to absorb relevant external knowledge, combine it with pre-existing internal knowledge, adapt it to specific needs and objectives, and exploit it for innovation purposes [9].

Therefore, e-Government education is of critical importance for the development of modern highly complex and sophisticated e-Government. For this reason public agencies, ICT implementers, students, and faculty are demanding e-Government education offerings with an urgency rarely seen before in academia. It is necessary, for a variety of e-Government-related roles occupations that have emerged, ranging from those requiring heavy technical skills in ICT and limited organizational knowledge, to those demanding extensive organizational skills and only modest technical knowledge (with many 'hybrid' ones that need considerable both technological and organizational capabilities). Previous literature has emphasized that the e-Government domain is a highly interdisciplinary. It combines knowledge from four main domains: the technological, management, economic and political sciences [7][10][11]. For this reason, the e-Government practitioners (in government agencies as well as in involved private firms, such as ICT or consulting ones) have their background in one of these four fields. In this regard, they need to acquire knowledge and experience from the other three domains, and then obtain the main knowledge of the e-Government domain. However, despite the abovementioned inherent difficulty and complexity of e-Government education, as well as its high importance, limited research has been conducted about it. Most of these researches describe relevant educational programs and initiatives.

According to Augustinaitis and Petrauskas [12], the interdisciplinary nature of e-Governance allows integrating a broad range of specialized knowledge, for instance knowledge from public administration, law, information technologies, communication, management and political sciences. In addition, significant percentage of students of such educational programs are primarily originated from these disciplines.

Janowski et al. [13] analysed seven e-Government graduate university programs. The results indicate that 29% of the programs train political leaders, 57% of them train government leaders, project managers and management staff, and 43% of the programs train technical staff. The focus on only one of the above roles in these programs is very limited (29%). The majority of the programs (71%) target more than one role, while none of them target all roles.

Concerning specific learning topics, the literature is mostly concentrated in country-specific studies, which provide different, but complementary results. Anohina Naumeca et al. [14] highlight the lack of learning courses concerning interoperability in the European countries. Interoperability related courses are essential, as they drive delivery of cross-border and cross-sectoral public sector services.

Biasiotti and Nannucci [15] argue that regarding Italy, master degrees on Public Administration (PA) and information technology organized by public administration schools, concentrate on technological issues (information systems, communication networks, tools and methodologies for public communication) and on legal instances of technological innovation in the PA (security, information technology law, internet law, etc.). Ganapati and Reddick [8] conducted a survey of Master in Public Administration (MPA) programs in the U.S.A. concerning the provision of e-Government related courses, as well as the importance assigned to such courses. More than a quarter of the respondents (29%) viewed such a course as "extremely unimportant" or "very unimportant", which indicates that a considerable share of MPA programs is not aware of some realities in public administration, associated with the high penetration and impact of ICT. Therefore, it has been concluded that the e-Government related education provided in the main U.S. MPA programs is not sufficient, and e-Government is under-represent in them, so they finally train a workforce unprepared for the digital world.

The needs for e-Government education increase, as government proceeds to the gradual exploitation of recent disruptive ICTs, and shift from solely looking to the support of administrative processes to a more ambitious purposes of supporting higher-level policy-making processes and functions.

These new objectives and directions of e-Government, and the above new technological advances, as well as the full range of involved disciplines, necessitates the development of corresponding new e-Government courses, and in general a holistic educational public sector digital transformation.

III. Research Method

The methodology undertaken includes the following steps: 1) the definition of the research keywords regarding the data collection of existing training programs related to e-Government, 2) the mapping of the geographical search areas, 3) the specification of a training programs metadata scheme and 4) the filtering and analysis of training programs focused on e-Government area.

Between February and May 2018, exhaustive Web search was conducted, using various search engines to analyse Web page descriptions of e-Government programs and course offerings by different types of educational institutions. Also particular web pages of universities reputed in the related literature or other publications to have an e-Government program were accessed. Also, all programs suggested from e-Government researchers and practitioners have been considered. Some established e-Government programs did not have a clear web presence or other did not provide the program courses. Identified e-Government programs include academic ones, executive training ones and various types of certifications. Most programs were at the master's level, but a few were available for undergraduates. They varied considerably in their focus, types of courses offered, and degree requirements. We chose only those programs that were described in detail on the web and came up with a total of 73 programs in May 2018. The total number of institutions offering e-Government education stood at 64.

We examined programs considering the following aspects: (a) Institution's country, (b) program's educational level, (c) provided courses. The considered courses were further classified in clusters. We used course titles and descriptions to place courses in categories. The classification scheme intended to provide a general picture of the types of courses offered in this area and an idea about the extent to which such programs give emphasis in each course cluster.

IV. FINDINGS

Seventy e-Government programs have been identified and considered. The most common strategy among these programs is to offer a concentration (or track or specialization) in a specific area of e-Government.

Institutions that offer e-Government educational programs are located in 32 countries (alphabetical order): Argentina 2, Armenia 2, Austria 1, Barbados 1, Belarus 1, Belgium 3, Estonia 1, Bosnia & Herzegovina 1, Canada 2, China 1, Colombia 3, Estonia 4, Germany 5, India 2, Italy 4, Mexico 5, Netherlands 2, New Zealand 1, Norway 1, Poland 3, Portugal 1, Romania 6, Russia 1, Serbia 1, Singapore 1, Slovenia 1, South Africa 2, Sweden 1, Switzerland 2, U.S.A. 10, Uganda 1, UK 3.

Figure 1. e-Government training programs categorized based on the certificate they award

Regarding the education level, there are eight executive training programs, eight undergraduate university programs, thirty postgraduate university programs and the rest of them are short course ones (Figure 1). The courses of e-Government related programs have been classified in the following clusters (each cluster is described, number of identified courses in parenthesis, course examples are provided in each group) (Figure 2):

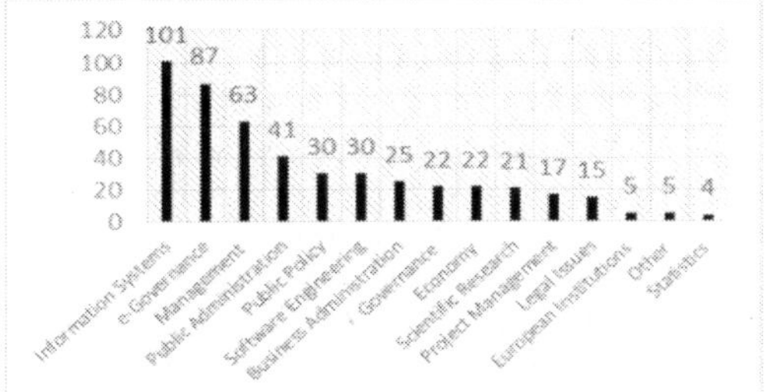

Figure 2. Course clusters and number of courses identified in each of them in e-Government related training programs

e-Governance (87). Courses in e-Governance category consider aspects such as the application of information and communication technology (ICT) for delivering government services, exchange of information, communication transactions, integration of various stand-alone systems and services between government and users, back office processes and interactions within the entire government framework, etc.

Indicative courses: Phases of e-Government and stages of e-Government development, Impact and measurement of e-Governance, Development of government websites.

Public Policy (30). The public policy category focuses on the systematic analysis of issues related to public policy and the decision processes associated with them. This includes training in the role of economic and political factors in public decision-making and policy formulation; microeconomic analysis of policy options and issues; resource allocation and decision modelling; cost/benefit analysis; and various applications to specific public policy topics. Public policy courses teach students policy analysis, policy studies, public policy, political economy, urban planning, public administration, public affairs, public management, etc.

Indicative courses: Sustainability and innovation in society, Public Innovation and Resistance to Change, Importance and Impact of Social Channels on Public Policy, Information Security Policy and Ethics, Information Policy.

Governance (22). Governance is composed of all processes of governing, whether undertaken by a government, a market or a network, over a social system and whether through the laws, norms, power or language of an organized society. It relates to the processes of interaction and decision-making among the actors involved in a collective problem that leads to the creation, reinforcement, or reproduction of social norms and institutions. Governance courses cover public sector, public organizations, and the concepts of leadership and governance. They study the features of the political structure of countries. They contain information on the institutional, procedural and value components of the political system and public policy in countries, as well as a description of the problems, contradictions, and prospects for the political development

of the country. They consider aspects such as the political system and regime, state institutions, political parties, civil society, directions and problems of economic and social policy.
Indicative courses: Government Enterprise Architecture, Democracy and Governance, Evidence, Institutions and Power, Risk Assessment and Governance.
Project Management (17). The project management category covers all aspects that are related to managing technology and innovation projects in the public sector. They include a variety of areas such as effort management, project portfolio management, program management, project risk management, project workforce management, etc.
Indicative courses: Project Management, Management of IT Projects in Administration.
Software Engineering (30). Software engineering courses consider issues regarding the systematic application of scientific and technological knowledge, methods, and experience to the design, implementation, testing, and documentation of software. Courses that are specifically incorporating programming, program design in their titles and that are technical in nature, such as web programming and security systems, are classified as software engineering.
Indicative courses: Introduction to Development in Cloud, Building interoperability and digital data exchange, Principles of Database Management, Data Warehouse and Business Intelligence, Mobile Apps: Application Development, User-Based Design, Spatial Data Capture.
Information Systems (101). Information Systems courses consider aspects such as management of information systems, design, implementation and development of information systems, systems analysis, data communications, database design, collection, organization, storage, and communication of information, etc. It also integrate topics related to business process design and automation, reengineering and transformation.
Indicative courses: Business Information Systems, Virtual Environments Usability, Information Management in the Public Sector, Information Systems Architecture, Information security in state and municipal government, Collaborative Systems in Administration.
Business Administration (25). Business administration courses provide a broad knowledge of the functional aspects of an organisation and their interconnection. They include all aspects of overseeing and supervising business operations and related fields which contain accounting, finance, and marketing. They also consider the performance or management of business operations and decision making, as well as the efficient organization of people and other resources, to direct activities toward common goals and objectives.
Indicative courses: Advanced Business Process Modelling and Automation, Transformation and change management, Start-up world & Prototyping ideas, Develop an innovative ecosystem, Digitally-driven Entrepreneurship.
Management (63). Management courses consider the administration of an organization, whether it is a business, a not-for-profit organization, or government body. Management includes the activities of setting the strategy of an organization and coordinating the efforts of its employees to accomplish its objectives through the application of available resources, such as financial, natural, technological, and human resources. Management courses provide a solid foundation in organizational behaviour, human resource management, labour-management relations, negotiation, conflict resolution, compensation systems, and organizational development.
Indicative courses: Human Resources Management, Leadership and Teamwork, Strategic Planning, Conflict Management, Impact Assessment.
Public Administration (41). Public Administration courses study the implementation of government policy and prepare civil servants for working in the public service. They introduce concepts whose fundamental goal is to advance management and policies so that government can function efficiently and effectively. They include aspects of economics, public finance, research methods/statistics, policy analysis, ethics, public management, leadership, program evaluation/performance measurement and human resources management.
Indicative courses: Public Sector Service Design and Implementation, State and Municipal Administration, Theory of the state and rights, Theory of Administration, Organisation of the Public Sector, Public Procurement.
Legal Issues (15). Courses in the legal issues category educate individuals in the principles, practices, and theory of law. This cluster of courses provides to the trainee, the knowledge and skills necessary for admission to legal practice in public administration. It also provides to current lawyers with advanced training or greater specialisation, or it updates lawyers on recent developments in the law. They include aspects such as understanding of the potential of e-Governance, the policies, the required legal and institutional frameworks, and insights into an engaging e-Governance involving different stakeholders.
Indicative courses: Legal aspects of e-Governance, cyber security & secure governance, Administrative Law, Legal Organisation of Public Administration, E-Regulation.
Scientific Research (21). Scientific research courses concentrate on the fundamentals of doing research, aimed primarily, but not exclusively, at the postgraduate level. These courses provide an understanding of research approaches and skills, and importantly an ability to deploy them in students´ studies or their professional lives. They aid those who have research as part of their postgraduate studies. Research methods courses prepare the student to design effective, ethical investigations. They teach appropriate frameworks and tools for qualitative and quantitative studies in e-Governance.
Indicative courses: Strategy and methods of scientific research, Research Methods for Process Analysis,

Investigative methods for e-Governance, Research on Public Management and Organizations, Quantitative Methods.

Economy (22). Economy courses include microeconomics, macroeconomics, econometrics, economic statistics, history of economic thought and political economy. They cover aspects such as microeconomic theory, macroeconomic theory, and econometrics.

Indicative courses: Public Finance, Public Budgets, Financing Programs for Digital Development, Health Care Finance.

Statistics (4). The statistics category is concerned with statistical methods, evidence-based reasoning, particularly with the analysis of data. Statistics courses study the collection, analysis, interpretation, and presentation of data.

Indicative courses: Statistics in Administration, Probability and statistics.

European Institutions (5). European institutions courses provide structured knowledge of EU fundamentals and focus on selected priority issues for an in-depth understanding and future-oriented approach to EU integration. The institutions of the European Union are the seven major decision-making bodies of the European Union (EU).

Indicative courses: European Integration and EU Institutions, European Administrative Law, EU Funds Management.

Other (5). The category "other" includes the rest of the provided courses.

Indicative courses: Physical Education, Ethics, Publicity, Mathematics for decision sciences, English for Science and Research.

V. Discussion

Not that long ago, e-Government related programs and course offerings were virtually non-existent, but today they are rapidly increasing. In this research, we identified 64 institutions offering either concentrations or majors in e-Government at different types of educational level worldwide. But even as more universities rush to market with such offerings, major controversies remain unresolved surrounding the need for, and the nature of, e-Government education.

e-Government courses have arrived as a significant element of public administration and technology schools. Educational institutions are scrambling to turn the study of e-Government into majors and degrees. However, the approach to offering such course content varies across institutions. Controversy highlights whether e-Government represents an incremental modification of the capabilities and strategies available to information technology or public administration areas or whether we are witnessing the birth of a new education area. Institutions of higher education are debating if they should "patch" e-Government perspectives into existing courses and programs or offer new courses and majors.

Though some researchers have contended that e-Government should be an integral part of the curriculum and that separate programs and degrees are unnecessary, others have argued for specialized programs in the area [16][17].

Schools with separate majors in e-Government aim to offer intensive study of e-Government and address what might be a new approach to reorganize and manage public sector. Other institutions are designing courses and programs that treat e-Government as an integral part of the broader public administration or information technology curriculum. This approach assumes that a basic grounding in fundamental public administration concepts and information technology aspects is still needed in the new type of government. e-Government facts and content may be obsolete sooner than students can finish a program. Integration of e-Government into established curriculums also may force students to examine the social, global, psychological, and ethical aspects of this approach to government.

Technical versus nontechnical focus aside from the debate on whether to integrate e-Government into a public administration program or offer it separately, there is also a lack of clarity concerning the extent to which such courses should emphasize technology aspects as opposed to functional public administration areas. Should courses emphasize the technology that enables e-Government or focus on the effect of technology on government strategy and decisions? Do e-Government capabilities require a technological foundation, or can students function effectively in e-Government environment without knowledge of the enabling technology? Who should initiate and "own" e-Government education- the computer information systems faculty or the public administration faculty?

In the current study, e-Government programs are being offered by both public administration schools such as Hertie School of Governance and, primarily, technological schools such as the College of Information Science & Technology in the University of Nebraska Omaha or the Institute of Business and Management Informatics of the University of Koblenz Landau. Findings suggest that technology could no longer be an afterthought to government strategy but an integral part of every phase of the strategy development. But what this means regarding the related education is not clear.

Education opportunities in e-Government field remain elusive for some regions and countries, in the developing countries. Only 6 academic programs are provided from institutions that are located in Africa or Asia. Therefore, it is also important to develop tailored e-Government training programs to support new public policy and technology professions to strengthen institutional capacities of developing countries in deploying digital government and digital services.

To design a complete educational e-Government program, the present study suggests fifteen main course clusters that lay a solid foundation for the creation of a comprehensive and coherent e-Government program. These clusters cover different aspects of e-Government needs. The majority of the provided courses belong to Information Systems (20,7%), e-Governance (17,8%), Management (12,9%) and Public Administration (8,4%) clusters.

These e-Government programs should be offered in a holistic way providing the opportunity to students to develop a high level of knowledge and capabilities in:

- an appropriate range of organizational tasks, management procedures, multi-stakeholder projects, legal and methodological concepts towards the efficient and effective execution of public projects;
- a wide range of technological skills (established and emerging ones), towards beneficial innovations, transformations and transitions in the public sector;
- a variety of different aspects of information systems (IS), that can be developed: IS that support internal processes, electronic procurement, digital information provision to citizens and businesses, electronic transactions between the government and citizens/businesses, interoperability, electronic participation, governance and democracy, utilization of social media, open government data, smart cities, etc.

VI. CONCLUSION

The growing interest of e-Government programs during the last years is significant. The debate on whether e-Government should be viewed as a new curricular area has not slowed down curricular innovation. The ability of universities to acquire faculty and technology resources and to continuously offer more innovative courses will affect the success and viability of these programs. This paper examines the nature of 70 e-Government programs and explores their content. It also sets the foundation for curriculum development in e-Government education.

Educational postgraduate programs need a structure that allows the inclusion of country-specific needs based on the maturity stage of the country and the developed governmental action plan. To improve the efficiency and effectiveness of e-Government projects the country's leaders must pay closer attention to the problems of increasing the "right" e-Government skills of civil servants.

Further steps to this study will be to identify, structure and describe the specific modules of undergraduate and graduate level educational programs. A possible research approach is also the identification of the needed micro-certificates interrelated with the appropriate skills from the ESCO ontology, which is a classification that identifies and categorises skills, competences, qualifications and occupations relevant for the European Union labour market and education.

ACKNOWLEDGMENT

This paper is a result of the project "SmartEGOV: Harnessing EGOV for Smart Governance (Foundations, methods, Tools) / NORTE-01-0145-FEDER-000037", supported by Norte Portugal Regional Operational Programme (NORTE 2020), under the PORTUGAL 2020 Partnership Agreement, through the European Regional Development Fund (EFDR).

REFERENCES

[1] E. Estevez, and T. Janowski, "Landscaping government chief information officer education," in 2013 46th Hawaii International Conference on System Sciences, pp. 1684-1693, IEEE, January 2013.

[2] https://www.iaria.org/conferences2019/filesICDS19/NGDG.pdf, ICDS 2019.

[3] http://www.icegov.org/track/workshop-3, ICEGOV 2019.

[4] http://hicss.hawaii.edu/#!future-conferences/ctld HICSS 2019.

[5] https://www.journals.elsevier.com/government-information-quarterly, GIQ 2019.

[6] M. Yildiz, C. Babaoğlu, and M.A. Demircioğlu, "E-government education in Turkish public administration graduate programs: Past, present, and future," Journal of Public Affairs Education, 22(2), pp. 287-302, 2016.

[7] T. Janowski, "Digital government evolution: From transformation to contextualization," Government Information Quarterly, 32(3), pp. 221-236, 2015.

[8] S. Ganapati, and C. G. Reddick, "An Ostrich burying its head in the sand? The 2009 NASPAA standards and scope of information technology and E-Government curricula," Journal of Public Affairs Education, 22(2), pp. 267-286, 2016.

[9] S. Arvanitis, E. Loukis, and V. Diamantopoulou, "Are ICT, Workplace Organization and Human Capital Relevant for Innovation? A Comparative Study Based on Swiss and Greek Micro Data," International Journal of the Economics of Business, 23(3), pp. 319-349, 2016.

[10] A. Grönlund, and T.A. Horan, "Introducing e-Gov: History, Definitions, and Issues," Communications of the Association for Information Systems, 15, pp. 713-729, 2005.

[11] H. J. Scholl, "Central Research Questions in e-Government, or Which Trajectory Should the Study Domain Take," Transforming Government: People, Process and Policy, 1(1), pp. 67-88, 2007.

[12] A. Augustinaitis, and R. Petrauskas, "Master studies on e-governance administration: the first experience in Lithuania," In International Conference on Electronic Government, pp. 453-456, Springer, Berlin, Heidelberg, August, 2004.

[13] T. Janowski, E. Estevez, and A. Ojo, "Conceptualizing electronic governance education," In System Science (HICSS), 2012 45th Hawaii International Conference on (pp. 2269-2278). IEEE, January, 2012.

[14] A. Anohina-Naumeca, V. Sitikovs, P. Goetzen, and M. Chmielecki, "Design of the electronic course on e-government interoperability essentials," in European Conference on e-Government (p. 649). Academic Conferences International Limited, June, 2013.

[15] M. A. Biasiotti, and R. Nannucci, "Teaching e-government in Italy," in International Conference on Electronic Government (pp. 460-463). Springer, Berlin, Heidelberg, August, 2004.

[16] P. T. Jaeger, "Building e-government into the library and information science curriculum: The future of government information and services," Journal of Education for Library and Information Science, 49(3), pp. 167-179, 2008.

[17] S. Kim, and K. Layne, "Making the connection: E-government and public administration education," Journal of Public Affairs Education, pp. 229-240, 2001.

**International Academy, Research,
and Industry Association (IARIA)**
412 Derby Way
Wilmington, DE 19810

ISBN 978-1-5108-8365-9

9 781510 883659

CURRAN ASSOCIATES INC.
proceedings.com

Thirteenth International Conference on Autonomic and Autonomous Systems (ICAS 2017)

Held at InfoSys 2017

Barcelona, Spain
21 - 25 May 2017

IARIA